TERRY HALLER is president of the Chicago Research Company, chairman of the Financial Communications Strategy Center, an editor of the *Journal of Business Strategy*, and a member of the Chicago United Way Communications Advisory Council.

secrets of the
master business strategists

Terry Haller

A SPECTRUM BOOK

Prentice-Hall, Inc., Englewood Cliffs, New Jersey 07632

Library of Congress Cataloging in Publication Data

Haller, Terry.
  Secrets of the master business strategists.
  "A Spectrum Book."
  Bibliography: p.
  Includes index.
  1. Corporate planning.   I. Title.   II. Title: Business strategists.
HD30.28.H34   1983   658.4'012   83–11005
ISBN 0-13-798249-6
ISBN 0-13-798231-3 (pbk.)

ISBN 0-13-798249-6

ISBN 0-13-798231-3 (PBK.)

This book is available at a special discount when ordered in bulk quantities.
Contact Prentice-Hall, Inc., General Publishing Division, Special Sales,
Englewood Cliffs, N.J. 07632.

A SPECTRUM BOOK
Printed in the United States of America
10 9 8 7 6 5 4 3 2 1

Prentice-Hall International, Inc., *London*
Prentice-Hall of Australia Pty. Limited, *Sydney*
Prentice-Hall of Canada, Inc., *Toronto*
Prentice-Hall of India Private Limited, *New Delhi*
Prentice-Hall of Japan, Inc., *Tokyo*
Prentice-Hall of Southeast Asia Pte. Ltd., *Singapore*
Whitehall Books Limited, Wellington, *New Zealand*
Editora Prentice-Hall Do Brasil Ltda., *Rio de Janeiro*

To my mother

Contents

preface

Our economic order teeters on the edge of frightening uncertainty. As goes the economy, so goes your career.

Some crystal-gazers, ignoring those occasional cyclical blips they regard as only brief respites, forecast a return of the Great Depression complete with dust bowls and soup kitchens. The more stout hearted foresee industry and society reaching new heights that will dwarf any former attainments.

We are in transition now, and it would be safe to say our destiny will be governed by our choices—and these choices will dictate the quality of our careers and lives.

Linking crossed arms, swaying to "We Shall Overcome" and with tears welling up, some will admonish the government—an organization strictly beholden to an electorate untutored in economic realities—to administer stop-gap measures that shrink the capacity of a nation to generate productive new wealth. A tearful concern for society's ills is fodder for the network news, but it doesn't solve, or even define for that matter, any of the problems.

The only sector with enough sanity to launch the new era of universal prosperity is the business community.

Then why hasn't it?

Because the system is not without its own faults—not the least of which is its errant leadership, whose appalling track record of late has resulted in a spectacular rise in managerial headrolling.

In place of these traditional "captains of industry" we need "field marshals"—people who can lead their troops into winnable battles, who can instinctively avert battles of attrition that have characterized the commercial theatre for too many years. In other words, we need *master strategists* whose secrets can release the free enterprise system from its current imprisonment in the old boom-and-bust cycle.

Now, before it's too late, we need strategies which allow our great industries to allocate their precious resources of talent, money, and plants to endeavors assured of success and to avoid those guaranteed to spell failure. We hanker for strategies that can create new wealth, provide new jobs, satisfy all reasonable human needs, and produce salutary profits in the process.

Strategy is a science. The master strategists know what they are up to. For the future of Western civilization, the rest of us must share in these secrets so that all of our business endeavors can be strong rather than marginal, and so we can "overcome" our chronic fiscal deficiency.

This book attempts to outline what is known about business strategy, what works, and what does not, and in the process make available to the average reader what few executives come to realize even by the end of long and glorious careers—namely, that business strategy can be approached like any other discipline, and that is has its own body of laws and principles.

acknowledgment

Several years ago I was waiting in Jakarta airport's forlorn international lounge for my plane back to the States. The hours passed slowly as flight time came and went. No changes in the schedule had been posted on the board. There had been a few announcements over the public address system, but not in any language I was familiar with; since nobody moved (there were four of us in the lounge), I assumed they did not apply to us. Eventually my patience expired, and when the next inscrutable announcement blasted over the P.A., I approached the other waiting passengers, all of them Japanese, and asked if that last announcement had anything to do with our flight. The most senior among them said it had, that there had been some delay, or something, and then looked at me with a patronizing grin and asked, "So, American not understand Indonesian, yes?" I have reflected on this encounter many times since, and it has taken on a disproportionate meaning for me. For one thing, it started me thinking on what it is about the Japanese that makes them better performers than we and what it is we should be doing about it. Subsequent wrestling with this problem, and more encounters with the folks from Japan Inc., led me to conclude that Japan's Achilles' heel is *strategy*—that it is *strategy* that will save us. So to that Japanese gentleman in the Jakarta airport, *arigato* and best wishes.

xiii

1

strategists
get the best jobs

Bronson and Clark graduated from the same MBA program and were hired by the same company. In his undergraduate days Bronson was a modest star on the varsity squad, while Clark was active in less physical pursuits. Clark got better marks. Both were sent to the sales field for a six-month training program, and both had hoped to get into product management when they returned to the head office.

In the field Bronson's boss evaluated him as a good candidate for product manager, and so that was what he became. Clark was encouraged to take a "promising" slot in the media department. So he became a media supervisor, which, let's face it, is just a staff job.

Clark decided to make up for the setback in his career. He applied himself diligently. He studied old files, searching for "truth," and looking for ways to do his job better. He read a lot. "God, is he smart!" said his boss. Soon he was promoted to group media manager on the company's most important brands—the ones with the big budgets. He was now policing the agencies on multi-million dollar expenditures.

Meanwhile, Bronson was having a good time. He didn't have to plow through the files because he was able to argue—along with most of his peers—that the past was no guide to today's market. He got along well with everybody. He often drew parallels between marketing and football and saw himself the team captain. He shunned

1

detailed discussions of research findings, packaging costs, ingredient changes, and even media spending. (He had a friend in the media department, good old Clark, who was only too happy to furnish him with whatever he wanted, including lengthy position papers geared to stifling all troublesome controversies.) He talked a lot about general things, speculated freely on what competition would do (who could argue with speculation?) and used as his secret model the marketing history of a laundry detergent that Procter & Gamble put out several years before his time, and on which he once prepared a paper in college. He had forgotten most of the facts in this case but had developed a kind of gut-feel about it. When it came to decision-time, his colon would ache until he selected the same path his favorite detergent once followed. At first he didn't think that was how he was supposed to do his job as product manager, but it seemed to work. He was always complimented on his reasoning when all he had really done was to scan a batch of rather obvious options and pick the one that got rid of an unpleasant feeling in his stomach. Since it worked, it became a habit.

His friend Clark labored late every night. Sometimes he even came into the office on Sunday. Bronson took it easy. Naturally he didn't leave the office right at quitting time, but he once confided to a drinking buddy, "I could really finish my day's work by noon every day." He spent his days in meetings with various staff departments at which little real business was done, but he got to know a lot of people and they got to know him. Since Bronson had exclusive access to current developments on his brand (nobody ever bothered to inform staff people about such things), he sounded to the staffers, at the age of 26, like someone much older in years and business experience. With such an easy audience he was able to practice at being a chief executive.

Ten years later, Bronson was president of one of the company's more exciting divisions. Clark was media director. Bronson made $135,000 a year, Clark $52,000.

Bronson was one of the lucky ones. He was a born strategist. Clark was a mere tactician. Bronson didn't really have to work at it. In fact, he wasn't actually that good at strategy, but he was able to pass off what was acceptable in his company as "current wisdom." His talent was the knack of appearing to be a strategist. By contrast, the harder Clark tried to excel in his job, the more he convinced everyone that he was just a tactician. He concentrated on detailed, well-documented expositions of his programs, but didn't feel the need—or the right—to address himself to the broad corporate issues like profit-optimization.

With a push in the right direction Clark could have become a better strategist than his friend Bronson. He had a better brain, was more industrious, and could absorb new concepts quicker and better. Bronson only had one guiding idea—that business was vaguely like football, and one exemplar—the P&G soap product he studied briefly in college.

Yet the company they worked for was right. Tactics don't count for much—not in the long run. The company and its strategy are really synonymous. Its strategy is its future and the progenitor of its profits. Bad tactics can be hastily abandoned and new ones put in their place. Strategies have long time horizons (5–15 years), so they've got to be right. Tactics are merely ways of implementing strategies, and the options are limitless.

Office cubicles are filled with tacticians. They are a dime a dozen. Few strategists abound. And they are in demand. As a rule, top executives are strategists, and they hire fellow strategists for key slots in their organizations. They are welcome guests in the director's dining room.

Strategists recognize strategists—within minutes of encountering them. But tacticians can seldom see any difference between strategists and tacticians. This makes them say a lot of wrong things in job interviews.

Tacticians do okay in specialty jobs—if making somewhat above average income is okay—but they don't usually rise to the top, except maybe in isolated industries like show business. Sometimes, in desperation, they start their own businesses. Problems ensue. They are basically only implementers, so they don't think long and hard enough about developing their own business strategies. If their businesses manage to survive, they usually do so at less than optimum profit levels.

In some jobs tacticians have more fun than strategists. It is probably more fun to shoot commercials, especially on location in the Caribbean, than to sit in an office planning a marketing strategy for a new soft drink. But try explaining to your kids that you want fun in your job and may not be able to send them to Harvard.

Strategists have always gotten the best jobs. They call the shots. This has been true all through history. The great generals and the great empire builders were strategists. It is true today in the business world, in politics, and in life in general.

In fact, the world has always imposed a kind of child-adult relationship between tacticians and strategists. Few people in power admire tacticians, but they use them and exploit them. The tactician is not the master of his or her own fate.

This book is dedicated to the proposition that tacticians can become strategists. They can undergo a metamorphosis. They can learn the principles and analytical procedures followed by the leading strategists. They can apply these to their careers, to their own businesses, or to their private lives. There is no trick to it. If the tacticians have more brains than their strategist counterparts (which is frequently the case), they can outwit the strategists at their own game.

"I thought you got by on charm. I didn't know you did homework."

MIKE DAVIS (BURT LANCASTER), ROPE OF SAND.*

how to recognize a strategy when you see one

This book is about strategy—what it is, how it works, and how to formulate it. But let's be candid: If you're a tactician (go ahead, admit it; it's okay), all you've seen of strategy up to now may be its culminating marching orders. You've probably missed out on the hard (and most fascinating) part—all the thinking that goes into casting and forging a strategy.

Admittedly, some corporate frauds, like Bronson, are able to foist off outlandish strategies on their companies without blessing them with the necessary work, and a lot of them get away with it. The real pros, however, do it right; this is the path I would like to put you on.

Strategy isn't something you can nail together in slap-dash fashion by sitting around a conference table with thundering corporate soothsayers, giving full weight to the first fatuous idea that pops up. While this may go over great at a PTA meeting, in the business world you're going to be held accountable for the strategies you concoct. If they don't cut it, your reputation will be badly shredded.

When most businessmen talk strategy, it is really only "street strategy" that comes out and not (for want of a better term) the sounder and loftier "gourmet strategy" that enhances reputations and builds careers through its more favorable win:loss ratio. Street strategy is the kind of strategy that lightweights can talk about

4

extemporaneously—with no preparation, with only a passing knowledge of the situation, and with a heavy sprinkling of platitudes. Gourmet strategy is the kind of thing you have to think about for a while; the qualitative difference would be similar to comparing the economic insights offered on "Saturday Nite Live" with those on William F. Buckley's "Firing Line."

Most of the business world, sad to say, doesn't really know what strategy is. Instinctively all businessmen, even those who are not prominently omniscient, sense that strategy is serious and weighty. When discussing it, they will speak through fiercely clenched teeth or through pursed lips in a vain attempt to convey assurance and brawny resolution, but their facial contortions belie their bluff. In fact, talking about strategy with the run-of-the-mill manager is like a dialogue with the stereotypical Hollywood "dumb blonde"; once you try to get her off fatuous subjects like her clothes, hair, and finger nails, her mind wanders. The wandering mind is a common *betê noir* in business circles.

The fear of its apparent, heavy thought content can throw a lot of people off the track of serious strategy. Most of us prefer to talk out decisions. We spend most of our time in meetings. It's part of the corporate culture. And it would be all right if we were accustomed to diligent preparation prior to these meetings, but *that* is seldom part of the corporate culture. People get away with little or no preparation; there are no sanctions to force deeper prefatory work in most companies. Without the necessary analysis and exegesis, the strategy formulation that is expected to come out of such meetings is short-changed. (This will become clear as you get into the subsequent chapters.) The foggy discourses that characterize most of these meetings conclude with resolutions in the camp of the street strategist.

not a fad

Strategy is always, perish the thought, in danger of being a mere fad. As Americans, the world's most professional consumers, we are easy marks for the fad-purveyors—even in management techniques. We love signing up for seminars that will turn us into crack managers in just 48 hours, almost as much as we love signing on for exhausting, strenuous physical-fitness programs—both of which we soon tire of and forget. Our fad-receptivity threshold is high, and we are suckers for easy solutions. It is downright American. But it is dismaying to think there really are people who believe strategy can be mastered at a two-day seminar. Notwithstanding my serious reservations about this, strategy, whipped along by the faddists, has risen, fallen, and returned time and again as the ultimate fulcrum. But its residual staying power has been shamefully transitory. Something else with more tinsel and ease-of-application—a new management style, some new personnel theorem, a one-minute problem solver, or an all-encompassing mathematical model—always comes along to replace it just as it is about to get reestablished. Many of these have helped build our present economic charnelhouse. In contrast to all of these easy-think prescriptions, strategy is not opinion but knowledge, not sentiment but conviction, not fervor but philosophy. Naturally, I think strategy *is* the ultimate answer. I know that's one of those motherhood statements, but what the hell. Obviously, if your strategies aren't any good, no amount of fancy execution is going to keep you out of trouble or make you rich. And strategy is about as far from being a fad as any management utensil can be.

strategy defined

Maybe this is the point to define strategy. I've already indicated what it is not. It's not the lockerroom game plan cooked up by the coach at halftime to honor the Gipper, nor what the eager salesman contrives while calling on his key accounts, nor even what the CEO devises over drinks with cronies at the club. Significantly, it has less to do with doing things right than with doing the right things, as Peter Drucker has pointed out many times. There is a big difference.

As we shall see, strategy is something that touches all facets of the enterprise. The definition that best conveys its far-reaching scope and nature is the one that Dr. Hofer gives in his book, *Strategy Formulation: Analytical Concepts*. "Strategy is the fundamental pattern of present and planned resource deployments and environmental interactions that indicates how the organization will achieve its objectives." There is more to this definition than meets the eye, as will be seen in due time.

the birth of strategy

Strategy isn't new. Some like to claim it all began with Hammurabi, or with guys like Alexander the Great and Charlemagne (whom historians refer to as the Great Administrator).[1] But in business it is a relative newcomer.

Although I don't wish to burden you with a lengthy dissertation on its origins, the background leading to it is important so you can understand why you must master it in order to make the most of your career.

In its brief history, organized business has gone through two major phases and is now embarking on a third. The first phase was the Era of the Entrepreneur, which went from around 1880 to 1950. In those days, strategy was pretty simple since the economic environment was pretty simple. If they needed a railroad in Kansas to get the produce or cattle to the eastern markets, a well-heeled robber baron came in and built one. Apart from the messy political intrigues that were usually involved, there was nothing very complex about it. The strategies were always very obvious.

After World War II, the second phase—the Era of the Professional Manager—got under way. Tactical things, like production technology and marketing methods, became very sophisticated, but strategy was still pretty easy. Markets were growing so fast, all you really had to do to be a success was to get into them. This pretty well sums up the 1950s and the 1960s. It was a big banquet, and we're still paying for it. One of the Professional Manager Era's mixed blessings was the emergence of really elegant marketing ideas. Rather than let the factory manager decide what to make, as in days of old, the marketing manager determined what people would buy, and ordered the factory to make it. Unfortunately this got out of hand and led to some very unprofitable situations, as inflation and high interest rates made it impossible to support the huge working capital outlay required by ambitious marketing programs that too often promised more than they delivered. This is where the Era of Professional Management ended up in the early 1970s: A lot of companies simply ran out of cash.

The third phase, the Era of Strategic Management, came to the rescue. (Since strategic management is still totally untapped, as far as most companies go, you can't blame it for our current economic plight.)

No one knows who invented strategic management. In all likelihood it was a lowly, frustrated tactician who was rewarded with being able to keep his or her job a while longer. Personally, I think it a poor commentary of all the tactician's well-paid, corporate proto-strategist antecedents that they didn't think of it sooner.

Strategic management was crying out to be discovered. Its premise is so simple that even a Junior Achievement participant might have framed it: "What causes profit?" No doubt an old-style entrepreneur would answer: "Profits come from making your product cheaply and selling it at a whopping high price." The professional manager would sound somewhat more sophisticated: "Profits are derived from huge sales volumes, loyal customers, and sexy products supported by impressive advertising compaigns." Any accountant would inform you that the answer is readily apparent in your Profit and Loss Statement. But all would be dead wrong.

Even early strategic managers didn't have the answer at first. But they were determined to find out the answer by studying a large number of different businesses. Some of these businesses they selected for perusal were making lots of money, others were average, and the rest were out-and-out losers. They pulled together as much information about these businesses as they could get their hands on, and they went way beyond the traditional accounting data that had previously formed the sole basis for solid business analysis. (I'm sure they chuckled at such quaint notions as the "current ratio" and the "acid test ratio" as they developed their bank of data.) They looked at market shares, market growth rates, product quality (what would their accountants do with that one?), R&D expenditures, productivity, vertical integration (the old make vs. buy issue), and lots of other things. At this point they were juggling so many factors that they had trouble keeping everything straight. So they reserved time on a computer. (In those days you had to beg the payroll, sales order, and accounts receivable people to let you have time on the big hulky machine over the weekend.) They plugged in a rather elegant multiple regression program, and let the circuits do the grunt work of digesting all this data.

But rather than bore you with an explanation of the math these early strategic managers used, let's just go straight to an illustration. I've observed that you can't go wrong if you keep your illustrations focused on old-fashioned rural values, so let's say you have this farm. Your county agent gives you some advice on how much rain, sunshine, seed, fertilizer, herbicide, and so on it takes to grow a good crop of corn. Now you know that you'll never get a perfect season—the weather is usually lousy. But a well-versed, multivariate analysis can tell you what to do if you get only half the required amount of rain or if you goof and dump too much fertilizer on the field. This analysis could tell you also what kind of outcome to expect with any other combination of these factors. Farming being what it is, though, you'd never be able to figure it out in your head because the relationships between all these factors are anything but simple. Instead, they're exponential. So, if you want to be a successful farmer, you really need that computer analysis. In like manner, the early development of strategic management was aided by the availability of a good, multivariate analysis. Many companies use this approach today to formulate new strategies, although it's not always necessary.

The first really good crack at strategic management, as far as history notes, was pulled off at General Electric. This company, which invented so many of the marvels of the modern age, also invented the first workable approach to the scientific formulation of strategy. All of this was based, of course, on trying to answer that first simple question: What causes profit?

GE found that there were, indeed, several ascertainable causes. It uncovered about 30 factors that play a part in producing profit. These factors seemed to have a universal application; it didn't really matter what business you were in so much as the way you happened to be in that business. You could have two different zinc mining companies, for example, with one making a lot of money because it had those 30 factors put together right, and with the other zinc firm losing money because its 30 factors were assembled incorrectly.[2] Or, conversely, you could have two quite different businesses—a chicken plucking service and an engineering design firm—both of which had the same return on investment because the factors, for each, were arranged in a given way. (It's just like putting together the magic combination of sunlight, moisture, and fertilizer down on the farm.)

Some proponents of strategic management like to use the following medical analogy to advance its cause: If a guy visits his doctor with an ailment, the doctor will perform many tests: from an analysis of these tests the doctor will be able to determine what is wrong with the patient and prescribe a cure. In the same vein, the business that visits the strategic management "doctor" could have its 30 factors tested and assessed and then be given a "prescription" for whipping itself into better shape.

This multifactored grist has worked its way into the strategizing mills of many of our top firms—even into those firms that long felt only simplistic elements contributed to their success. For example, take the Coca-Cola Company. Coke's chief financial officer, Sam Ayoub, proclaimed, "I don't want to criticize previous administrations (of this company), but in all honesty, there was a period when this company was dominated by purely marketing and operating people, and the financial side was neglected. Now there is a realization that there has to be a balance."[3] Today, it is almost impossible to do business without being fully cognizant of the interplay of the vital factors that constitute a business strategy. Only pure luck will get you the success that a thorough factor-scan can produce. It also follows that personal experience, without such redoubtable analysis, isn't going to be much good.

why strategy cannot be based on personal experience

There is no reason why you should let yourself be intimidated by the rank amateurs who currently may wear the strategy crowns in your firm. For most of them the sustained rigors of actually boning up on the laws of strategy would be too great a mental strain. As you have probably noticed, they seldom read your memos. Living fulfillments of Marshall McCluhan's media-is-message theory, they probably don't read much of anything. Instead, talking a lot and listening a little, but on the whole intellectually apathetic, they think you can create business strategy like Bronson—at first with gut feelings and later based on experience. They are mistaken.

Strategies, you see, happen to have very long time horizons. From introduction to maturity, a new consumer product can take up to five years. The struggle to get a new nuclear generator on line could take an electric utility over 15 years. How many people do you know who stay in the same job as long as that? And how often do strategies go from inception to natural maturity and eventual demise without being altered, aborted, or pummelled beyond recognition by competition? The fact is that personal experience is not much good here. Even CEOs in major corporations would have lived through only a few unfractured strategies during their careers. Not enough to make even them experts.

A lot of what passes for experience is flawed recollection. Often this comes pretty close to being sheer fiction. To the strategist, who lives by documented results, truth is not only often stranger than fiction, but also *truer*.

Even if his or her memory is good, the Bronson type of armchair strategist who falls back on experience for guidance is often guilty of drawing on *matched-dependent-behavior*—a pretentious psychological term that describes the drive to do things based on past experience because those strategies succeeded in the past. But as the brat who holds his breath to get his own way eventually must discover, past behavior does not always succeed in later life. In business, a perceived strategy that once worked may have done so because the enveloping circumstances were entirely different than those in the present. That's why master strategists churn together all situational factors before they forge workable strategies. Succumbing to the lure of past experience is as fey as assuming that your boss will be as permissive as your parents if you try jockeying your way to power by holding your breath.

Many fogbound companies are, of course, run by iron executives who impose their ancient and often fuzzily recalled experience at every strategic crossroad. If the iron executive is a bloody genius, the company might do quite well, but generally, as an iron executive's business picks up an elevated level of complexity, its chances for success dwindle along with its spirit. "That to live by one man's will became the cause of all men's misery."[4]

The incubus of a dependency on past experience in strategy formulation can get you snagged on the burrs of another psychological phenomenon, *selective perception*, which I'm sure most readers have been gudgeoned by more than once: Selective perception is at work when a vital project fails to leave the drawing board because the boss finds it too complex or too boring to think about, or where a new product is allowed to go national even though it flopped in test market because of someone's personal commitment to it and a refusal to accept major changes in the economic environment (the cardinal sin of U.S. auto and steel folks).[5] Above all, the master strategist's are objective and resist the beckoning call of their personal investment in a project, lest it becloud the analysis of factors impinging on their forging of sound strategies. Moreover, strategists must arm themselves against the importunity of those basing their judgments on superficial appearances or misinformation received from self-serving manipulators.

strategy and economic rot

Someone recently said that the United States can't really be much of a democracy when we all feel so powerless. No one can be totally oblivious to the economic malaise gripping the Western world, but few like to admit how deep the rot has gone. It's far beyond the point where an economic cure can be effected by spurring our workers to perform like Mitsubishites (the morning set-ups and so on) for the rot now infects our mental equipment, enfeebling our wills and management styles so badly it shows. Some Americans remember, with nostalgia, how they used to receive celebrity treatment on foreign business trips. Now the Europeans, who once doted on their every word, no longer bother to listen, and the Japanese listen only out of culturally induced politeness.

Lulled by the heavy traffic of past glories, U.S. business languishes in an introspective funk. Few external, corrective measures have appeared to alter its destructive, rag-tag, inward-looking complacency. It is ominously reminiscent of the old American Catholic Church, so aptly described in *Bare Ruined Choirs*: "In the small world of rectory and convent, the intellectual level kept sinking....There, in the dark, oddities of belief were bred." How similar this is to American business, whose inward bound, tactical wheel-spinning has produced "oddities of belief" about what it takes to be successful and a ghetto mentality regarding any other country that happens to be propelled by more artful strategies.[6]

Our strategic superficialities, our hussar impatience with trying to hone that final edge of strategic excellence, have driven us, as the British might say, into a sticky patch. I'm sure few readers want to devote their careers to trying to beat the Russians, but it's always in the back of our minds. So, should we be encouraging them? This is what our dithering and fumbling, our declining standard of living, and our sputtering tax base are doing. Time is running out. The managers who look good right now are just executing a mopping-up plan extending from the halcyon days of a rich but prodigal past. In parts of Smokestack America this has already run its course; in others the end is nigh. The mopping-up managers have duped themselves and others into concluding that it is their management acumen that produce the success rather than the fallout from an accidental and fortuitous

1950-1973 congruence of strategic factors that may never occur again *without* definitive human authorship. The human author we have in mind is, of course, the master strategist to whom we present the puissant task of reordering our economy and saving the free enterprise system. Is this being overly dramatic? We'll see, but I don't think anybody else is going to have the answers.

failure bound

It bothers me when my kids say they wish they could have lived in the 1960s. When I was a kid, everyone looked forward to an exciting future. But already many of us have given up. Some are desperately hoping to grab the golden ring on the next roundabout in the Industrial Revolution. "Space, telecommunications, information," they think, "all this high-tech stuff, that's what's going to save us." This assumption requires a tremendous suspension of disbelief, as if a new technology and a few new products cannot be copied by hungry offshore competitors or rendered obsolete overnight by even more advanced technologies. Others are simply content to blunder ahead, reinvesting in doomed industries, like the steelmakers who have dumped billions into an industry that was generating a return on equity of only 6 percent or so. Others seek salvation in diversification, fitfully hoping to escape the clutches of industries they know only to fall into the jaws of industries they know nothing about. Regardless of the scenario, those who are victims of inadequate strategic analysis will all fail.

Our fear of the Japanese peril is justified only so long as we fail to pull up our socks and start being more professional about strategy. Japan is not, it should be pointed out, the consummate strategist of the world; in fact, Japan, in a very real sense, has succeeded not through the superiority of its own strategies but by exploiting the weaknesses found in ours, as this book will make clear.

basic concepts of strategy

Strategy formulation is no job for those who prefer to get by—as many have been—performing roles instead of functions, by being visibly active rather than productive. It does require extensive, concentrated analysis. But it's basic concepts are not as hard to learn as high school algebra. All you have to do is get away by yourself and think things through before you can hammer out the best possible strategic plans. But before we go further, let's return for one minute to the continuing saga of the development of strategic management; that'll help establish its conceptual foundation.

We were talking about GE and the factors it unearthed with direct sway over profitability. GE learned that if a manager knew which factors were weak and was able to fix them (i.e., develop a new strategy addressing the weaknesses), the manager's business produced better results. Shortly after GE made this discovery, the Harvard Business School convinced GE to grant the school's Marketing Science Institute the right to use its findings and methods as a research tool. Eventually a group called the *Strategic Planning Institute* came out of this. The SPI is a nonprofit organization supported by several corporations who feed it all their critical business data. With hundreds of separate businesses in its data bank it can do a lot of profound and useful contemplation about strategy. Its PIMS Program is one of the most definitive statements on how strategy works, (and from time to time I'll be referring to some of its findings). There are now, of course, many other strategy data banks, but the SPI's research staff is the most industrious, and one can have a high degree of confidence in its work and pronouncements.

There are two basic things that all of the advanced strategic analyses depend on and which we should keep in mind when tackling strategic problems:

First, the factors that are associated with profits work in teams, never alone. For example, in my chapter on marketing I will discuss how market share and market growth go together (i.e., neither one on its own being a sole determinant of success) and, as you will see, the way they mesh is often rather surprising, perhaps even startling, to those choosing to disregard it.

Second, *basic* strategies can be put together only for business units, not for the whole corporation. The reasons are obvious. One is that you can take a different direction in some units than in others, so you have to have different plans. If you make both space-age telecommunications equipment and rural crank-style telephones, you'd obviously be spending rather aggressively on the former, and probably milking the latter. Apart from some very general kinds of statements, there is no such thing as a basic corporate strategy; there is only business unit portfolio management (see Chapter 13), and once you know how to formulate strategies at the unit level, the so-called corporate strategies become rather obvious.

strategic business unit

Because of the ground rules formulated through advanced strategic analysis, a new term crept into the jargon, *strategic business unit*, or *SBU* for short. An SBU is a lot like a product group or a market segment. For example, Kelloggs would probably consider their Frosted Flakes as part of the presweetened SBU and regular Corn Flakes as part of the regular breakfast cereal SBU. Meanwhile, Quaker Oats would say there was yet another breakfast cereal SBU, the one in which their hot oatmeal brand belongs. Size of market has nothing to do with this. Each SBU has to be discrete. It must be able to have its own set of strategies, customers, and assets. Usually you can recognize an SBU on sight, but sometimes there will be quite a loud debate about it. The key thing is the SBU's strategic independence from other business units.

rivals on strategy road

You may be wondering if you have what it takes to become a strategist and what kind of competition you are going to be up against.

There is always going to be competition; you will have to step on some toes, but the roadblocks aren't going to be that tough. If you want to be a world-class strategist, if you wish to shuck the encumbrances of tactical dithering, all you require is the will and a modicum of effort and application. Your competition probably won't be very sophisticated. Closely paralleling Long John Silver's characterization of his fellow pirates— "We're all foc's'le hands, you mean. We can steer a course, but who's to set one?"[7]—their most strategic opus is rehashing the game in their Monday morning quarterback sessions, where their emulations of famous coaches, players, and managers totally miss the fact that there are few great teams and even fewer competent managers, the majority being little more than marginal windbags. The allusion is intentional: It is marginal performance that has become the accepted standard in business and has turned us into a borderline nation of elegantly groomed supervisors, with laidback charms and easy solutions, who prefer cutting deals to hard analysis and vigorous planning. Your competitors in the contest to usurp control of corporate strategy-setting have risen to the top echelons with little more than native survival skills, with only some vague, inner vision powered by a low wattage bulb, which the rational strategist would be able to snuff out with a few minutes of critical analysis.

strategists and the national purpose

Only through the strategist can American industry turn around and regain its sense of purpose. Only the strategist has that clear-sighted view that can rescue the nation from its narrow-viewed doldrums.

Many of our best companies are managed by tactical volkerwan-derungen—mass-migrating short-termers wandering from company to company, failing to garner any worthwhile, personal strategic insights available through the application of the principles of strategic management, and never identifying with any company they serve. They lack the mind-set to chart their companies' courses. In private, over drinks, most executives talk like they are not even part of the company they work for. Though they may have virtually unlimited jurisdiction over their bailiwick, they refer frequently to "them" rather than "us," and assume a rather defeated air complete with shoulder-shrugging about the "hopeless" situations "they" face.

Lacking a mature strategic orientation, some fall into one of the most pernicious of all the traps awaiting the decision maker: the bigger the problem, the less likely the intellect will be called on to solve it. It has been this way all through history. Man invariably becomes less rational as the problem gets more serious. He'll fall back on tradition ("That's the way we've always done it."), defensiveness, and anything else that comes along to spare him the burden of applying his intellect.

So much of our nation's business is in the hands of the uncommitted, short-sighted decision makers who often squander their energies on inconsequential matters, letting the most vexing problems drift. With this as our defense, we must fight off the invading army from industrialized nations who seem not to have our problems of will, organization, and strategy.

Master strategists offer approaches that can help us avoid these mistakes. Their strategies are capable of addressing the issues, separating fact from opinion in the process, and seeking the highest possible long-run returns without regard for any personal, emotional involvement. In so doing they can produce strong fiscally solvent corporations that serve the national purpose in an infinite number of direct and peripheral ways.

any tactician can become a strategist

The tactician has a chance to become a strategist. Strategy is no longer regarded as the province of gridiron game planners and company politicans. It now belongs to anyone who wants to do the thinking and analysis required of it. If you make the effort and learn the formulas for high profits, you're going to be in much better shape than the joker who does not. And most of your rivals, for all of the reasons mentioned above, are not going to move their butts to acquire this knowledge. You don't even have to worry when they try to block your efforts by denying you entry into their meetings, since you can develop strategy on your own. All you need is the raw data and a knowledge of the laws of strategy.

The following chapters are going to give you most of those laws.

*Rope of Sand, a Hal B. Wallis production, directed by William Dieterle, screenplay by Walter Doniger, released by Paramount Pictures, Inc., 1949.

1. John P. Fitzgerald, "The Three Levels of Strategic Choice," *Journal of Business Strategy*, 1, no. 4 Spring 1981, p. 52.

2. Sidney Schoeffler, Robert D. Buzzell, and Donald F. Heany, "Impact of Strategic Planning on Profit Performance," *Harvard Business Review*, March-April 1974, p. 139.

3. John Huey, "New Top Executives Shake Up Old Order at Soft-Drink Giant," *Wall Street Journal*, November 6, 1981, p. 1.

4. Richard Hooker, *Ecclesiastical Polity, Book I*, 1553-1600.

5. Mortimer Feinberg, and Aaron Levenstein, "How Do You Know When to Rely on Your Intuition?" *Wall Street Journal*, June 21, 1982, p. 14.

6. Garry Wills, *Bare Ruined Choirs*, (New York: Doubleday, 1971).

7. Robert Louis Stevenson, *Treasure Island* Collins' Clear-Type Press London, no date, p. 82.

3
failsafe marketing strategy

"How quickly the silver tarnishes. How quickly a conquest turns heavy."

TOADY (PETER LORRE), ROPE OF SAND

the shopworn marketing concept

The art of shaping strategy in sales and marketing used to be kid stuff. Back in the 1960s you were anointed "master strategist" if you followed what they called the "marketing concept." The idea was that the consumer's wants and needs had to serve as the basis of all your efforts from new product development, through manufacturing and packaging, to advertising and promotions. Fortunes were spent on market research discovering what consumers really wanted. Pandering to their needs became your strategy.

The marketing concept is still around and occasionally flashes down as new-found illumination upon the small towns of America via the easy-think luncheon club circuit. It has an intuitive, face-value appeal. Actually, there's nothing terribly wrong with giving consumers what they want, as far as it goes (and obviously, unless you work for the government or follow Jane Fonda, you wouldn't go out of your way to do the converse). But the marketing concept has a nasty habit of riveting your attention. It takes your mind off other things that are more important, like making a maximum amount of profit or assuring **17** a nice, steady, positive flow of cash.

In fact, a lot of companies, both big and small, got into a lot of trouble because of being shackled to the shopworn marketing concept. Take Chrysler for example; they tried to match G.M. and Ford car for car, model for model, color for color. Or just stroll through any supermarket and look at the rows of toilet soap. Even Hollywood fell victim to the marketing concept; most TV stations have film libraries stacked with cans of recent look-alike movies that had no box-office appeal. If everyone gives the consumers what they want, then everyone ends up making virtually the same product.

This is precisely what the marketing concept strategy did. It ended up with a world-wide spate of "me too" products. As if that wasn't bad enough, the economy conspired to make such a strategy totally impractical. Soaring inflation and its burden of high interest rates made the working capital commitment on all those models, sizes, colors, and packaging variations unaffordable. Costs per unit shot up, and the marketing concept was booted out the window wherever good strategists had their way.

the strategy of restraint

There is a smarter way to market your product or service. I call it the *strategy of restraint*, because in many regards it requires that you tell yourself no, to hold back, to go only into certain segments of the market, or go with just certain products. It tells you what criteria to look for and what goals to shoot for to make more profit, rather than simply, and wantonly, to court the consumer. With the strategy of restraint you can become better at marketing than the glamour boys of the go-go 1960s. It's like the old racetrack metaphor about the mule and the thoroughbred. Both can get around the track, but the thoroughbred does it more efficiently. By harnessing the strategy of restraint, you can end up with a better bottom-line for a lot less work. If Chrysler had employed the strategy of restraint, they would not have had to drag their shareholders and employees through so much fiscal agony.

The strategy of restraint eschews the muscle-flexing associated with the overtly aggressive marketing postures of the moribund marketing concept. Instead, its foundation is a healthy appreciation for laws of marketing that extend, by the way, far beyond the stalwart, agrarian virtues and precepts embraced by conventional, lumbering corporate decision makers. These laws may be different from what you expect and may involve getting in tune with a few things you've not worried much about before. Of course, the factors that go into these laws will be familiar, but the way they relate to one another may be new and even innovative. I speak of factors like market share,

market growth rates, pricing, product quality, R&D, product differentiation, new product activities, market segmentation, and "value." I'll
cover the first two in this chapter and the rest in later chapters.

profit and market shares

Let's begin by taking a close look at market share. Market share is
your sales as a percentage of the total market. And it's of monumental
importance. It closely governs your financial performance. For the
average business the market share will be double its return-on-
investment, so as market share climbs so does ROI. It is an immutable
law that market share and profits are inseparable.[1]

There are many reasons why this happens. The most obvious is
economy of scale—a share increase usually means a volume increase.
But there is a lot more to it than that. Hidden factors are at work here.
Big market shares signify a loyalty from your customers that lets you
get away with fewer expensive sales inducements than your less
fortunate competitors with their burden of fickle patrons. Distribution
is also easier to get and keep, since the trade can't afford to disappoint
their patrons. Accordingly, fewer trade allowances are required. In
other words, while your smaller share competitors live only to grovel
at the feet of their benefactors, you can go through life in cavalier
fashion.

Perhaps the key reason why share and profits are so closely
linked is the *learning curve* effect. Any business with fairly alert
management will notice that, as its volume increases, it finds better
ways to run its operation. Hence, unit costs go down. Someone even
found a formula for it: Every time sales double, the per unit, added-
value costs drop 20 to 30 percent.[2] So not only does the big share
business benefit from sheer sales volumes relative to its punier rivals,
it also grows more efficient in the process by an almost universal and
protracted learning curve effect.

It has taken a long time for the diehards in the world of finance
to recognize the awesome role of market share. But even Wall Street
security analysts, who once contented themselves with columns of
accounting data, now demand to know a company's market shares.

You may not be lucky enough to work with people who have yet
learned this. You may be under pressure from reckless bottom-line
artists who want you to sacrifice market share (by cutting out your
advertising, for example) in order to show a quick profit. If you permit
your share to drop—for any reason—earnings will eventually suffer.
Not only do you have to fend off the quick-profit seekers, but you
better make sure your pals in manufacturing can guarantee you
enough factory capacity to serve your future needs. Even a tempo-

rary bottleneck will cause your share to plummet as competition moves in to take up the slack. Speaking of competition, you'd better keep your eye on competitors too. Don't let them lure away your customers with product improvements. Keep this in mind: it's easier to keep your market share up than it is to let it slip and have to claw your way back up. Diminished profits await the unsuspecting who are lulled into disregarding the cardinal importance of market share.

don't be fooled by growth markets

Another crucial profit control item is how rapid your overall market is growing. Almost everyone instinctively feels that a fast-growing market is nicer than a slow-growing or declining market. Crude thinkers are attracted to the growth market like lizards to the sun. But they are useful only for very long-range pursuits. For now, in order to support your operation today, you should learn to love and appreciate the unglamourous slow-growth market and use it as an opportunity to support your future schemes.

This is best demonstrated by taking a look at an interesting method of combining the two factors we've just discussed: market share and market growth. Figure 3-1 illustrates it best.

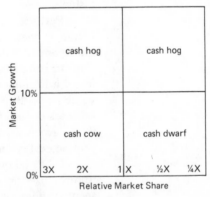

FIGURE 3-1.*The Market Matrix*

Growth is usually defined here as a past five-year average in constant (i.e. removing the effects of inflation) dollars. Relative market share is your product's share as a proportion of the biggest of your competitor's. This is know as a *market matrix*. It is used for SBUs or product categories (like dog food), or market segments (like dry dog food), and seldom for entire industries (like pet food). If you are in charge of several different kinds of products, you can chart them all on this matrix. Borrow your kid's colored pencils to keep the different categories straight. Don't worry about getting all the numbers exact. Approximations are fine.

The market matrix is used to calculate (or predict) the most important of all financial goals: cash flow. (See Chapter 8 for a discussion of the vital nature of cash flow.) It was developed originally by the Boston Consulting Group[3] but is used as a quick, handy tool by a lot of business strategists. It embodies a compelling logic about markets, marketing strategies, and responding to competition. If you can memorize the principle I am about to unfold, you will demolish your opponents whose subjective air-and-blather will be no match for your powerful strategic thrust.

The matrix is divided into four squares. Note where the cut-lines are. One is at 10 percent growth, the other at market share parity. These aren't just arbitrary divisions. Experience shows that cash flow and marketing success are governed by laws that change from one square to another. Where your product falls on the matrix determines what kind of business strategy you should have and what your cash flow is likely to be.

cash cow

Since they are so different, let's look at each square one by one. First, the best one: the lower-left square. Punchline: This is the only square that gives you a positive cash flow. Why? You will recall our contempt for the knee-jerk executive who worshipped at the shrine of market growth. What this corner-office cipher never stopped to think was that working capital needs (cash, accounts receivable, raw materials, inventories, etc.) would grow faster than customers would pay off their accounts because of the built-in time delay. This time delay can be a real threat when the market (and presumably sales) grow at a menacingly rapid rate. Hence, this executive would have cash going out faster than it was coming in—in other words, a negative cash flow. Now you can understand why the "mature" market is nice to have around. But it's not much use to you unless you dominate much of it. Most markets will only support three contenders, and the rest of the pack will be able to live only on hope and not on a positive cash flow.[4]

So it is the combination of big market share and slow growth that provides today's success and pays its bills. Boardroom Neanderthals may not think that this is the sexiest of pairings, but if they give you any trouble, ask them what they think they would do without a positive cash flow. Borrow until their debt-to-equity ratio sends an alarm over the tickertape? Sell a new issue of company stock with only a dim hope of fetching a decent price? If the cash isn't coming in faster than it's going out the door, like the poor soul in the Federal Express commerical, he's out of business. And having a product in the lower-left square is the only salvation. By the way, the name the master strategists give such a product is a "cash cow." Speaks for itself, doesn't it?

Obviously it is *de rigueur* to try to breed as many cash cows as you can. If you don't have any now, it's probably too late to go in for creating them in mature markets. It's wiser to start in a growth market (I'll cover that in my discussion of the upper-left square). Meanwhile, if you have a cash cow currently, here's what you should do: Be defensive. That's all. Just protect yourself. Don't go for a bigger market share (unless you can do it for free). Remember, this is your big chance to fill the corporate coffers. Don't blow it. Spend money only to ward off competition. They're going to be sniffing around because they know you've got a good thing going and not all of them are sophisticated enough to understand the folly of such behavior and the ruinous consequences to their own cash streams. You are always going to have to contend with the primitives inside and outside your own organization. But to be successful, you should live by the laws of strategy. Avert competition with just enough spending to make competitors feel uncomfortable. Play dirty. Announce a major plant expansion to convince them you're in this business to stay. Their instincts will tell them you'll stop at nothing to protect your turf and allow this "new plant" to hum along at optimum capacity. Make them believe that any attempt to lead your cash cow to slaughter would be futile and dangerous.

A case of a fumble, a recovery, and some interesting unintended side-effects in this square is seen in the soft contact lens business. When Bausch and Lomb brought out the soft lens in the early 1970s, they had the market virtually to themselves and were able to command very high prices (about $300 a pair), but they had a habit of treating the retailer rather highhandedly, giving an "in" for competition to gain distribution. When Bausch responded to these competitive inroaders with some applications of hardball marketing skills, this incipient competition was hurt quite badly. But, instead of folding up their display cases and stealing away silently, they sought refuge in the arms of large corporate acquirers, like Revlon and Ciba-Geigy, who had the financial and technological weapons to confront Bausch in a fairer fight. Hence, what could and should have been a nice, fat cash cow for Bausch (what with all the marketing activity going on) became a touch-and-go growth market with an insatiable need for cash support when retail prices plunged to $100 a pair and lower. Still, the long-term goal of making the business into a cash cow rested on Bausch's ability to hang onto its still impressive market share until the market matured. "Market share is a religion with us," said B&L President Dan Gill. "We will defend that market share on a global basis."[5]

high share cash hogs

Meanwhile, don't go to sleep. Think upper-left square. This is your future, especially if you don't presently have a cash cow. But even if you have, they're all going to die one day. All markets expire. It may take years or decades, but eventually they all collapse. So get busy on the cash cows of the future. Don't let opportunities slip through your fingers like the old Saturday Evening Post did back in 1939 when Bill Paley, in need of scarce depression era financing, begged them to buy out his fledgling CBS network. The Post scoffed at such a suggestion from this upstart. Today the Post is dead (a new magazine later used the Post name) and CBS is a vast cash fountain—a herd of cash cows by anyone's standards.

You could breed your cash cow by inventing a whole new product category, or by coming in fast on the tail of someone else's invention. The easier route, however, is to "segment" a market. This means taking a current product category (like breakfast cereal) and creating a new subcategory (like presweetened breakfast cereal), which, with proper promotion, you can make into a market segment with its own discrete set of characteristics.[6] If you are successful in establishing the new segment, you will be able to claim your spot in the market matrix's upper-left square, since being first grants you automatic market share leadership. You can't live long in the hope you'll occupy this spot in the sun all by yourself. You can't see them yet, but over the horizon is an army of sharpshooters on the march. They are gunning for you. This is the square where your most aggressive instincts must bear fruit. Fight off intruders with heavy advertising and flawless activities. Expand your distribution network. Use irresistible trade incentives if necessary. Spend like mad. Your goal is market share.

This is a cash hog square, however. Don't expect to see any profit or a positive cash flow for a while (until growth slows). Like sex, it's better if you wait.

If you just missed being first and already have competition, now is the time to try to build up your market share. If the growth in this market segment is exciting and its volumes generous, it will attract more contenders than it can actually support. Soon there will come the dreaded shake-out phase. The weaklings will withdraw or be told to get lost by the trade or the consumer. If you survive the shake-out and hang on a bit longer, you'll have yourself a nice, healthy cash cow once growth drops to below the 10 percent line. Then you'll have the cash stream to do it all over again with another new venture. This is the square where you have the most fun and attract the most attention from top management. It's worth doing well.

A good object lesson in the art of performing fancy footwork in this square can be shown by tracing the progress of Atari. Back in 1972 the pinball machine business was a mature market with its cash cows and cash dwarfs. Atari burst on the scene by creating a new, coin-operated market segment: a coin-operated video-game called Pong. When its success attracted the usual horde of competitors, Atari's share fell to 10 percent. But Atari's boy-genius founder, Nolan Bushnell, simply side-stepped pending doom by entering another market segment: a home version of the (dedicated) video-game. And then, when this market waned, Atari quickly pulled off a dramatic marketing coup by introducing a programmable game guided by a changeable semiconductor chip. To ward off competition, they did something that was considered extremely unorthodox for the toy industry—they advertised year-round, not just prior to Christmas. In 1979 Atari had a whopping 80-share of a booming growth market, and a product that fulfilled a dream of Gillettean proportions—a continuing, razor-blade-like consumer buying pattern for cartridges, on which there was a 50 percent operating margin.[7] Today, the Atari dream continues, but when this fast developing market will mature is anyone's guess.

low share cash hog

But you can't always have things work out so nicely. What if you find yourself with a business or product in the upper-right square? It's another cash hog situation that makes you a prisoner of a negative cash flow. And if you keep doing what you are doing now, the future is bleak; when the market's growth rate moderates, you'll drop down below, where you're likely to continue to experience rotten cash flow. There is still hope. But it will require strenuous effort. Back in the 1930s a guy named Chester Carlson had a product that would have been positioned in this square. It was a novel electro-static printing process that he tried to peddle to the rapidly growing mimeographic firms. Bloated with success, they were not interested. So Carlson started his own company—and Xerox became a diverse portfolio of many cash cows. Carlson followed a strategy that any deserving, upper-right square product can use to get across the line onto the left-bank and later into the cash cow's pasture. (Today its competitors are using the same medicine against Xerox.)

Product differentiation was Carlson's central strength. Customers won't notice a "me too" business, a product, or a service that doesn't have a meaningful point of difference vis-a-vis all the other nonentities in the same category. So find a way to make yourself unique. Better quality (lemonade vs. lemonade-with-a-cherry) may be one way. Better packaging is another. Sometimes a cleaner, more elegant appearance works. Study your competition. If you can afford it, do some market research with their customers to uncover their underlying weaknesses. Then go to work on creating the ultimate, invincible answer to these weaknesses. If you still have any money in the budget, you could go back to the customer group and have them assess your creation. If they give it high marks, put together a marketing plan that exploits your advantages in the strongest possible terms. Be prepared to spend heavily on this. Xerox did it. So did a lot of others. You can too. But be coldly objective. Don't get personally involved. Be ready to drop your pet ideas if you don't get a glowing customer response. Lastly, if you start to taste success, keep the spending level up and don't let anyone pressure or urge you to take a profit until the market matures.

the cash dwarf

Now to the bad news. What if you're in the bottom-right square? You didn't buy this book to learn how to be mediocre. But that's what being in this square means. Everlasting mediocrity. Low market shares and mature markets are the hallmark of innumerable companies with feeble P-E multiples. Somehow they manage to survive, but they never produce outstanding returns. Market segmentation and spin-off strategies are almost the only ways you can improve your fortune. Going overboard on trying to improve your present product or service in a slow-growth market isn't a very attractive scenario because your high share competitor (the cash cow) isn't going to let you get away with much. Unless you have an inspired idea that the cash cow can't copy, you'd better seek a new market segment to improve your financial performance. As far as the current business goes, even the master strategists would struggle in vain against the odds of ever turning it into a cash producer. You should try to dump it. It could go as an acquisition to a company seeking synergy, or to someone just plain dumber than you. No one will be able to make it perform any better than you, but that's not your problem.

If you can't find any takers, then your next best strategy is to harvest. Harvesting is when you withdraw all marketing support and let the business die a slow, lingering death, during which time it will throw off some cash that you can invest in something more promising.

There is only one time you can justify holding on to a business that is in the lower-right square. That's when your learning curve has produced a situation where you have been able to exact an exceptionally high ROI despite your small share of the market. This doesn't happen very often, but you will see it occasionally in very old companies with ancient assets. However, when it comes time to renew their operating equipment at today's prices, they are in for a shock. The long-term prospect of the average occupant of this square is fading profits.

In the next chapters I'll continue discussing strategy in marketing and sales. I'll get into some additional considerations—like product quality, R&D, new products, "value," and pricing—that you need to know in order to work your way into the sweet pastures of the cash cow.

notes

1. *Basic Principles of Business Strategy* (Cambridge, MA: The Strategic Planning Institute, 1980), p. 23.

2. Bruce D. Henderson, *"Perspectives: The Experience Curve - Reviewed; I - The Concept,"* no. 124, (Boston, MA: The Boston Consulting Group, 1974), p. 2.

3. Bruce D. Henderson, *"Perspectives: The Experience Curve Reviewed; IV - The Growth Share Matrix or The Product Portfolio,* no. 135 (Boston, MA: The Boston Consulting Group, 1973), pp. 1-7.

4. Bruce D. Henderson, *"Perspectives: The Rule of Three and Four,"* no. 187 (Boston, MA: The Boston Consulting Group, 1974), pp. 1-4.

5. H.D. Menzies, *"The Hard Fight in Soft Lenses,"Fortune*, July 27, 1981, pp. 56-60.

6. There's more than one way to segment a market besides just product innovation. Product attribute appeals can be employed on a regional basis where customers differ geographically in what they seek in a product. For example, it is reported ("Business Bulletin,"*Wall Street Journal*, November 14, 1982, p. 1) that Texans emphasize horsepower and acceleration in their cars, while Californians go for reliability and comfort. Accordingly, G.M. makes its souped-up Buick Regal Grand National for folks like the Texans and markets the same car as the high-fashion Somerset Regal in sunny California. Even the concept behind the U.S. Football League is a form of segmentation. Planning an "off-season" (March–June) is strategically tantamount to attempting to create a whole new segment of fans.

7. P. W. Bernstein, "Atari and the Video-Game Explosion,"*Fortune*, July 27, 1981, pp. 40-46.

4

strategic pricing

So far we've seen how market share and market growth rates have a decided mastery over your forthcoming financial success. These two factors are the basic foundations for your overall business strategies. But, as you've probably thought to yourself, the growth rate of the market is a "given" you are powerless to change, and market share is merely a goal that (despite the strong intuitive appeal of what was outlined in the last chapter) you may have difficulty in pursuing. So, the question on your inquiring mind is: "How do we get where we want to go?"

The marketing strategy that leads you to the land of hyper-profit is leavened with a great deal of pragmatism, and its route map is annotated with many strategic considerations involving product quality, R&D, new products, "value," and pricing. In this chapter I will cover pricing. Occasionally I will stray into the quality/new product/ "value" regions, because these factors ultimately must be linked up, but I will reserve my intensive treatment of these factors for following chapters.

While pricing isn't as dull a subject as the marketing texts have made it, it still isn't much fun. The chore of having to determine the selling price for a product or service can give you an attack of colitis. Nonsupply-siders may deem this a psychosomatic reaction to our irrepressible greed, but our visceral rumblings are surely easy to

27

vindicate. We justifiably fret over the possibility of pricing ourselves lower than necessary and thus missing out on the obvious accolades and security and opportunities provided by generous profits. In the interests of your long-term survival, that kind of blunder may be even more agonizing than the other kind that also provokes gastric upset—namely, pricing yourself so high as to put yourself beyond the monetary or psychological reach of the consumer. To placate our stomachs, and as an anodyne for intracorporate criticism, what we usually end up doing is to observe what competition does and price ourselves accordingly. That, as we shall see, is just about the dumbest thing we could do and the thinking behind it is based on nothing more than an economic myth.

As with all matters in the business world, the armchair strategists invariably fail to follow the best course. They are protean tacticians, but narrow and misguided strategists; their pricing gambits rarely make any sense whatever. In general, they are neither concerned with nor successful at achieving the final edge of excellence that the implementation of sound pricing practices can produce.

goals

the two general strategic goals of pricing

Before we get into some of the principles of pricing strategy, we should take a brief look at our objectives. Borrowing from the concepts in our last chapter, we can arrive at two general pricing goals: pricing for growth and pricing for margins. Clearly, there are no other reasons for having a price policy; although sometimes it is necessary to straddle both goals at once.[1]

Pricing for growth forces us to have Jovian patience and a longer view of things. It makes us embrace a long-range commitment to the business and to stoutly resist that ardent and often feverish temptation urging us to syphon off any immediate positive cash flow. It lets us nobly use price as a means of engineering a more rapid growth in our sales (perhaps even in the overall market) and in our market share. The payoff is an eventual cash flow that will be more salutary than otherwise, once the market settles into its mature phase.

Pricing for margins is the flip-side of this. It emphasizes the short term and gives you the quick thrill of a positive cash flow, even though you will ultimately suffer—and maybe strangle—for not having seized the market share level your product had the capacity to attain.

This is a political world and such goal-setting realistically requires a look at your company's growth objectives, as well as its profit requirements, before you lock in on your goal. (If you are fairly low on the corporate totem pole, you probably have been told already what your goal is.) Additionally, you have to look beyond the confines of your own operation to see what is happening in your market and even beyond. Technology and consumer lifestyles constantly change. If your assessment is that such changes are going to occur rather quickly, you may not have the time to play the pricing-for-growth game; there'd be no point to investing your immediate gains back into the business if the whole market will soon be rendered obsolete by new products or new processes. The fashion industry would be, and usually is, an obvious example of where you may as well take the money and run. In a less frenetic industrial environment, a reinvestment plan makes sense. Hence a good analysis of the entire macro-environment is an unavoidable and imperative preamble to price policy decisions.

These goals, of course, are simplistic in nature; as we shall see later, the price plot thickens and, in order to have a successful pricing policy, there are a number of things we must incorporate into our efforts in this area.

basic ground rules

using price to intimidate competition

As discovered in the last chapter, your productive capacity, and the effect it has on the decisions of your competitors, can often determine the market share profile of your whole industry. This is a critical element, and it bears heavily on some pricing decisions. Market shares, as I have belabored previously, can be very sticky. Your attempts to dislodge them with a price-cutting strategy may provoke a similar form of retaliation from your competition. But, if you have ample surplus capacity and a fairly competitive cost structure, you hold a giant whip. Your competition knows that, if they decide to invest the necessary funds to expand their capacity, you could inflict severe pain on them by lowering your prices and (if price means anything at all to the buyer) elevating your market share just enough to make your rivals impotent to utilize the extra capacity they have just installed. So, if they are canny, they are going to be very apprehensive about building that new plant and see it sit idle while the customers take advantage of your largesse. Of course, if you want this nasty little strategy to work, you need to have an effective communications system that makes your pricing intentions crystal clear to both customers and competition. Your sales force can be the vehicle for this. They're always crossing paths anyway with the competition's representatives, and this gambit would give them something worthwhile to chat about.

If you adroitly execute this strategy in a growth market, soon there will be a welcome shortage for your product and then you can raise your prices with impunity. That experience curve you have been building up (it only takes average managerial acumen to get something good out of this concept) will now culminate in your becoming an invincibly efficient producer who can fall back on aggressive price slashing and trade deals whenever competition appears on the brink of increasing capacity. In the small town where I grew up, the local hotel owner warded off competition completely for over 20 years with this strategy. As long as you frustrate your rivals' hankering for capacity expansion, you can master the market. Your market share will grow and your costs will decline. So, in one sense it is your productive capacity that lets you control prices and even the investment practices of the whole market.[2]

experience curve complexity

because the experience curve may be employed in your pricing decisions, a few added words about it are appropriate here. If you have a complex product, you may actually need to take a composite look at several different experience curves. For example, if your product uses different components, some of which you make, others which you buy outside, you'd have to plot the sales volume trends separately for each component before you could ascertain what was going to happen to your overall costs. Depending on how this factors out, a healthy increase in your overall output should offer you a predictable decline in your operating costs. This exercise tells you how much scope you will have for playing around with your prices. In like manner, you should be able to make a rough assessment of your competitors' experience curves to determine just how much they are going to be able to retaliate if you decide to cut your prices.

the role of market share

market share as a sweeping principle in pricing

So far I have established some of the broad theoretical underpinnings of pricing policies, but we still don't have enough to work with. It's nice to set broad goals and play with experience curves and flex your capacity muscles to intimidate the less intrepid competitor, but I'm not sure I have yet prescribed an efficacious remedy for your price-induced colitis. You need some more insights on this before you will begin to feel confident that you are going to endow yourself with the best possible price.

The trouble with all this is that your selling price does not function in a vacuum. It's tied in with just about everything else you do and with everything that happens to you. There is always going to be some exception or grave reservation about any generalized statement. As Professor Kingsfield told his class in *The Paper Chase*, "There is always another question." But as I go through the rest of this chapter, I think I can put some order to the chaos and remove most of the contradictions. So let's start off with a sweeping principle; later we will try to see how we can work with it in a diversity of pricing situations.

This principle is this: If you have the biggest market share, you can usually set the highest price. Now, we're not saying you should do this, but only that you can.

Your dominance of the market makes it rough on even your biggest competitor. Under normal circumstances, the Number Two brand cannot put his price up without shooting low-odds crap with his own market share. In some markets the trade is very resistant to any attempt to abridge its margins, especially on runner-up brands. And there are some product categories where intra-segment price differentiation simply isn't tolerated at the retail level, often because it simply cannot be enforced. The cigarette market is subjected to such intra-segment pricing restrictions. In other markets, consumers are highly disloyal and will switch brands at the first sign of a pricing disincentive, particularly when the brand is not supported by the quality of marketing effort that usually accompanies share leadership.

Even the most determined and skilled marketers can run into problems on this. It happened to Philip Morris. After buying Miller Beer in 1969 and using its incomparable know-how to bring it all the way from seventh to second place in sales, PMC grew concerned that their return-on-beer-assets was running at only 10 percent, which was scarcely better than what they could have gotten from a certificate of deposit. In 1980 they elected to jack up the price of Miller High Life 6 to 7 percent in order to get a better return rate. Unfortunately, this occurred during the lengthy reign of the "king of beers"; Budweiser held firm on its price and no doubt chortled as Miller's sales curve flattened like stale beer. After years of frothy growth ranging from 20 percent to 30 percent a year, their unilateral price hike called a halt to an almost unprecedented run of market success.[3]

Though it shouldn't happen to a dog, PMC also got caught in the crossfire between two giants in another product category. In 1978 they had acquired Seven-Up. Everyone then thought, "Wow, these are the people who turned Marlboro from a no-account lady's cigarette into the mightiest macho brand in the world. Now they're taking on the Coca-Cola Company, and they'll probably give them a good run for their money."

But, instead, they found themselves smack-dab in the midst of a vicious price-cutting and trade-dealing war between the two leading brands, Coke and Pepsi. Both colas were making extremely generous offers to steal distribution, shelf-space, and brand loyalty from each other. Philip Morris didn't believe in that sort of thing. "It cheapens the brand image and erodes brand loyalty," they surmised. Meanwhile, there was so much discounting going on in the soft drink market that Seven-Up's president, Ed Frantel, confessed, "I don't even know what 'regular price' is anymore." The price war between the giants raged on, and with no intention of retaliating in kind, Seven-Up's share began to slide, not much, but just enough to hurt. For a company with PMC's track record, any share decline is a corporate crisis.

The lesson here is that, if you aren't the market share leader, you are pretty much forced to follow the pricing policy of the leader, unless you have something uniquely appealing to offer. Seven-Up apparently didn't—even though some marketing dogmatists would claim that lemon-lime and cola don't compete directly. When the noise of a price war gets loud enough, notions about discrete market segments don't always matter to the consumer.

While all this was going on, Frantel claimed, "Had we been operating in a more conventional market, we would have fared better than we are today." Maybe so, but if you aren't the boss of the market (Seven-Up only had a 5.4 percent share, Coke 24.3 percent and Pepsi 18.0 percent) you normally don't call the pricing shots and a "more-rigid-than-thou" attitude just won't work.[4] There is no place to run and hide. You have to join the battle. Sitting on the sidelines means you're going to get beaned by a foul ball.

Why should this be? Why is market share so crucial? What do we know about the nature of market shares that we can use to establish a sound pricing policy? For one thing, most business analyses show that these market leaders usually have the "best quality" products—or, at least, the customers regard them this way. In many cases that is one reason why they got the biggest share in the first place. (Quality will be discussed in considerable detail, with full emphasis on its profit producing ramifications, in the next chapter.)

A rather fascinating article in the *Harvard Business Review* entitled "Market Share: a Key to Profitability" untangled part of this phenomenon by discovering that the high share-high, quality-high price triumvirate was most pronounced with infrequently purchased products.[5] In other words, the triumvirate did not apply as much with high frequency purchases—refrigerators vs. cigarettes, for example. The reasoning is that the low frequency item is usually a durable, commanding big bucks. So there is a fairly large dollar risk associated with buying it. This precipitates such anxiety that some buyers are glad to pay a premium to get the comforting reassurance of quality. Rightly or wrongly, they assume you get what you pay for.

The article also revealed another triumvirate uniting share and price with the overall number of customers in the market. When your market has only a few buyers, and when they are rather concentrated, they have much more effective bargaining power and they know what thumbscrews to tighten to keep prices down. Accordingly, your mammoth share won't help you a whole lot in maintaining high prices. But when there are many customers, and they are all spread out, they lack this power and they can't do much to influence you. Hence, your high share can be used to support high prices.

These are the general principles that apply here, but it's all relative, of course, and we have some rough and rocky terrain to traverse before we can hope even to begin to understand the intricacies of pricing strategy.

declining market shares

But what if you're not the market share king, and your share, in fact, has been slipping a little? Wouldn't a price cut be a good way to arrest the decline? You know the old story: cut prices, boost volumes, and— even though margins will suffer—you make a lot more money. Yes, this does make some sense, but the catch is that it's a crude strategy, and it might not work as well as some other things. For one thing, you don't have that experience curve effect enjoyed by the market leader. If a price cut is all you had in mind, the market leader could wisk you off like a speck of lint. Without the leader's impressive marketing and advertising backup, you might end up as one more "me too" item in a field of wimp competitors. Moreover, price cuts don't work in all industries anyway. Classic economists insist that some prices are inelastic, and the modern marketing expert realizes that this can be complicated immensely by the consumer's imponderable irrationality. A clumsily executed, sudden price cut can suggest a drastic lowering of quality. "I wonder what they're leaving out?" asks the suspicious customer. In many industries this halo effect can be a very treacherous and strong sanction against unelaborated price cuts.

It is therefore incumbent upon us to search further for the right way to use pricing to halt a market share decline.

There is a better way, using a combination of pricing and quality. When you offer a fairly high quality product at a relatively or unexpectedly low price, you give the consumer "value." Studies show that it is more likely that you'll gain share using a value-enhancer strategy than by going for a plain price-cutting strategy. Later in this chapter, I'll produce some data from these studies showing the pivotal role of value in your pricing strategy. For now, just remember that simplistic price-cutting is not the best road to travel if you want to bring a halt to a declining market share.

share vs. margins

Regardless of his or her background, and not entirely without reason, the average marketing executive is obsessed with market share. So am I, and after the big plug I gave it in the foregoing chapter, it's going to seem duplicitous to even suggest that such an obsession can deteriorate to a dangerous and single-minded fixation. But it can, and often does. I don't like to be a killjoy, but some marketing people have to be reminded constantly that they're still supposed to be running a business in which all knowledge doesn't emanate from Madison Avenue. Margins cannot be ignored.

I like the story Bill Stiritz, president of Ralston Purina, tells of his days at Pillsbury. It seems that a bright, young product manager in the grocery products division figured out a way to get his angel food mix share up. He cut his prices 20 percent. He was smart enough to try it first in a test market where he saw his sales volume double. Unfortunately, he was not smart enough to assess accurately the results of this test market. Flushed with success and with the eloquence that often accompanies it, the brandman sold the company on going national with his pricing recommendation. But this time competition was ready, and competition included Duncan Hines, made by Procter & Gamble, a company that would never be so foolish to try to sabotage a competitor's test market. Also, as we've said, market leaders call the shots. So when Pillsbury went national with their 20 percent price cut, competition matched them. Naturally, everyone's profits plunged. Pillsbury didn't get its share increase. And the product manager was fired. Bill Stiritz, who had observed the entire saga, was taught a lesson that many product managers never seem to learn: Respect profit margins, even at the expense of market share, unless you are in a growth phase of the market. "The end isn't just selling goods," Stiritz said, "but rather to earn an adequate return. That goal sometimes gets lost."[6]

I realize all this may sound terribly infantile to the small business owner who would be astonished that anyone could ever take eyes off margins, but it can easily happen in a large, high-powered corporation where the level of sophistication is so astronomical that commonplace matters are overlooked.

Let's carry our concerns about margins a step further: Margins receive a heightened importance during an inflationary period. We will now examine this at length.

coping with inflation

Being obliged to set prices in an inflationary economy is an easy way to end up in Ulcer Valley. Though insistently assured by our elected representatives that inflation will soon be brought under control, I somehow lack the necessary faith to peddle a book about strategy without addressing the problem, regardless of how long this book might be around. Even if I am wrong and the government does sort out this economic mess, all is not lost be reading this section, because there will always be an inflationary economy somewhere on the face of the globe where you can travel to apply the following principles.

Start off with this thought: Unless you are awfully lucky, or working for the mob, the profits your prices allow don't really keep up with inflation. You may be deluded into thinking that your ROI is fine if your asset base reflects book values. In only a smattering of companies has replacement value accounting caught on at the business unit level. General Electric has made it part-and-parcel of its everyday business planning, but few others seem willing to make the effort. But let's be realistic; you're going to have to replace all your assets one day. And if you are forced into accepting a price level that doesn't deliver enough cash to buy new assets at their highly inflated prices (many times the current book value) then your business simply is not very appealing. Alas, most businesses face this gloomy outlook today, and some see it worsening during periodic recessionary cycles that put the squeeze on cash and depress product demand so much that even the hint of a modest price increase is out of the question. With a general economic deepfreeze, and its low industrial capacity utilization, you cannot contemplate a price increase that does anything more than keep pace with inflation until demand begins to outstrip supply.

On the brighter side, the stronger your presence in the market, the better off you'll be in trying to combat inflation. Even then it won't be easy or necessarily very rewarding, but if you are weak, you will surely suffer more. For one thing, your low share makes you the high cost producer, which in turn gives you skimpy margins. To keep going, you have to finance your operation not only from earnings, which are clearly not sufficient, but also from long-term debt. So now you've got yourself saddled with the burden of high interest expense to intensify your agony. As a result you can't derive as much good from your price increase as your stronger cohorts. Now, you do have a few options. They aren't very attractive, but it's all I've got. One option is to curtail your growth plans. No more expansion. Raise your prices and suffer a decline in market share. The danger is it may be permanent, but meanwhile it will give you extra cash and help you hold on for a while. If you are one of those people who like company when in misery, you can take some comfort from knowing that even your strongest competitor won't be able to extract much enjoyment from its dominance over you. Assuming its capacity slack is not large, in order to pick up the business you are voluntarily dropping, it will have to expand. Unless the competitor jacks up its prices faster than inflation would dictate, whereupon you might gain back some of that lost share, it will have to enlarge its debt base and incur a big interest penalty. No one really benefits.

Strategic Pricing   We all know that inflation hurts everybody, but if there is any solace in it, there is one finding that may help until it all blows over. Several analytical studies have shown that certain aspects of the Profit & Loss column are more sensitive to inflation than others. I previously made a point of underlining the critical role of margins—even to the point of suggesting they should take precedence over market share—in your strategic planning. Margins loom larger than ever during periods of galloping inflation.

Picture your P&L as a vertical series of percentages with total sales as the base (i.e. 100 percent) and all your expense items and subtotals, and whatever profit is left over down at the bottom, percented to that. (See Table 4-1.)

Table 4-1. Proposed profit & loss statement (business unit)

	%	%
Gross sales	102	
Cash discounts	2	
Net sales		100
Variable costs		
Raw materials	30	
Labor	20	
Other	3	53
Variable gross profit (VGP)		47
Marketing expenses		
Advertising — media	6	
Merchandising — consumer	4	
Merchandising — trade	3	
Marketing research	1	14
Net direct profit contribution		33
Marketing administration	2	
Sales expenses	3	5
Marketing profit		28
Production period	9	
Technical research	1	
General expenses	4	
Bonuses, etc.	1	15
Operating income		13
Interest expense	1	
Interest income	0	
Provision for income taxes	6	7
Net income		6

Now, in pure percentage terms, all expenses increase with inflation, but your interest expenses will increase somewhat faster than anything else. That is brought on by the large borrowings you have to make to finance negative cash flows looming out of the higher cash outgo for things like raw materials, packaging, inventories, and accounts receivable.

If your accounting system is set up at the business unit level to help you as well as your bookkeeper, you will have two types of costs: fixed (i.e., fairly constant at any sales volume level) and variable (i.e., goes up when sales rise and vice versa). Since it is only the variable costs that you can manipulate with any facility, your system should also print out a line giving your variable gross profit (VGP) so that you have a governable target to shoot for. Forget about what comes after that (fixed or period costs and finance charges, etc.) because, during inflation, it won't have nearly the impact on your bottom line or on your cash flow prospects that your variable costs do. In other words, there is a very urgent need to maintain your variable gross profit when inflation strikes.

(To those readers who have all this down cold and detect that I am talking down to them, I must apologize. But I have seldom seen business-level accounting systems that provide these breakdowns and I am aiming this at those who have to toil in the dark in the hope that they will be able to persuade their accounting people to install a more useful system.)

VGP maintenance (settle for simple *margin maintenance* if your accounting system is not geared to this split-level reporting mode) through a surgically applied combination of cost reductions and price increases is better than just relying on price increases alone if you wish to stay above water when inflation lurks. It is worth voicing the obvious here—namely, that cost reductions will magnify your profits without gulping down a big dose of added working capital investment. Many of our marketing-oriented brethren overlook this point. Underlying the obvious a bit further: If you engineer your cost reduction via a savings in component or ingredient costs, you automatically slice off a big chunk of your inventory expenses. The upshot of all this is that a cost reduction produces a more favorable cash flow than a price increase of the same magnitude.

So, in getting back to our initial proposition—that financial performance is more sensitive to changes in VGP than to any other single expense element in your financial projections—it is imperative that your selling prices and variable costs be permitted to rise only in concert.

In one typical analysis that I studied in a multiproduct company where the discounted cash flow return rate goal was set at 27 percent, the financial sages determined that, if variable costs and prices were both increased during the same periods at, say, 9 percent (the inflation rate projection they used), over a 10-year period they could achieve the company's goal. But if they allowed costs to rise at the 9 percent rate, and prices only at a 6 percent rate, the return rate dropped sharply to only 4 percent. Even worse, when they let prices offset a 9 percent cost increase on a straight one-for-one dollar basis (rather than percentagewise), the return rate fell to 0 percent. Naturally, it would always be nicer to increase prices faster than costs on a percentage basis, but your customers might not cooperate unless you seduce them with some highly compelling compensating incentive. This is hard to do when you are trying to cut costs.

When faced with a pricing decision in the midst of significant price jumps, you should conduct studies like the foregoing before attempting to see which strategies will help you maintain your VGP. This is the key, and your pricing strategies must be formulated with this in mind, even if it means putting a temporary bridle on your quest for growth.

pricing the new product

pricing in anticipation of future costs

The likelihood of any new product providing an adequate return in the future will depend on its ability to maintain its variable gross profit in the face of inflation-driven mounting costs. But with new products you have to balance this requirement with another one: playing the market matrix game outlined in my last chapter.

That chapter told why it is important to go after quick mastery and supremacy in a new market. Pricing is one way to accomplish this. What you want to do with your pricing on a new product is to make it highly unattractive for your rivals to gain any meaningful market share that lets them obtain the benefits of riding their own experience curves and becoming entrenched with both the trade and the final consumer. You should use your pricing strategy to reach the top rung on the volume ladder, and then you will be rewarded with both an impressive cost advantage over competition, which they probably won't ever be able to equal, and with a fervent following among the buyers that makes it more economical (on a per unit basis) to market and merchandise your product or service.

Therefore, do not set your introductory prices to reflect your initial cost pattern. This is too short-sighted. Even if you don't really have much to contend with in the way of competition when the market for this product or service is new, you might encounter it later on. Moreover, by setting a high introductory price at the outset, you might just put a check on the rate at which this new market could take off and grow to a colossal magnitude. Set your prices low enough (even if it means incurring a loss at first) to anticipate what the experience curve is going to allow you to price your product at later on to deliver a profit when you achieve reasonable volume goals.

Naturally, this demands that the market for this product be around for a while. I'm not talking about Rubic cubes or anything of an ephemeral nature here. Things like that do not need and, in fact, defy long-term planning. They also require extremely high margins at the outset because there is no afterwards, unless you include the Bargain Huts and so forth that are strewn on the highways leading into our provincial towns.

fine-tuning your prices

market research of little value

The above principles can lead you into the correct pricing ballpark for long-term planning purposes. Further finessing is needed to fine-tune your prices. Since we have already ruled out the easy course of parity pricing as retrograde (we will have more to say on this later on), getting your prices precisely correct can be a ticklish problem. I know that many companies resort to consumer surveys for this, but I personally don't like using marketing research to guide my pricing strategies in consumer goods, although it seems to work fairly well with industrial products where there is more of a rational basis for purchase decisions. In consumer goods pricing, research has to rely on interviewing actual consumers, and they are too tormented by the scorpions of psychological bias to respond reliably to pricing issues. Too many of them feel they have to save face and never appear "cheap," while others (e.g., fans of Ralph Nader and subscribers to Consumer Reports) bend over backwards to sneer at anything that smacks of twentieth century marketing.

Of course, the test market route is always available if you wish to overcome the interviewing bias, but few companies can afford the luxury of having test markets for each and every marketing variable, so in actual practice it becomes impractical to test everything in this manner. And, as we said before, test markets don't give you an answer on what kind of response your best competitors will come at you with, since truly sophisticated competitors seldom tip their hands in your test market.

Marketing research can also impede the process of strategic pricing. It will only give you a reading of an immediate value and can't provide any insights into the long-term market matrix implications of your pricing decisions.

Fine-tuning, then, is a task that requires some rather detailed thinking. First, let's consider a typical problem that I and many others have seen over and over in the business world, and then, finally, I'll walk you through some rather advanced concepts in pricing decisions. Successful, bang-on pricing strategies are not easy to arrive at, but let us press onward.

Pricing is often implicated in an extended scenario that crops up with dismal frequency in many businesses. Faltering sales automatically lower the capacity utilization of the business and consequently make its ROI very bad. The common solution: Cut prices and get capacity utilization back up at all costs. While this is going on, heads begin to roll, tempers flare, and a pernicious executive mind-set is established. Not only do we see a very desperate pricing decision being made, we also see other signs of *management angst,* purchasing decisions are made too readily, often at unfavorably high prices, because everyone is scared to hold up the operation and watch the lugubrious utilization level decline even more. Productivity may also drop as management seizes any opportunity to ward off labor problems. They may acquiesce to an overly charitable wage package out of a desperate fear of a strike of any duration. So things continue to blacken, and then, gripped in a cost-cutting frenzy, management examines the discretionary parts of the P&L proforma; inevitably, they suddenly realize they can save mega-bucks by simply cutting out most sales and advertising expenditures. (By now everyone in the executive suite believes the Vice President of Finance, who has always considered this to be economic waste anyway.) And so, what we usually witness is a further slump in sales. The price cut, which didn't help in the first place, now looks awfully stupid. Unfortunately it is too late to do anything, and no one can turn back the clock.

This scenario can take many different forms, but the major propellant is a kind of executive response that grabs at pieces of the picture and tries to solve what is a basic overall strategic problem by using periodic, piecemeal approaches rather than a complete overhaul.[7]

price as a reflection of more than just product

Sensible pricing decisions cannot be made in this kind of hysterical environment. Doing so can cause permanent damage to your long-range prospects. Prices are not something that can be set or changed without a considerable amount of study and a mature appreciation of where they fit in the strategic continuum. It's a complex game, like chess, and no move can be made intelligently without a thorough cognizance of how the move can affect, or be affected by, a whole host of other factors.

On a very elementary level, prices must be set to reflect not just your product but also its accompanying services, its packaging, and its image. These are all part of what the customer buys. Their relative value varies by product category. Your marketing and advertising may also give significant added value to the product, which you should not overlook when you set the price. Axiomatically, if you have an article that can justify a premium price, your advertising and promotional efforts should reflect this. Price is not only an objective matter. You have to keep the psychology of the user in mind, even for industrial products. Price and quality can be inextricably linked. The number of products with only an average level of true physical quality or utility value that, nonetheless, manage to thrive with (or because of) a premium price is legion. Of course, this won't come as news to the average soap or HBA product manager. And even Tetzel, whom Martin Luther attacked for his traffic in phony relics and exaggerated indulgences, knew the value of a strong advertising claim in guaranteeing the success of high prices.

By the sheer force of advertising, packaging, design, and pricing, the consumer perceives them as superior in quality. Designer jeans would be an obvious example of this; the halo effect of the famous designer's name makes them *de rigueur* to the fashion-conscious consumer and tends to overcloud and even enhance the product's lack of real structural departure from the mundane brands. Yet, if designer jeans had come on the market at regular prices competitive with Levi's and Wrangler, they would never have pulled off their market segmentation coup, despite their glandular advertising. Accordingly, you should set your prices with all of the strategic considerations I have outlined, but, at the same time, do not overlook the fact that your product is more than just its physical attributes. You might be able to elevate your prices without anyone being the wiser about its true physical conformation.

the analysis of price

Finally we can move on to a higher plateau of thought. Even if I have not yet found the universal cantrip for all pricing dilemmas, we can at least examine some of the most refined work in this field to round out our picture. Armed with this, you can at least feel confident that you are equipped to tackle the pricing issues in your own business better than people who base their judgments on superficial thinking and past experience.

By vigorously analyzing the raw data in its PIMS Program, the Strategic Planning Institute found out many interesting and useful things about the effect of pricing on financial performance and how we can use pricing as a navigational aid in the marketplace. These findings add an extra dimension to what I have so far covered. But, keep in mind that all business strategies are dependent on the skillful orchestration of many elements; when I focus on only two or three at a time, I do so to highlight certain underlying principles. It won't be until all these elements have been thoroughly digested that we can arrive at a unified view of business strategy. Hence, do not be overly troubled by the appearance of seeming inconsistencies at this time; they will evaporate as we go along.[8]

To begin with, these studies demonstrate that if you couple a tiny market share to a premium price, your odds of getting a decent return on your investment are quite bad, which is pretty much as we have been saying. However, your return rate almost doubles if you price yourself at the market average or below. Previous discussions on the nature of market share should explain why this would be so. On the other hand, if your market share is middle-of-the-road or higher, pricing won't have much effect on your ROI. True, there is a slight edge if you choose the premium price route, but the difference between that and a low price choice is not really very great (see Table 4-2).[9]

Table 4-2. Share, price and ROI

(ROI%)	MARKET SHARE		
	Low	Medium	High
Average price	11	14	24
High price	6	16	27

Source: Strategic Planning Institute[10]

This is not necessarily in conflict with my previous comments on the linkage between high shares and high prices because the above incorporates all the different rates of market growth.

Now, this is a start. But what if you aren't too happy with your market share? Can a pricing strategy help you build share? And what kind of pricing moves can work best here? The data in the PIMS Program show that the low-price choice will, as a rule, generate market share gains greater than the higher price choice. However, this pricing benefit may be illusory; it can only be fully appreciated by cross-tabulating it with your product's relative quality level. High quality can give you a souped up rate of market share increase at all price levels, since quality and price combine to form the concept of "value" that has a strategic life all its own. I don't want to get into the question of quality and the derivative concept of value any more than I must until the next chapter, but there are a few incidental points I want to cover on their role here.

As we will see, the use of product quality (relative to competition) is a paramount vehicle for the achievement of outstanding business success. Pricing naturally plays a part in parlaying quality into its highest profit-producing capability. Your hunch, based on what I have said up to now, is probably that high quality can demand and get a premium price. But, as you will recall, at the beginning of this chapter I outlined two price-setting goals. One of these was to get yourself established in a market with a strong share position as this makes life so much more pleasant later on. I also said that dominant brands can command a higher price than their competitors. So, going back to a previous question and hoping to put more light on it, what if you just want to grow and get a bigger share and not necessarily become the dominant brand? The answer is that you can parlay your high quality into a bigger market share gain if you go up against competition via the lower-price route. For example, in the PIMS Program, out of the hundreds of separate businesses that were studied, it was found that the average gain in market share would be 7.7 percent with a high quality-low price approach and only 4.9 percent with the high quality-high price approach (see Table 4-3).[11]

Table 4-3. Price, quality and share change

| | RELATIVE PRICE | |
Market share change (%)	Low	High
Low quality	2.0	2.7
Average quality	5.0	3.0
High quality	7.7	4.9

Source: Strategic Planning Institute[12]

Okay, you say, that's nice if what you want is a gain in market share. But what if what we are really looking for is a better return on our investment? What then? The study continued to show that there is not much of a penalty one way or the other. The ROI for the former approach is 32 percent and for the latter, 28 percent (before taxes). (See Table 4-4.)[13]

Table 4-4. Price, quality and ROI

| | RELATIVE PRICE | |
ROI (%)	Low	High
Low quality	15	14
Average quality	21	16
High quality	32	28

Source: Strategic Planning Institute[14]

Remember that this table covers all rates of market growth and does not distinguish between the products' current share levels.

In Table 4-3 you can see that, believe it or not, a high price gives more of a share gain than a low price among low quality products (2.7 percent vs. 2.0 percent), and that the results are only slightly reversed when you consider ROI. If your product quality is average, the improvement in both market share and ROI is even more pronounced with a lower-price strategy.

Value is an issue that grows increasingly important as our dollar depreciates in buying power and consumer living standards plummet. Value delivery is indeed rewarded. To begin with, it helps get you

trial. Thereafter, when the buyer finds the quality roughly comparable to the premium priced alternatives, his or her delight leads to an
increase in frequency of purchase and maybe even to "loyalty" for the
product, thus giving it the bigger market share increment. True, the
high quality-high price combo generates good results, too, and thus we
can logically say it follows a successful strategy in being priced at a
premium. But the high quality product that chooses to offer the
customer an outstanding cost-benefit value gets an even greater
reward from the buyer. Palpably, all of these statements, being based
on samples of experiences, are not absolute conclusions. They are,
like most of our business decisions, based on mathematical probability, not certainty. But that should not deter us from incorporating
them in our decision-making process, since guesswork—even when
based on many years of experience—has even a lower likelihood of
being right.

premium pricing vs. discounting

Although your pricing task will always have to address the two overall
goals (margins vs. growth), the formulation of business strategy is not a
simplistic pastime, and you may have to occasionally disregard some
of the aspects of these goals as you attempt to get the best components
together for that vast exponential equation that reflects the way your
business can achieve its highest levels of attainment.

Most studies in the field tell us that parity pricing is out,
regardless of what other strategic elements are present. However, for
premium pricing and discounting the situation requires some further
detailed examination to extract a total understanding of some impressive opportunities offered by each of these under different sets of
conditions.

The Strategic Planning Institute found by establishing a "success index" criteria based on a combination of ROI and market share
growth[15] that some rather astonishing conclusions emerged (see Table
4-5).

Table 4-5. Price and success

		Discount Prices	Equivalent Prices	Premium Prices
(Success index: share growth + ROI)	Low	22	-8	17
Advertising/promotion expenditures as a % of sales	Medium	20	-8	8
	High	-29	-19	3

Source: Strategic Planning Institute[16]

- A business that wants to pursue a policy of premium pricing will do
well on the success index when it has a heavy advertising and

promotional spending program working for it. By heavy we mean at least 1.5 percent of sales. The big ad spenders do a lot better if they remium price than if they have a parity or low price. (The apparent difference between the 3 percent for the premium-priced big spenders and the 17 percent for the premium-priced low spenders is not statistically significant.) There may be a number of reasons for this. You frequently find that a company that devotes a large amount of its cash to a serious advertising program is much better at writing marketing plans in the first place, which means they know how to position a product for maximum advantage. Their past successes in the marketplace give them the confidence to trust in the benefits of elaborate marketing activities. Also the halo effect, mentioned earlier, may apply here and work against the discounter. Any implied claims of quality or superior performance in the discounter's advertising simply may not be very believable because of its low prices. Seems unfair, but that's often how things are.

• At a low level of marketing effort there does not seem to be any difference in success by pricing strategy, unless you are still interested in looking at parity pricing, which here gives you the same disappointing results most of the others studies foretold.

• The same is true if your promotional effort is just average. It would seem then that, all things being equal, if you don't plan to devote a big chunk of your budget to marketing, you would be well advised to focus all your effort on sales force activities and stop worrying about things like ad copy and trade deals.

• A distinctive product does better with a premium price, and this, of course, reinforces one of my key points in the last chapter—namely, that product differentiation is often the key to critical customer acclaim. But now we can add to this a rather salutary point: Your creative work in bringing a meaningful difference to the marketplace can be visibly recognized in a higher price. The more difference you build into your product, the less knowledgeable your customers. They will have to rely to a large extent on the price you set to tell them something about your product's probable quality. Discounters, on the other hand, perform better in product categories where the product traits matter less, such as in a commodity business. It is there that discount pricing can really pay off in terms of both building share and enhancing ROI. I believe this would have an intuitive appeal.

• One last conclusion: If you keep a big inventory of finished goods, you can do better on the success index with a premium price. Many customers are going to be a lot happier dealing with you, even though you charge more, because you can deliver the product when they need it. Waiting costs them money. This, no doubt, seems rather obvious.[17]

What about discount pricing? What is associated with the discounter's position on the success index? This may come as a surprise, but the discounter can only perform better than the premium-priced competitor if the discounter is relatively free of the grips of a union. The payoff here can be dramatic (see Table 4-6).

Table 4-6. Price and unions

% employees unionized	Discount Prices	Equivalent Prices	Premium Prices
Low	42	3	13
Medium	-41	-3	-4
High	-19	-28	15

Source: Strategic Planning Institute[18]

Given a low level of unionization (fewer than 36 percent of employees signed up), the discounter gets a success score about three times greater than the premium pricer with the same unionization level. However, if the discounter has to contend with a high level of emplyees in unions, it doesn't do very well at all; whereas the discounter's premium-pricing cohorts do just about as well as they would when they were less unionized. Many people are puzzled by this at first, but the rational is that the work rules and wage rates that you have to swallow to keep the union happy give you less control over your operation. (You see, it wasn't just a nasty capitalistic myth!) Hence, you simply cannot control your costs as well. If you are a discounter, the one thing you need above all else is exceedingly tight control over costs.[19]

Not too surprisingly, since it pervades many strategic scenarios, the discounter can also benefit from offering a high-quality product. Once again, value works.

watch that cash flow

Now don't forget about your cash flow just because everything else looks so wonderful. Increasing your market share, especially when done via a discounted price, is always going to create a cash slump. There is no way around this, within reason of course. So the lessons on the experience curve and the market matrix still have to be applied to the long-range implications of your pricing options. However, with the foregoing you have a better idea about your options, and you can build all of this into your overall plan.

international price competition

As the world continues to shrink and the Industrial Revolution enters a new phase—the global spread of technology—innumerable industries in the United States and in Europe face stiff competition from the developing nations that can produce equivalent, (or in many cases, superior) products at much lower prices. What kinds of strategies, for example, can the steel, chemical, shipbuilding, and textile industries employ to combat the combination of sporadic, worldwide overproduction and fierce price competition from the LDCs?

We are getting to the point in history where the next phase of the Industrial Revolution is beginning to emerge in some industries. Robotization lowers the labor cost and other *avant garde* production, and distribution techniques make it possible to set extremely low prices. For most industries, though, that answer may be a long way off. One presently plausible course is to export your labor, but this has been used many times before and is not a permanent solution to the problem for several reasons—one of which is that eventually the LDC to which you sent your work may become your future competitor after you've supplied all the job training.

A better solution is to do something interesting to your product. Make it different or, possibly, more specialized. Seek out some kind of improvement. Operating in your favor here is the fact that the marketing people in the LDCs are not as sophisticated (yet) as in the developed nations, so this kind of approach (which is really just a variation on the market segmentation strategies we talked about in the last chapter) has a high probability of success. It allows you to start a whole new ballgame and to go through all the pricing strategies that this will entail.

In the next chapter we will continue with our look at marketing strategies, concentrating on some other factors that can help us to achieve either a high market share or, barring that, an acceptable ROI and a healthy cash flow.

notes

1. Charles Hofer and Dan Schendel, *Strategy Formulation: Analytical Concepts* (St. Paul, MN: West Publishing Co., 1978), p. 134.

2. "Industrial Pricing Policy and Market Share," (Boston, MA: Boston Consulting Group, 1978), p. 2.

3. Gwen Kinkead, "Philip Morris Undiversifies," *Fortune*, June 29, 1981, pp. 62-65.

4. Janet Guyon, "Philip Morris's Seven-Up Co. Slips, Beset by Price Wars and Trouble with Bottlers," *Wall Street Journal*, October 2, 1981, p. 25. Seven-Up's share later began to rise when it used a "caffeine-free" strategy in its advertising beginning in March, 1982, as a way of differentiating itself.

5. Robert D. Buzzell, Bradley T. Gale, and Ralph G.M. Sultan, "Market Share—a Key to Profitability," *Harvard Business Review,* 53, no. 1 January–February 1975, pp. 97-106.

6. David P. Garino, "New Ralston Chief Says He'll Sacrifice Sales to Keep Company's Profit Margins High," *Wall Street Journal*, July 2, 1981, p. 23.

7. Sidney Schoeffler, "The Unprofitability of 'Modern' Technology and What to Do about It," PIMSLETTER, (Cambridge, MA: The Strategic Planning Institute, 1978), p. 5.

8. Don't miss the point here. Your own SBU may have these characteristics yet not obtain the same ROI results as are shown here. In citing these data, I am trying to show relationships, but there are some caveats that must be made: 1) strategy embodies more than only two-factor combinations. By examining only two at a time we purposely shove them under a microscope and blow up their impact for maximum dramatic effect;

2) all of these relationships are based on probability, and extreme anomalies can and will occur; 3) the absolute numbers will vary through time as many different economic factors exert their influence, but the relative values should remain fairly constant, and that's what you should focus on. It should go without saying that successful strategies are built up only through a painstaking assessment of all the strategic factors discussed in this book, and no self-respecting strategist (certainly not a master strategist) would dare concentrate on only one or two of them.

9. "Selected Findings," (Cambridge, MA: The Strategic Planning Institute, 1976), p. 9.

10. Ibid.

11. Mark Chussil and Sidney Schoeffler, "Pricing High-Quality Products," The PIMSLETTER on Business Strategy (Cambridge, MA: The Strategic Planning Institute, 1978), p. 2.

12. Ibid.

13. Ibid., p. 3.

14. Ibid.

15. Stephen Land, "How Price Premiums and Discounts Affect Performance," The PIMSLETTER on Business Strategy (Cambridge, MA: The Strategic Planning Institute, 1978), p. 3. The SPI also weighted the index used here in favor of businesses that were able to build market share in a growing market where the long-term payoff was greater. This produced the same overall conclusions, however, as are cited in the text.

16. Ibid.

17. Ibid., pp. 2-5.

18. Ibid., p. 4.

19. Ibid.

5

quality:
guillotine of public opinion

Maybe we can blame it on strong leadership. Entire industries are expiring. Consumer cynicism is rampant. Our instincts tell us much of our output is pure crap. We have assumed we could go on forever selling the sizzle, even if the steak were leathery.

And what does declining product quality have to do with strong leadership, pray tell? Well, it's just an observation, and there's never going to be any statistical data to back it up, but I think you might agree: Over the past several years, we've had an especially big presence of strong, forceful managers who have enforced the effectuation of constant bottom line improvements. You know how they operate. They demand an X percent cut in costs one year, Y percent the next, ad infinitum, to make their operating profits swell with predictable regularity. But there's only so much fat to cut. By a kind of creeping degradation, each product's quality is whittled away, bit by bit, in stages that are imperceptible from one to the next; but in the aggregate of time, everything becomes <u>indeterminately shoddy</u>. This chapter will not advocate replacing the strong leaders with wimps, but with smarter leaders. Smart leaders are those who understand the

49 strategy of quality.

Americans are not alone here. We once used to regard British craftsmanship as the best in the world, until that became the kind of joke exemplified in the old Beatles' movie, *A Hard Day's Night*. When the villain's gun jams, he bemoans, "Of course, it's British. ... It should have been a Luger." Now, perhaps, we have only West Germany and Japan to look up to for genuine quality, bringing to mind the quotation from Emerson that appears above. To survive in the global competition with countries like those, we only can hope that our sales prospects quickly tire of their diets of caviar and come home to us. Some hope!

Quality, as it turns out, is more than an artifact of the Puritan Ethic; it is the very soul of business, a progenitor of success and fiscal reward. The election to ignore quality (even if only through a gradual, creeping distortion invisible to the consumer in the short term) brings swift punishment to the perpetrator.

Perhaps all this has finally become obvious. We can't ignore the scores of industries fleeing our shores for foreign lands where our own inventiveness is augmented, refined, and returned in goods our citizens prefer to their own.

The story of quality as an ingredient in your marketing strategy contains many interesting facets. Quality is one of the more powerful and more direct causes of ROI. As such, it can be analyzed in some depth. And the results of this analysis can be used to help you formulate business strategies that can use quality in the most salubrious manner. The subject of quality is the vital raw material to be processed by a powerful imagination. No single aspirin will cure all the headaches of our welfare economy, but this one is of the extra-strength variety.

even dogs prefer quality products

Years ago, I consulted on a dog food marketing project in France. My client had a reasonably healthy presence in the market; his brand was in third place with a 16 percent share of a market that was growing around 30 percent per year. I was dubious about the quality of this product; I'd been out on field interviews and heard many dog owners say their mutts didn't relish our product. Apparently, it provoked those hang-dog modes of nonverbal communication that unmistakably meant Bowser was asking if he could please eat something else. Unlike his favorite brand, which Bowser would bolt down without chewing, ours underwent excessive mastication. I convinced the marketing department to do some blind tests.[1] This showed that the

50

client's product lost badly to rival brands and provided me (or so I thought) with the ammunition to get the client to launch a serious product improvement program. But my pleas fell on deaf ears. The head Gaul pointed out that his market was growing so fast his plants couldn't keep the pipeline filled; so, as far as he could tell, there was *no* problem. I tried to point out that markets do not grow forever, that France was way behind most of the rest of the civilized world on dog food feedings, that it was catching up fast, and would shortly level off. Once that happened, I argued, he was going to end up with *oeuf sur la face* because his sales volume right now was coming mainly from trial (rather than loyal users), and when the growth stopped, he'd lose share. Suddenly he no longer understood English and imperiously informed me my French was unacceptable because it bore the trace of an American accent.

All consultants love showing the world how perspicacious they are, and this time the verisimilitude of my forecast was immaculate. By the time the next Nielsens arrived, the brand had slumped a full two points in face of a sudden surge in the French inflation rate. The next two months saw a further two-point decline in the Nielsens; so did the following period. Those French mutts had had enough of our pedestrian victuals, and their owners were forced to migrate permanently back to brands that turned their pups into clean-plate rangers. These, of course, were the brands that soared over ours in terms of sheer quality.

"we make good things for living"

General Electric is one company that, very early on, discovered the integral role of product quality. It has remained an important part of the company's strategy and is one factor that helps it stay successful even during periods of economic malaise. "GE traditionally has gained share in periods of economic uncertainty," says Carl Yankowski, who is the general manager for GE Housewares. During such a time, the consumer becomes more careful, even cautious, and looks for top value. "By value," Yankowski says, "we mean knowing the three parts of an educated purchase decision: the cost of the purchase, the benefits of owning, and the cost of the usage. Nothing is more expensive than a product bought on price alone that doesn't perform as expected or that stops performing before expectations." GE's constant quest for a quality image in its products keeps customers loyal, as can be seen in Yankowski's consumer research. "In answer to the question 'Which brand are you most likely to buy?' a significantly greater number of those in the market are responding 'GE.' The preference for GE has been high. It is now higher still."[2]

In fact, other surveys suggest that, as far as consumer products go, quality, and not price, is gaining ascendance and may be the paramount sales message needed in the effort to entice consumers. Faith B. Popcorn, president of the New York ad agency, Brain-Reserve, Inc., says that buyers will be more and more interested in something she labels "integrity buying."

"People will buy products for their integrity rather than status," she says. "Quality will become the new status."[3]

The Philadelphia marketing research firm, Consumer Network, notes that, while people are grudgingly becoming accustomed to paying higher prices for food items, they are "very suspicious about quality." They asked consumers in a national survey where they'd like to see food processors invest more money, and the multiple-choice answer selected by most responses was "better quality at the same price." This outscored "larger sizes at the same price," "smaller sizes at a lower price," and "lower prices even with less quality."[4]

Another Gotham ad agency, Leber Katz Partners, ascribes the heightened increase in quality-consciousness in the United States to a phenomenon it calls the "Europeanization of America." Laurel Cutler, executive vice president of this ad shop, sees Europe as a kind of test market for what is going to happen in the U.S., given that they had to face up to the energy problem, inflation, and high taxes long before we did. She thinks that U.S. consumers will "develop the values that characterize Europeans: respect for the old, the traditional, the tried, and the true."[5]

One can easily nitpick any of these observations. Europe has never been the consumer economy that the United States is; choice in almost any product category is severely limited, and, with a few minor exceptions, shopping in Europe is an exercise in annoyance and inconvenience. Moreover, the American consumer has not discovered quality just recently; it has always been a hallmark of the successfully marketed product. While it is true they are giving it a higher priority today than before, profits have always been correlated with relative quality. But, nitpicking aside, what these surveys and commentaries say to me is that the time may be right to more fully exploit a quality strategy.

quality not understood

Quality, however, is not readily appreciated or understood as thoroughly as it should be. When I was new to the business world and employed by Procter & Gamble, I just assumed that all corporations took the same care and pains to make sure their products were acceptable to the consumer. Eventually, I revised that notion. By rubbing shoulders with associates who had been groomed in a legion of other corporate environments, I learned that P&G was exceptional—it had no peers when it came to the art of assuring product quality—and that most of its competitors were merely deluding themselves when they depended on less thorough procedures, including consumer research, to inveigle themselves into the belief their products were preferred by consumers. I realize that the unintentional arrogance of P&G alumni can be maddening, but this claim of superior quality is not due so much to something Procter knows that no one else can share as it is to a pervasive company attitude that few other companies would have the patience for. No product leaves the plant without concrete evidence that it is highly favored, both overall and on the basis of individual attributes, against competition. New products and formula changes on old products are thoroughly tested in what must be the world's most elaborate and painstaking system of blind product testing. Even the company's consumer research techniques themselves are repeatedly scrutinized, and revamped if necessary, to assure that the best possible methods are being applied. New products *must* trounce competition. New formulas either must beat or tie with the old. The consumer is the final judge, and the company brooks no exceptions. P&G marketing managers are never allowed to underestimate the tastes of the consumer but must adhere closely and precisely to defined definitions of what the consumer wants in a product before they can get approval for their marketing plans. P&G never lets its managers wing it on gut feelings or operate on instinct alone. Critics are quick to say that this stifles creativity, but even a casual review of the company's history belies this allegation. The energies of the so-called marketing genius in this particular corporate environment are channelled into areas where creativity and subjectivity count, but scientific impartiality rules the roost wherever it can be imposed.

Pampers. Procter & Gamble's pursuit of product quality, manifest in all of its brands, can be typified in its disposable diaper, Pampers. It took four years of intense R&D preparation before this brand made it to its first test market in late 1961. At that time, there was nothing new about paper diapers; they had been around for several years (Chux, Drypers, Kleinerts, K.D.s, etc.) without exactly becoming barnstormers. The whole group of extant paper brands never amounted to more than 1 percent of the disgusting mound of diapers used in the United States each day. The disposables were expensive. Besides, most mothers didn't think they did as good a job as cloth diapers. (I trust you can do without the details.) Needless to say, the large baby market of the 1960s was too big and obvious to pass up, and many paper product companies of the time were desperately hunting for the key to a successful disposable diaper entry. Instead, P&G looked for problems. Problem one: the paper diapers of the 1950s were not all that absorbent. Problem two: the effect on the neonate was also unsavory; they left babies awash in permanent wetness. What Pampers offered (but only after arduous testing and development) was a unique, triple-layer construction of a flexible, outside plastic sheet to keep the wetness in—an exceedingly absorbent wadding that spread it about evenly to prevent any one spot from getting soggy. But the real P&G coup was the third layer, the one next to the skin; it worked osmotically to pick up the moisture, send it on to the wad, and hence permit the user to live a fairly dry life. All this for only six cents each. Pampers was recognized by consumers as a clearly visible advance in quality and led to a huge expansion in the formerly dormant disposable diaper market, which it easily came to dominate. Such triumphs never come easily. Said one engineer who had worked on the initial stages of Pampers manufacturing: "I think it was the most complex production operation the Company had ever faced. There was no standard equipment. We had to design the entire production line from the ground up. It seemed a simple task to take three sheets of material ... fold them in a zigzag pattern and glue them together. But the glue applicators dripped glue. The wadding generated dust. Together they formed sticky balls and smears, which fouled the equipment. The machinery could run only a few minutes before having to be shut down and cleaned." But the earnest pursuit of relative quality advantage persisted, and Pampers went on to return many times over the investment it had incurred.[6]

Heineken Beer. By no means is P&G the only company with a heart of quality at the center of its every business strategy. Quality is usually the mainstay of most any venerable and enduring brand that survives long after others have expired. Heineken is this country's biggest selling foreign beer with around 40 percent of the U.S. import market. Freddy Heineken claims, "I make the Rolls-Royce of beer. How can I make a super Rolls-Royce? It doesn't exist. A Rolls is a Rolls, a Heineken is a Heineken." The source of its high quality dates back to 1879 when Mr. Heineken's grandfather engaged a student of Louis Pasteur to isolate a special yeast, which has been carefully cloned down to the present. Using the same yeast over and over gives them a known constant in the brewing process and, therefore, quality control. Of course, there is more to Heineken's successful quality control than just that. There's also the company's unshakeable insistence on slow brewing (eight days) and long aging (six weeks). This compares to the more prevalent three-day brewing time and one-week aging time of the vast majority of breweries.[7] Meticulous quality control may be more crucial in the brewing industry than anywhere else. One of my ancestors ran a once popular brewery whose cidrous workers carelessly neglected certain procedures, thus allowing the yeast to turn. Undetected, bad brew went out on the market. Beer drinkers talk a lot. What resulted was the most rapid word-of-mouth campaign ever witnessed. Propelled by this, sales declined and the brewery went under.

sword of damocles and halo effects

The quality issue harbors jumbo-sized dangers, which can ensnare the unwary, the nonvigilant, the lazy, the self-satisfied, and the intellectually sloppy. The fight for successful exploitation of product-quality superiority is not singularily one of engineering, nor of a focus on the product's physical attributes and performance features. It is, in fact, a struggle for the consumer's mind. Few products exist that neither benefit nor falter from some extrinsic association with factors having little physical bearing on performance. Yet these associations contribute mightily to their quality images in the minds of consumers (as we saw in the previous chapter). If you are a professed Pepsi patron, you know how embarrassed you feel when you can't detect that you've been slipped a Coke. The more adamant you've been about the virtues of Pepsi, the more your friends laugh at your inability to demonstrate real, organoleptic discernments. Blindfolded, few smokers can tell what brand of cigarette they are smoking. The brand name itself creates an aura that engulfs the product's physical attributes. Consumer perceptions of quality are not wholly objective, to put it mildly.

If you neglect to reinforce your product's positive associations with effective advertising, with connotative packaging, and with other marketing mix elements, you will fail to project to consumers the ultimate benefits of your product's physical advantages. Even when your actual product is physically inferior to your competitors, these extraneous aspects may generate an opportunity to engineer superior consumer perceptions. Complete strategists utilize the so-called halo effect to penetrate beyond the screen of immediate, concrete considerations about their products and services into a whole view of quality.

industrial halos overlooked

Most consumer products, by design or by accident, are marketed in cognizance of the halo effect, but the industrial sector gives it too little attention. Industrial buyers are supposed to be close representations of "economic man": coldly rational, more critical, better informed. But they are human after all and not immune to the ravages of biased perceptions. There are halo effect opportunities abounding, even with the most seemingly mundane industrial goods. One example, over-used but still good, is the paper board manufacturer who offered its corrugated box line in various pastel shades. Users discovered that aqua resulted in greater productivity from their shippers than the regular brown color because workers thought the cartons were lighter and easier to handle. Car drivers will believe a vehicle with a softer accelerator pedal has better pickup. These cunning little tricks won't save America in the battle for the World Cup quality laurels, but they are peripherally important as enhancements. However, quality is most often a result of some kind of innovation. A business can go too far in abusing its manipulation of the halo effects inherent in its products. And so, lest we get carried away with the assumption that the halo effect alone will produce a victory on the quality front, we should point out that the Strategic Planning Institute has some data that shows that fully one-third of businesses with higher-than-average-quality products will be backed up by some inventive element protected by patents or trade secrets, contrasted with a mere 15 percent of those with below-average-quality products. All is not form over substance—not by a long shot.

greater flexibility in marketing

Quality leaders are the gentry of their product group, and like society's gentry, they are more lithesome in their choice of behavior. They have infinitely greater flexibility at their disposal. The phalanx of lower-quality competitors will be hard pressed to lure away your loyal customers in any product group where esteem dictates brand choice on a more or less systematic and continuous basis. Low-quality competitors may be able to induce the occasional spate of temporary consumer wandering, but if they don't have the goods, your superior quality will prevail in the end. As we saw in Chapter 4, you can charge and enforce higher prices without too much fear of losing your customers, providing you don't get too grabby. This of course lets you do a lot more marketing hocus-pocus than competition, and it permits you to maintain your margins better.

Given its prolonged, contextual grip on your attainments, prod-uct quality is something you should want to carefully monitor and document. Usually you have an inkling on how you stack up against competition, but you should not be satisfied with this. Get it confirmed with appropriate product testing and market research studies. Be wary of becoming dependent on the people who were involved in developing or selling a product for a determination on how it compares to your rivals' products. Their criteria will probably be quite different from your customers.

Though self-interest is the best incentive for ameliorating the quality of the nation's output, there are sound, altruistic reasons for promoting this for the good of the country. I would only be echoing many writers who tell us we deserve to lose markets to foreign competition, that some of us are only trustworthy at running fast-food joints for the rest who earn a living fiddling with information. It would be for the general economic good to regain preeminence in automobiles, cameras, small appliances, stereos, motorcycles, bicycles, tires, calculators, and televisions and overcome our growing hamburger/communications cultural fixation. Or do you really believe the governor of your state is going to be able to transform the entire labor force into high-tech producers?

habits need to change

To stimulate a heyday of quality products, we must overcome many habits of thought and deed. As much as you may admire and appreciate its contribution, modern marketing alone is no substitute for producing a quality product. Much of what has happened to our once prosperous business community can be traced to our old, myopic love affair with the applied leeches of the marketing concept that we were slinging darts at in Chapter 3. Like sparrows who have come to owe their existence to the droppings of a horse, we have been pinning our hopes on secondary characteristics; we must return to the basic, cardinal virtues of product excellence.

The old Singer Sewing Machine Company is a case in point. Singer is widely credited with having invented the sewing machine, and, almost single-handedly, this company put a sewing machine in virtually every home. Worldwide, its name is still synonomous with the product. For decades, Singer was the undoubted leader, with the dominant market share and the level of quality, reliability, and ease of usage that allowed it to maintain its position without fear of serious competition. But then some marketing guys (who else?) must have climbed on board and imposed their inimitable view of business that became so prevalent in the 1950s and 1960s. Building a huge chain of retail establishments, they promoted heavily and expensively, seeking quantum volume increases with deals and rebates. Their very advertising seemed to ignore the product and its marvellous qualities; accordingly, since it no longer seemed so important, the product itself began to sputter and fall behind that of competition, which was not equally cursed with "sophisticated" marketing talent. In particular, **57** the Europeans came on strong with super quality. Pfaff and Necchi pounced on the upper-crust segment and captured big chunks of it with more advanced, more reliable machines. Then the Japanese leveled their sights on the cheaper segments, walked in, and established a handsome franchise with lower-priced machines that were in some cases technically better than Singer's. Today, as most readers are aware, Singer is a broadly diversified outfit, but it's having to get by without its sewing machine cash fountain—all because it felt its marketing know-how could gloss over the fact that the product it offered had fallen behind the technological standards of the times.[8]

quality defined strategically

Putting it in simple planning terms, your quality strategy goal is to fill a need such that its value to the user is greater than your costs. Thus, your profit can be seen as the difference between your product's value (symbolized by the price it will fetch) and your costs of getting it to the user. Clearly, then, your long-run fortunes rest upon your ability to come up with a product or service better than your opponent's in delivering value. Not exactly profound advice, but it's an organized start.

It's the rare product that doesn't have some characteristic you can work on for value enhancement. For one thing, you can make it more useful. Digital watches that just tell time are already passé after only a brief history. Now they must, at the very least, incorporate a stopwatch function, tell the date, have an alarm, and maybe even a calculator. Some have very specialized purposes, like the jogger's watch that reckons your speed and distance. A watch that only tells time is now a curiosity, or merely an expensive piece of jewelry. Wristwatches have become more useful and, therefore, have a lot more value even though the costs involved in such impressive value enhancement appear to be minimal. Importantly, value enhancement doesn't always have to be expensive. What did it cost the dairy industry to come out with homogenized milk or to add Vitamin D?

Well, the function route is one way of doing it. Ease of use is another. Conceivably, there may be a market for a digital watch that is easier to set. (I suspect many who receive the more elaborate versions of these timepieces as gifts don't bother to read the instruction booklets.) Another market may exist for the digital watch that doesn't fall apart when you try to change the energy cell. Sliced bread is the time-honored example of enhanced value via an ease-of-use strategy. Premeasured portions (tea bags being an early illustration) have added value to many articles, though sometimes they fail to excite the consumer (e.g., laundry detergents have tried it and failed).

There are many other ways to make your product better than your rival's. You could make it more reliable, easier to repair, more readily available. In some industries the possibility of immediate delivery could be a value-enhancer. For example, interior decorators who order furniture direct from the factory, unlike a furniture retailer, may keep their clients waiting several months for delivery; hence, the manufacturer that can produce items as soon as the orders are received (the industry holds a finished goods inventory for only the most standard items, not those occult pieces decorators fancy), instead of waiting six months or more for identical orders to mount up, could carve out a handsome niche in a badly fractionated business.

There is always an opportunity to jack up your quality, even in the most staid and tired old industries. Federal Express did it by putting together its own airforce. The folks at Emory and Airborne, prior to the birth of Federal Express, had been providing a fairly viable service for over 20 years, keeping down their capital needs by using scheduled airlines as their shipping vehicles. Federal Express felt it could conquer a big slice of the small package business by guaranteeing faster delivery, but to do so it needed absolute control over the aircraft and a more efficient routing. By picking up the customer's package, flying it to a central hub in Memphis to sort and reroute in the small hours of the morning onto outbound planes, Federal gets almost all of these packages to their destinations overnight. At the time that Federal began, Emery was managing to do that only half the time.[9]

product differentiation vs. torpor

When you get right down to it, the most efficient driving force in your struggle to achieve superior product quality would be the intention to present your product as meaningfully differentiated from the rest of the pack. With "me-tooness" there is little basis for artful competition; with glaring differences competition can be intensified. The greater the difference, the more competition there will be. The whole idea behind the free enterprise system is for the strategist to locate those market segments he or she can dominate via significant forms of differentiation. The competitive advantages thus obtained help secure generous market shares which in turn produce the returns needed to continue. In circular fashion, the intensity of competition will also determine the amount of differentiation each market segment will have as greater competition leads to more differentiation.[10] It should go on forever, but when the spurs are withdrawn in the race for product differentiation, as we sadly have seen in many sectors today, the system stagnates, consumers become disenchanted, production declines, and torpor grips the nation.

When Procter & Gamble announced it was buying the small, private label citrus processor, Ben Hill Griffin Inc., analysts speculated that some interesting forms of new beverage differentiations were just over the horizon. Hercules Segalas of Drexel Burnham Lambert Inc., for one, thought that P&G probably had some application of its new desorbate technology in mind. This was a patented discovery that let Procter extract more of a commodity's true flavor than any previous process. P&G had developed the process for its coffee business, but if it were to be applied to the fruit drink business, brands like HI-C and Hawaiian Punch would face big league trouble: a competitive fruit drink tasting more like the real thing, rather than some watered-down, kid's birthday party punch. "They don't want to go into the juice business without a differentiated juice," Segalas said, putting it in strategic focus.[11] (At time of writing, P&G has put its Citrus Hill orange juice into test market with the claim it is "made in a unique way that maintains the natural good taste of fresh oranges.")[12]

No product category should be considered sacred. "Fake Food: To Dairymen's Dismay, Imitation Cheeses Win Growing Market Share," said the headline in the Wall Street Journal on July 20, 1981. Considered as illegal as counterfeit currency in Wisconsin, where state agents seized a shipment of the synthetic dairy product, the product's national market share in 1980 was 5 percent and was forecast to grow to 50 percent by the end of the century. The ersatz cheese is made from casein, a milk derivative not yet produced in the United States (possibly because of opposition from the dairy lobby?), vegetable oil, and flavoring. Some brands are said to come pretty close to the real thing, but that's argumentative. Apart from its lower price, the elements of product differentiation worth writing about are its low-calorie, low-cholesterol features, plus the fact that it has the same nutritional profile as real cheese. If all goes well, it will proceed down the same path as margarine (which also used to be illegal in Wisconsin, giving rise to the "oleo run" between there and Illinois), ersatz coffee creamers, and whipped toppings. Despite the wrath of dairymen, it is generating a following and usurping scarce shelfspace in supermarkets principally because of its successful differentiation strategy.[13]

Clever and relevant differentiation lets you establish niches that may be totally insulated from direct competition. If this helps you build a loyal consumer franchise (or at least a group of customers whose choices are not merely stochastic, as they often tend to be in nondifferentiated segments), you can expect its preferences to more or less override its customary price sensitivity. In other words your prices do not have to be set principally on the basis of costs.

Axiomatically, this will work only for products where differentiation is possible; but if you consider all of the facets of quality, this could include most everything that is mined, grown, processed, or manufactured. I will concede that there are a few, lone commodities that do not lend themselves to this kind of strategy. Perceptions of certain chemical compounds are not easily altered by image advertising, and unless the magic extrinsic factor can be found (delivery efficiency, corporate reputation?), the experience curve notion won't apply—barring, of course, the rise of new technologies that could change the whole game. Where costs solidify and opportunities for differentiation do not arise, competitive relationships stabilize.[14] But this kind of thinking can go too far. Many commodity producers work under a cloud of perpetual discouragement, which deters all new thinking. The phantoms of age-old failures are resurrected to block all efforts by the visionaries to inseminate the product line with life and excitement. When you stop to think about it, almost all our popular consumer products were once no more than faceless commodities. Soap used to be sold in bulk by grocers until a guy in Cincinnati decided to prepackage it; when one of his workers left the paddle stirring a batch of soap during the lunch break, thereby inventing the floating soap, he didn't pass up the chance to exploit this unusual point of differentiation. Morton Salt could have continued as a commodity product but elected instead to differentiate by iodization and anticlogging. History shows that the most commonplace articles have been turned into thrilling new brands time and time again as differentiation progresses from one triumph to another.

Even with industrial products and services your differentiation strategy will be buoyed up by marketing tactics designed to work along with it. It goes without saying that your advertising copy should complement this, but even your media plan can assist by reaching the very audience that would be most interested in the heterogeneity you are purveying.

product positioning

Marketing positioning may also complement your effort to shape customer perceptions. Positioning entails presenting your product as uniquely separate from your competitors. Good positioning will make your product seem like it occupies a wholly separate market segment. In the early 1970s Winchester Little Cigars did just this. The brand looked more like a cigarette than a cigar. Indeed, it almost smoked like a cigarette. It's Ph level, used by the Treasury Department to delineate cigars from cigarettes, was about as close as it could get to that of a cigarette without actually crossing the line (which would have subjected it to a much more severe set of excise tax regulations). Lastly, Winchester was advertised just like cigarettes; instead of being positioned as a "little cigar," which was a tiny, unexciting product category, they were positioned closer to (but not quite in) the cigarette category. Winchester became the largest selling cigar in the world (in units), obtained close to universal distribution, and even when measured against the enormity of the U.S. cigarette market, its share was well beyond the threshold of success.

Positioning is not always that productive. The soft drink Seven-Up tried it back in the early 1970s in an admirable attempt to divorce itself from the cola-dominated portions of the market. But, as we mentioned in Chapter 4, this attempt eventually failed to produce substantial, lasting share gains. For most products and services, positioning should be viewed as an adjunct to a broader program of product quality and differentiation and not as a strategy by itself.

limited by consumer vocabulary

Not many people like to talk about this, but one thing that can trim back the attainments of a differentiation gambit is the impoverished vocabulary of the ultimate consumer. In the consumer goods world, the accepted wisdom is to make sure most new product ideas are vetted with consumer panels in their preproduction conceptual phases. In reality, however, many of these concepts die simply because the consumer cannot talk intelligently about them. In fact, without the right words in their meager vocabularies, they can't even think about them clearly and logically and, therefore, when asked, cannot make useful decisions regarding them. Perhaps this is one significant explanation as to why new products emerging from the stables of our most sophisticated manufacturers often seem rather trite. The far-out ideas are killed in the concept test stage. Truly unique, genuinely differentiated products sometimes have to be introduced on faith, and their advertising must furnish the tongue-tied consumer with a workable vocabulary. Naturally, the needs such a product is slated to fill should still be researched prior to product development, but only to the extent that a fresh, new vocabulary is not needed to render a pragmatic assessment. For more down-to-earth products, naturally, consumers can cope quite adequately.

THE ANALYSIS OF QUALITY

Even though quality is an intransigent constituent of the profit equation, little has been written about it. Economists largely snub it, or, when addressing the issue at all, pine for that unattainable "perfect" world where all products are equal in their consumer appeal and compete only on the basis of price. Our top corporate moguls, eloquent in their major public pronouncements, boast of their company's quality products, but their attestations often sound more like Old Testament injunctions than careful strategic analysis.

So, in order to advance to a higher plane of thought on the subject, we find that we must look once again at the hard data generated by the cerebrations of the Strategic Planning Institute, wherein we can come up with some numbers that give us an unmercifully rigorous inspection of product quality's role as a profit mover. Unlike most of us, who can be swept along with the fervor of our own beliefs, the Institute categorically eschews fervor for fact. Therefore, it can be a prudent source of objective and reliable information that cuts through all the myths and shibboleths crippling so many attempts to devise intelligent product strategies.

"How can you analyze the role of quality," you may well ask, "when no one can tell me what quality is. Isn't quality just a mattter of taste; or, as the French say when watching American tourists pouring catchup on their *boeuf bourguignon,* 'Chaque`a son gôut?'" Even without the obvious, foreign dirty talk, that's a good question; so, before I get into this, let me first satisfy those who detect a note of futility in trying to be impartial about an issue that many still consider totally subjective. Strategically, quality is always assessed relative to directly competitive products. The assessment of a product's quality (this roughly follows a process outlined by General Electric when it first began to study the components of successful business strategies back in the 1960s) consists of an aggregate of judgments as to how the end user would appraise your product vis-à-vis competition. Quality control test comparisons and other laboratory examinations would play a small part in this. If you had reliable consumer surveys, they would, of course, take precedence over other data. The SPI mobilizes a simple formula to express the outcome of these judgments: For a given business you try to come up with a reasonably close estimate on what percentage of your sales revenue consumers would regard as superior to competitors; then subtract from this the percentage regarded inferior. This gives an input integer for a multivariate model that, when plugged in, will proceed to do whatever is required of it to illuminate the clout of quality on business results. When you get right down to it, most business people know how they stack up against competition, and, in actual practice, I've never encountered much controversy in arriving at the quality integer.[15] It will come as a relief to those who still have some misgivings about this that most of these computer programs used in strategic analysis don't demand a high degree of precision here, so no one really has to worry about being off by a few points. It wouldn't make any substantive difference in the results.

Now on to our analysis of quality as a strategic component. Since it is going to be a bit lengthy, this preview may be useful: The data will reveal six momentous things about product quality.

- The higher your quality, the higher your ROI.
- The higher your quality, the higher your market share.
- It makes no difference what your business is, quality always counts.
- Improving your quality improves your market share.
- High quality lets you get away with higher prices.
- "Value" is the ultimate execution of a quality strategy.

Naturally these are all probability statements. Don't get upset if you come across an exception now and then. As I'm sure you know, the probability theory governs all of life's judgments and decisions; few things are 100 percent certain.

These, then, are the key findings about the strategic role of product quality, but I presume you would like to have more details for your planning needs. The rest of the chapter will be devoted to each finding in turn.

return on investment

The lackluster business that produces lower-than-average-quality products or services will experience a smaller return on its investment than the firm producing products of average quality, but the differences won't be very large—a matter of only a few percentage points. The bumper difference in returns occurs for that gentrified business with the higher-than-average-quality product. Its returns will probably be well over twice the magnitude of the lower-than-average-quality purveyor. For those who like to think while they read, I hasten to add that the same thing applies when you examine *return on sales:* the lower your relative quality, the worse off your returns. (In one analysis of hundreds of different SBUs, the SPI showed that, with low-quality products, the ROS was only 6 percent; with average quality it was around 8 percent; with high quality it soared to 14 percent.[16] The exact numbers can change with the times, as they are easily shoved around by inflation and demand intensities, but the relationships are going to remain constant.) On the strength of this analysis alone, we can appreciate the sway of product quality. Clearly, it is no myth. Its importance as a magnet in drawing and keeping a clientele is unquestionable, except to the most cynical. However, working it into your overall business strategy requires more than just this limited appreciation.

Next, we must look at how quality entwines itself with other factors in fostering profits. Quality superiority helps get you a heftier market share, and in previous chapters we've written at length on how this can generate fat profits. The skeptics have the right to ask, however, if this is merely market share talking and taking quality along just for the ride. In other words, we may have deluded ourselves into thinking that quality strategies work when, in fact, all we are witnessing is a benefit of a big market share.

The short answer is that there is no illusion involved here. Picture a nine-cell chart with low, medium, and high market share breaks across the top, and low, average, and high quality breaks down the side. This would show that the skeptics are correct only in a limited sense: Whenever you have a high market share (regardless of quality level), you get a better ROI than you would with lower shares. But the skeptic's argument loses support thereafter. The same thing happens to be true when you focus on quality: Wherever it's high (regardless of share level), the ROIs are better than otherwise. The ultimate answer to the skeptic is given at the place on the chart where high share and high quality coincide. Here you get an ROI higher than anywhere else; it's at least three times the magnitude given by low-share/low-quality product situations, and about one-third larger than any other.[17]

As though their survival instincts were unerringly wrong, we see with abhorrently high frequency businesses that, failing to carve out a substantial franchise in the market, elect to bastardize their products and make them as shoddy as possible, hoping to boost margins. Then there they sit, stunned, as profits dwindle, seeking to find someone to blame. They sack first the poor sales manager, then their marketing managers, until shortly the entire management group is ransacked and replaced. From the very beginning, it was a simple misunderstanding about customers' respect for quality that was at the root of the trouble.

You can see the helpful union of share and quality much more clearly if you were to examine the quality *composition* of different levels of market share. Among businesses with low market shares, almost half will have low-quality products—not even one-quarter will have top quality. Moving right along to the medium share businesses, you would see a fairly even split; roughly a third will have high quality, a third medium quality, and a third low quality—not great, but an improvement over the first group. Finally, when you get to the high share group, you find that it's a perfect reciprocal of the first group: fully half have high quality, and less than one-quarter have low quality. Enough said.[18]

65

Palpably, other strategic factors affect profitability, too. Quality isn't the only thing to worry about, but it is one of the more intrusive factors in the strategic spectrum, and the strategist that elects to ignore it makes a colossal strategic mistake.

your business is not different

In spite of the mountains of evidence that deny it, most managers still think their case is different. "Yeah, well that may be true in the breakfast cereal business, and it might even apply to the auto business," they are wont to plead, "but my business is unusual."

Not true. As with all the strategic elements so far covered, quality transcends the idiosyncrasies of specific industries. Maybe we can use the SPI's data to put this red herring to bed once and for all. Among consumer products the average low-quality item gives you a 15 percent ROI, and high-quality items, 32 percent. With capital goods the relationship is 10 percent and 21 percent. With raw materials it is 13 percent and 35 percent, and with components it is 12 percent and 36 percent. In all cases quality pays.[19]

Still, not every reader will be convinced. Some will argue, "My business isn't different because of what I make. It's different because I've had to invest more heavily in it. So I can't afford to put more quality in the product."

In response, we can say the fact still remains that these relationships pertain regardless of whether your business is capital intensive or not, and whether or not you are vertically integrated. So, even if you are in the habit of regarding your business as unique, it is at your peril that you allow your product to drift onto a market that will not regard it with high esteem.

growth markets are the one exception

Quality, as I said, helps you achieve greater increases in your market share, but rather than belabor that point, I would prefer to spend some time exploring one important exception to this.

Quality's contribution to market share increments is really only applicable in a market where there isn't much growth. In the growth market, quality advantages do not help you much if you are seeking advances in your market share.[20] I suppose this has an intuitive appeal to it. Look at it this way: In most cases a growth market is a *new* market, or at least one that has recently undergone some kind of revitalization (like personal radios upon the advent of the Sony

Walkman). You may be able to slink by with relatively un-distinguished quality while the market is surging ahead, simply because the customer has not had time to formulate his or her own, private criteria as to what constitutes quality. At first there was only the Sony Walkman; then, shortly thereafter, many knockoffs appeared. By the time the market had gone into its second and third years, brands like Proton had appeared, offering substantially better audio characteristics than their forerunner. Among the teenagers in my neighborhood, it took many months before they collected their thoughts and were able to make confident assessments about the large number of brands then becoming available. In the beginning kids were hesitatingly willing to concede the quality laurels to Sony (because of its overall image), but later judgments splintered widely. So, while the segment was getting off to a fast start, quality per se was not too important; as growth tapered off, however, it became a prime factor.

I don't feel this should give the low-quality producer much solace. While quality may not be too instrumental in a fast growth market in helping to carve out a satisfactory market share, it is absurd to neglect it for long. When the growth rate cools, the low-quality producer will be left high and dry (just like my French dog food client). Some markets mature awfully fast, so there's often not a lot of time to let this one go unattended.

not too late to go straight

Question: What if you are one of those nefarious, low-quality producers; you made a lot of mistakes, sewed the wild oats, and have a bum product. Now you are contrite, and you've got a few notions on how to expiate your perversity by securing drastic improvements in your product's quality. Is it worth it? Is it too late? Will you only end up as a martyr to some lost cause?

Answer: Well, in this *one* sense, it is a forgiving world. You can put your errant past behind you. With honest product improvements you can orchestrate a veritable crescendo in your market share. Now it's going to cost you some money (The world is not quite so forgiving that your atonement should be free.) In the short run, your earnings will suffer. That will be your penance. But, if you're in it for the long haul, your aggrandized share position will more than make up for the initial damage. This is a reprieve and, ultimately, if you continue to go straight, your complete rehabilitation will be achieved. What the data show is that, regardless of where your quality level is when you first trod the path of righteousness, any improvements will get you a share increase of from 0.7 point to 1.0 point over a four-year period—the former being awarded to the relatively low-quality product that hoists itself up by the bootstraps of quality, and the latter going to the already high-quality paragon that manages to make itself even better. There isn't all that much difference, and these are only averages, so there's room for maneuver. The conclusion: Everybody wins share by setting a course on a quality beacon.[21]

one more look at pricing

In the last chapter I announced that I would resume our study of the question of value in a later chapter. This is later.

Since price is one side of value (the other side, in case you've forgotten already, is quality), let me preface this with a few comments for background. As I said at the beginning of this section, the top quality products can charge a higher price. Here are some SPI indications of how this pans out: On an indexed basis with 100 being the average price, the lowest quality products have a 99, and the highest a 107. Naturally this doesn't mean that they necessarily carry it off (I mean, you can charge any price you want, but the customers don't have to buy), but their respective margins suggest that they do manage to make it carry through into the P&L statement; the inferior product has a gross margin of only 24.6 percent vs. the superior product's 32.3 percent.[22]

value

Finally fulfilling that promise, we come to the subject of value. Value, to reiterate, is a function of price and quality simultaneously relative to competition.

Now, given that a product with a high relative quality can usually fetch a higher price than its inferior quality competitors, it logically follows that, if it chooses to offer itself at a price lower than its quality could demand (or even if not so hot on quality, but prices itself below other products of equal quality), it offers the customer the almost irresistible temptation of value. We all live in an ongoing information vacuum. Our physical nature attempts to impose itself and have its needs satisfied, and concurrently, our intellectual nature gropes for the right knowledge to allow us to function in a reasonable manner. The information vacuum is nicely filled by the value concept because it transcends so many different physical and mental issues and can be quickly and simply compacted into a handy, manageable, easily expressed *raison d'etre;* it can satisfy the needs of both the pushers and the pullers, of both supply and demand sides of the transaction; it is basic to our economic beliefs as consumers, and melds well into that conscious system of behavioral justifications that should precede, and follow, all transactions if enduring commercial relationships are to be secured by the industrial sector.

Value is often one of those things you have to see and feel in order to understand. The implementation of a value strategy may require some faith. In a world where all your business judgments come home to roost, it takes real moral courage to offer your product or service at a price lower than you know it can command. Nonetheless, under many specific circumstances, it is the best way to go if you want to have a high ROI.

I believe your faith can be strengthened by looking at some of the findings on value from the SPI. Value strategies help immensely when you are down and out and suffering the ignominy of low market shares. Since this is the lot of *most* products, the findings should have some relevance to many readers. Value strategies offer the low share product much comfort, and, while even the high share brand can enhance its ROI with a value strategy, it cannot get as much concomitant market share gain as its low-share cohort. When they decide to give their customers higher value, the low-share folks gain market share at twice the speed of the comparable brand offering only low value. Moreover, the ROI for a low-share/low-value product will be a crummy 9 percent before taxes, but its low-share/high-value complement will get roughly twice that much. Worth going for, wouldn't you say? The gains in ROI decline when you look at the medium share business. With low value they will get somewhere around a 20 percent ROI before taxes, but high value brings them up to only 26 percent, which is still worth shooting for but not as dramatic as with the low-share value strategy gains. When you have a high-share product with a low value, your ROI starts off higher than any of the other groups at 28 percent (a determinant of the high share, of course), but a high-value strategy will only bring it up to 33 percent. Still very pleasing, but the impression of improvement on the bottom line seems less spectacular, which must be considered in career planning. The overall lesson, however, is that, whether your share is big or little, you can improve your ROI by assuming the cloak of value, and that, for those of us who are cursed with perennial low-share brands, there is much to be gained—both for the business and for the career—in taking a long, serious look at a value strategy.[23]

Back a few pages, when I was discussing quality and growth markets, I pointed out that the older your product category, the more discerning your customers in their appraisals of your quality level. This, of course, will apply to the question of value, too. In the early stages of your product lifecycle, folks aren't in any shape to recognize value, but as things move along, they smarten up. Hence, if your product category has advanced into its middle or late phase, it is now timely to consider a value strategy, for this is when it will do its job. The average ROI for a low-value product in the early growth stage of the lifecycle is around 22 percent, while the high-value product does slightly better with 28 percent. As the market matures and growth slows to a crawl, however, the low-value product finds itself now getting only a 17 percent ROI while its high-value counterpart earns a 27 percent. Then, when the market goes into its grand finale, the low-value products will have a 12 percent ROI and the high-value ones will have almost double that (22 percent). So the message is crystal clear: A high-value strategy can help you maintain a decent level of returns through your product's entire lifecycle, whereas a low-value approach gives satisfactory returns only at its very inception and causes ROI to shrink if allowed to persist. Accompanying this is another finding that will appeal to all those frustrated marketing directors who have experienced the setbacks that go with trying to forge any market share gains during periods of market stagnation or decline: If you execute a value strategy, your share will grow about three times as rapidly as that of your competitors who offer lower value.[24]

Along these same lines, value can help you improve your profits when you are a bit tardy getting into a market. In fact, with a deft execution of a value strategy, you can come damn close to earning the same ROI that the pioneers are getting with a similar high-value strategy. Here's what the analysis shows: The low-value pioneer has around a 23 percent ROI vs. the high-value pioneer's 28 percent. This is just about the same relationship between value levels that we saw in the early phase of the market's lifecycle. In addition, the pioneers will not experience much difference in returns from their value effects as the market matures; their ROIs will stay about the same, or at most, go up a few points if they improve their value. But the product that is introduced quite late in the game can choose between a 6 percent ROI via a low-value strategy and a 24 percent ROI via a high-value strategy (some choice!); or, in other words, though it sounds unfair, a late market entrant can achieve almost the same ROI level as the pioneer without having to go through the back-breaking agony of the pioneer, who had to educate the customer base, talk it up with the trade, deal like mad to get distribution, and indulge in all the promotional exertions that trailblazing demands. The latecomer can walk in, assume the high value stance, and do almost as well as the innovator. As we all know, under normal circumstances, the Johnny-come-lately treads on thin ice, and few of them ever make it. But if they seize on a high-value strategy, they can flourish. It goes without saying, then, that you better watch out if you think your late-entry product can succeed by offering low value. You are dealing with a group of customers who, probably through bitter experience, know quality when they see it. A low-value approach will kill you with its savings-account level of returns (i.e., the miserable 6 percent reported above).[25]

Value, then, may be the ultimate form of differentiation, though the opportunities for product variation need not end there. It can augment and bolster the product differentiation that gave you that minimonopoly where you can set your own price and become virtually insulated from competition. A high-value strategy here gives you added defense against the inroads of rivals who, in order to inflict harm upon you, would need to invest heavily in R&D to discover a means of out-differentiating you—and then, once that had been accomplished, to engage you in battle in a market where the price level you have established may be totally unattractive at the moderate volumes they could realistically expect to achieve.

Hence, most of the key factors involved in prudent marketing strategy formulation come together: price, quality, differentiation, and market share. Once the proper balance of these ingredients is struck for the specific market context in which your product or service seeks its fortunes, the task of devising the executional tactics should become a fairly simple matter. Just make sure that whomever you assign to work out the tactics sticks to the strategy, particularly if part of the task is delegated to an advertising agency, as they are notoriously unable (or unwilling) to knuckle under to the restraints of any strategy not of their own making. In a sense, it is all very simple. Though we can analyze it to death, the subject of quality has probably changed very little since man has been bartering. The master strategists have always known that the secret to success is partly one of projecting value in the eyes of the beholder. In our tactical elaborations, we often lose sight of this fundamental truth.

Quality as a business strategy has a joyous and more universal side to it. It gives brightness to the commonly perceived gloom and cynicism of toiling for a profit. It is good public relations in a world made miserable by vocal misfits who use the media to tear it all down—who argue, darkly, that nothing we do in business makes any sense, that our lives have no purpose, no meaning, that all is as depicted in *Waiting for Godot*. Here, in the quality and value of our productive efforts, we demonstrate to the contemporary mind that there is a good side to our technological society that even the most disinterested can see and appreciate. It should help us keep our ramparts unbreached a while longer.

NOTES

1. Not as foolish as it sounds. In the U.K., I had tried testing a dog food using regular market (identified) containers and got a different result than when I later tested the same product blind. Of course, those were English dogs, and understandably more literate than the Gallic canines, but I didn't want to take any chances with my French client.

2. "GE Expects to Hit High Note in a Flat Year for Industry," *HFD-Retailing Home Furnishings,* December 28, 1981, sec. I, p. 22.

3. Bill Abrams, "Research Suggests Consumers Will Increasingly Seek Quality," *Wall Street Journal*, October 15, 1981, p. 25.

4. Ibid.

5. Ibid.

6. Oscar Schisgall, "Pampers: How P&G Created a Market," *Advertising Age*, January 18, 1982, p. 50.

7. David B. Tinnin, "The Heady Success of Holland's Heineken," *Fortune*, November 16, 1981, p. 158.

8. T. O'Hanlon, "Behind the Snafu at Singer," *Fortune*, November 5, 1979, pp. 76-78.

9. G. Colvin, "Federal Express Dives into Air Mail," *Fortune*, June 15, 1981, pp. 106-8.

10. Bruce Henderson, "Perspectives: Competitive Differences and Competition," no. 222 (Boston, MA: Boston Consulting Group, 1979), pp. 1-2.

11. Margaret Yao, "P&G Is Buying Ben Hill Griffin Citrus Business," *Wall Street Journal*, August 19, 1981, p. 8.

12. Bill Abrams and Paul Ingrassia, "P&G Plotting Big Move into Orange Juice," *Wall Street Journal*, October 8, 1982), p. 25.

13. Dale D. Buss, "Fake Food: To Dairymen's Dismay, Imitation Cheeses Win Growing Market Share," *Wall Street Journal*, July 20, 1981, p. 1.

14. Charles W. Hofer and Dan Schendel, "Strategy Formulation: Analytical Concepts," (St. Paul, MN: West Publishing Company, 1978), pp. 138-39.

15. Robert D. Buzzell, "Product Quality," *PIMSLETTER*, no. 4 (Cambridge, MA: The Strategic Planning Institute), p. 11.

16. Ibid., p. 3.

17. Ibid., p. 4.

18. Sidney Schoeffler, Robert D. Buzzell, Donald F. Heany, "Impact of Strategic Planning on Profit Performance," *Harvard Business Review*, 52, no. 2 (March-April 1974), p. 141.

19. "Product Quality," *PIMSLETTER*, no. 4 (1978), p. 5. While the exact figures could change with various economic forces, we would not expect to experience any substantial variations in the relationships.

20. Ibid., p. 6.

21. Ibid., p. 8.

22. Ibid., p. 9.

23. Mark Chussil and Steve Downs, "When Value Helps," *PIMSLETTER*, no. 18 (Cambridge, MA: The Strategic Planning Institute, 1979), p. 4.

24. Ibid., p. 2.

25. Ibid., p. 3.

6

new products
and a little bit of R&D

There isn't much in business strategy to get emotional about. But the Research & Development part of it comes close.

Now and again everyone *thinks* his own professional group gets a raw deal. But R&D almost always gets the shaft. Since the first caveman invented the wheel, the R&D people have been responsible for everything that has carried technology forth; they are the legitimate custodians of its future, yet they seldom bask in the corporate limelight. As a consequence, we have fallen on bad times, and many are asking if this is the end of the American adventure.

Even if we muster our resources and set forth on a strategy of product quality, sounding the drums with the added dual enticements of supervalue and unchallenged differentiation, few of us would be bubbling with optimism. We in the beseiged part of the industrialized world no longer have any assurance that foreign copycats won't duplicate our efforts. The evidence suggests we're no longer the best end-result of the Industrial Revolution. In fact, as self-doubt mounts, many ask if we have become the reactionaries in this revolution. How do we guide the destinies of our businesses through the global thicket? There's no protective shield against competition of that sort, but it sure would be nice to find something that makes the sting of it less **73** painful.

In many industries, and for many individual companies, the answer is to be found in enhanced applications of Research and Development and in bolder, wiser new products programs. Though there has been ample activity on the new product frontier, much of it has lacked wisdom. To quote Zbigniew Brzezinski, "Stupidity generally tends to be more widespread than insight."[1]

Much of the mindlessness can be traced to issues we have discussed in previous chapters. Knee-jerk attendance to the marketing concept is one culprit. Accompanying this is a depressing display of ignorance about the economics of markets—of what it takes to produce a positive cash flow, of the true nature of competition, and so forth.

our disastrous new products scene

With more serious reflection on new product strategy, our nation might have ended up happier and richer. Our performance in the new product area is the shame of the world of commerce. But don't blame the technical geniuses who invented all the new products. Blame those inveterate tacticians who impose their wills on our corporations, the silver-tongues who ensnare us all in their insane short-term gambits to fiduciary moonscapes.

Most of them know nothing of the past. It has become quite common for an American company to see the technology it developed, and eventually rejected, rebound as an impressive new product from a foreign competitor. (Many of our consumer goods are rejected because marketing managers cannot warm up to any innovation not easily communicated in a 30-second commercial.) Today Detroit is forcing itself to eat crow and learn from the Japanese, but in many cases what they are learning is that some of the technology that is so successfully implemented by the Japanese is technology Detroit itself developed, but rejected, years ago. Example: Nissan's two-liter engine with its *novel* hemispherical combustion chambers. Not really new. Chrysler first had it back in the 1950s. Surely all the high-tech ideas of the past are still stuffed safely away in shoe boxes somewhere in Michigan. Why did it have to be Nissan that revived it?[2]

Neglect and complacency have allowed massive industrial dislocations to take place. But, being a nation of extremes, there is also a flipside to the insanity. In some sectors, high-tech has become the lunatic's religion; without cowled theologians to form it, with no comprehensive thought structure, with neither coherent goals nor systematic strategies, we tithe away finite resources serving a cause that in the end, may be as ruinous as the Crusades. There is a high-tech bandwagon, and its drivers don't have road maps. A study by

Booz, Allen & Hamilton[3] confirms what has been evident to many of us for some time, that while the United States still has the best aggregate of technical brains, we lack the guts and long-range thinking to capitalize on our concepts in the marketplace. We squirm and make little fists in our pockets as the Japanese "wow" our populace with sci-fi products. William Sommers, executive vice president of Booz, Allen, puts a finger on the problem when he says, "It's no trick to hire scientists and engineers for technological innovation, but a company will fail to benefit much unless their efforts mesh with business objectives." Our industrial elfland needs more than magic to make it click.

The Booz, Allen study identifies some characteristics of companies that make high-tech pay. The first is that the technical staff gets to see the top dogs now and then; i.e., they are not forever banished to some out-of-the-way laboratory, occasionally allowed back to beg for funds and called on the carpet to account for being unable, for example, to turn riverbottom sand into semiconductors with minimal capital investment. In brief, they are regarded as part of the team, are even allowed to fail now and then, and are roundly appreciated for their role in the corporation. Honored as major contributors to the company's progress, they work in an environment that encourages good, two-way communication. Contrast that with the more typical company, where even the most brilliant chemists and engineers, with strings of academic degrees making management seem like high school dropouts, are belittled when they can't explain their creations to the ad agency in terms understandable to people who sport $250 Gucci footwear and whose spans of attention are so attentuated that all they can recall afterwards are the technical guy's Hush Puppies. Even more appalling is the groveling attitude technical people feel obliged to affect in the presence of marketing people. Visibly nervous, they stammer and grow inarticulate, even though on their own turf their eloquence is close to poetry. Their servile instincts are a function of the corporation's distorted perspective. In some companies the misplaced power of marketing is ascribed to the technician's allegedly narrow outlook, but many have a vastly broader general knowledge than many of their marketing counterparts whose instincts may be more suited to the court of Louis XIV than to the modern world of recessive economies and industrial dislocation. (As I said at the outset, R&D is the only place on the strategy spectrum where it is tempting to get agitated.)

Strong medicine is needed. A few companies seem to have the right approach.

Donald Hammond, director of Hewlett-Packard's physical electronics lab, advocates promoting a degree of entrepreneurship among company scientists: "We encourage our people to take about 10 percent of their time for under-the-bench projects."

Occasionally their pet projects can be transformed into viable new products, but marketing has to be restrained from hoisting up their not-invented-here roadblocks in the early stages of germination. Hammond mentions one such success: a new paper plotter concept for calligraphy and printing industries that was so successful it had sales of $50 million in year one.

B.F. Goodrich has also seen the light, which may come as a welcome surprise to observers long convinced the rubber industry was a throwback to the days of Dickens. In truth, there was a time when the old rubber company's executive set was pretty well sheltered from the scientific plodders, but no longer. Technology management has become an integral part of its five-year plan. Inescapably, this gives R&D heightened visibility. Its progress is carefully documented, and its funding is adjusted to meet current needs and to ensure that R&D and the company's long-range goals fit each other hand-in-glove. Gone are the old days when Goodrich simply allocated an arbitrary percentage of the past year's sales for R&D. It is now part-and-parcel of the company's overall vision of the future.

Companies like these are exceptions in our land. Most readers are only too aware that, when it comes to giving R&D concepts the breath of life, it's the Japanese who are the only gods on Olympus deserving one's full obeisance. At the risk of antagonizing the die-hard Babbits, Vince Lombardi look-alikes, and Willy Lomans, I'll even put it stronger: When American industry does flex its new product muscle, it usually comes a cropper. Let's look at the evidence: "Major new product successes haven't been the lifeblood of most large food companies," sums up a gargantuan study on the subject conducted by the New York ad shop, Dancer Fitzgerald Sample.[4] Taking the whole of the 1970s as its timeframe, a decade you could view as especially active in new consumer products, and concentrating on a grouping of industries that have been widely regarded as making the American dream come true, the agency counted over 5,000 new supermarket products. Using a rather modest standard (too modest I think, but never mind) of $15 million in retail sales as a success criterion (it's pretty hard to get national distribution and dealer support with anything less), Dancer found only 93 winners—a success probability of only 0.2 percent. With odds like that you'd be better off playing the horses.

To be perfectly fair and above-board, other studies have shown higher success rates. The highly reputable Conference Board gives new products a two-out-of-three chance of success. The world's largest market research firm, A.C. Nielsen, reports it is one out of three. But these analyses have a less rigorous success standard than the one DFS uses; they either accepted the manufacturer's word that its product was a success or judged a new product successful if it were still on the market after a certain period of time. As strategists seeking a maximum return on our investments, we have to have a more concrete objective in mind. For national products the DFS $15 million in sales cutoff is very conservative, so the agency's study is worth looking into more closely. (Later, in an in-depth analysis, we will explore the impact of new products and of R&D on ROI.)

What kinds of products failed? Here are some examples: When meat prices sky-rocketed in 1973, a lot of "meat-extender" products appeared on grocers' shelves. Made mostly from soybean and a little bit of seasoning, these products looked pretty promising for a while— until meat prices came tumbling back down. So, could you say that here was a good concept that met up with an unfavorable economic climate, or that it was introduced without a cautious study of the history of meat prices, which is punctuated with roller-coaster swings? During the 1970s at least five major food companies tried frozen sandwiches. All failed. Could the post mortem argue that this was the sort of idea that does well in a concept study but has to be priced so far above the cost of making a sandwich at home that it lacks practical merit? Are sandwiches so easy to make that a frozen sandwich has little convenience to offer? Another example: Early in the decade Campbell Soup introduced a pizza-flavored sandwich spread. It flopped, but this did not serve as a deterrent to other food packers. By mid-decade, Libby, McNeill and Libby had introduced its own pizza spread, which also failed. Then, in 1978, Corn Products Company introduced another one. You can always count on one thing: It isn't just the good ideas that get copied. Could you argue that the 1970s found food manufacturers misjudging the appeal of pizza, that they were not aware that restaurant pizza is preferred by consumers to the in-home frozen variety, and that, if pizza spreads couldn't even match the appeal of frozen pizza, it didn't have a chance (i.e., it had no *reason why*)?

Throughout the 1970s there were only 32 companies that came out with any new food products with sales over $15 million. Only a dozen companies had more than one winner. Most had whole stables of losers. Beatrice foods, to give just one example, in just two, short years (1977-79), brought out 59 floperoos! Beatrice's only triumph for the entire decade, according to the DFS study, was Shedd's New Spread margarine. Just to give you the flavor of new food item failures, here are some Beatrice fizzles from that era:

- an apple-cinnamon flavored eggroll (yes, an eggroll!)
- a yogurt bar with a pina-collada flavor
- a toilet bowl cleaning tablet (very "me-too")
- canned sukiyaki
- a dog treat called Glad Wags.

Some companies got so badly stung in the 1970s that they almost have adopted discouragement as the official corporate philosophy.

CPC, for one, claims to have just about given up on aggressive new product entries. CPC is more inclined now to focus on its overseas markets where the food industry still grows at an encouraging clip and marketing costs are not as high as in the United States. Eric Haueter, vice president for commercial development at CPC, says that "the inherent risk in any new product launch in the United States is $20 million to $25 million; even for a company our size [close to $4 billion], that's a pretty big risk."[5] Small successes are not good enough in a large company. Fred Lamont, formerly of Procter & Gamble, now spearheading his own New York consulting firm, says that "only major new products can make a real impact on a company; little products take almost as much effort as big ones and frequently can be a problem even if they succeed, because they are too small to develop."[6]

Enough of these recriminatory details. The moral is that the marketing concept, where we seek and satisfy human needs, is a trap. Only 93 out of 5,000 new products studied were able to whomp up enough sales volume to make the effort and the investment worthwhile. These examples of failure are typical manifestations of new-product planning. Not enough hard thinking is going on to formulate the most efficacious new-product strategies.

industrial products just as bad

The new-product failure rate transcends product categories. It's just as bad in the industrial sector, though not so glaring as it receives less public attention and isn't tracked internally as carefully. When new industrial products fail, they can go undetected for years. In fact, another Booz, Allen study[7] (different from the one previously cited in this chapter) found that one-third of all companies, incredibly, do not take a formal measure of the performance of their new products. That alone is a terrible indictment of American industry. Furthermore, what most businesses call a "new product" isn't new at all; most are just spinoffs or line extensions. Only 10 percent are what Booz, Allen would classify as "new to the world." These were the ones most likely to be successful—which takes us back to our comments in Chapter 5 about differentiation. Bold, new ideas give you a better crack at the new-products sweepstakes.[8]

Those who have turned their backs on new products, or who try to mollify shareholders after a string of failures, often argue that the numbers on innovative exploits aren't very attractive anymore, that cranking up the old plant to produce new products is simply too damn expensive today. The analysis, however, shows that the opposite is true. Capital investment, viewed as a percentage of the total cost of bringing out a new product, has actually dropped from 46 percent to

26 percent since the late 1960s. Now, admittedly, part of this is due to rising marketing costs, but (other things being equal) it does suggest that the ROI for new products should be better today than it was several years ago. Moreover, the experience curve drives down the cost of new product activities as a company gets more knowledgeable at how to go about it. The Booz, Allen study shows that every time a firm doubles the number of new items it develops, its costs per introduction drop 29 percent.

Monetary incentive plans have become quite commonplace in American industry (I'll have more to say on this in Chapter 11), but it is significant to point out that very little is done to encourage the birthing of new products; ninety-five percent of companies studied have no incentive plans to induce anyone to excel in this area. The guile of short-term performance serves as a rigid barrier to new product creation. For inspired scientists and tinkerers there has to be a greater reward than just getting to keep their jobs, especially when they are bound to be contrasting their contributions with the contributions of those who implement their ideas and reap the biggest rewards; to the scientific community it must seem that the implementors are getting the lion's share of the kill for a very minor intellectual expenditure. Not exactly the way to keep important people happy.

threat of generic products

Continuing with this gloomy valuation of our muddling, let's take one last look at consumer goods. Here is where our abysmal performance in new products and the concomitant ennui of consumers meet head on. You don't have to lift many rocks to find the disasters. The mounting decline in the integrity and desirability of brand names is one such disaster. When the brand aegis is not vigorously maintained by hyperdifferentiation, when value is not given, and when new product effort fails to renew a brand's aging appeal, generic products come along that do a "me-too" number at about two-thirds the price and walk off with a sizeable chunk of the business. Generics are reported by A.C. Nielsen as having an overall 1981 share-in-stores-stocking of 12 percent. The Selling Areas Marketing Index (SAMI) reports that total generic dollars amount to 1.58 percent of all food stores sales, or $1.4 billion annually. Generics tend to do especially well in upper income neighborhoods (where the harbingers of future mass consumer behavior dwell), suggesting rather strongly that it is the dearth of really desirable and inspired new products, not inflation, that has impelled droves of consumers away from the branded products long considered part of the American Way of Life. Twenty-five years ago the grey-flannel suit set would have scoffed at anything predicting the demise of brand marketing. If the generic craze is allowed to run rampant, it would set most of us back a hundred years. Clearly, renewed emphasis on making R&D and new-products efforts more successful is mandatory.[9]

the mounting japanese peril

Our failure to get our new-product plays right makes us eligible to warm the bench while Nippon wins the trophies. "But," you think (depending on how soon after its publication you read this chapter), "we can trounce the Japanese in the new information technology." Let's hope so, but I think even that is becoming more and more a big "maybe." The Japanese have an entirely different scenario in mind: By the end of the decade, they intend to be the first to introduce the ultimate generation of computers—ones that think, and speak, and make decisions just like humans. If they make it, and if they can keep the momentum going thereafter, it's good-bye to the Good Life for us. Once again we'll be the Colonials, and Japan will get to play England. We'll be sending the new Mother Country our crops and natural resources, while "she" sells us, at outrageous, monopolistic prices, all the electronic gadgets we can afford.[10]

strategic laws governing R&D

You can beget an innovative product line with strong R&D endeavor or replications of someone else's creative effort. Both work when done right. But developing the new-product strategy involves more than just hope; there is a time for valor and a time for calm surveillance.

As before, in order to debunk the subjective pontification that clouds men's minds so they can't draft workable strategies, we will visit the data bank—again the SPI—to withdraw a few facts about the R&D component of business strategy.

As we start sifting through the numbers, the first thing we come across is rather discouraging.[11] (If you're making moves to get your company to support a heftier R&D program, you may be tempted to keep this piece of information under your hat.) It says that, once you get beyond a certain R&D level (i.e., anything beyond a "low" R&D expenditure of 1.4 percent of sales), the more you put into it, the more your ROI drops off. But it is misleading to construe this as an indictment of an ambitious R&D effort per se. Naturally, you're always going to find situations where no amount of R&D will do much good. At one extreme there are companies that resist every urging of their young lions to get on the new-products bandwagon. To them R&D is just a useless expense, even though they might allow it to continue. Going to the opposite extreme, there are companies that spew out new products based on every strange smudge they find stuck to the bottom of a test tube. They aren't going to fare well financially either. So there are a couple, albeit exaggerated, cases where large dollops of R&D will obviously hurt profits.

However, except in these extreme cases, it would not be fair to indict R&D as the real malefactor. The linkage of low ROI to "high" R&D spending (3.0 percent of sales or more) is accidental. The kind of business that commonly indulges in heavy product development efforts can have other traits that lower its ROI potential.[12] For one thing, any active new-product program lowers operating profit—though not, one would hope, for the long term. This business might also have had a higher-than-average investment intensity (sales divided by assets) and may have been lured on its R&D voyage to discover ways of spreading those assets over more rent-paying products out of sheer desperation. Once established, an R&D installation can be self-perpetuating, even if it seldom makes any significant breakthroughs or even if management lacks the imagination to know how to market its discoveries. (Poor marketing will easily cut the success rate of any R&D program down to size.) Another characteristic of the big R&D spender is a tendency to have only average-quality products. All of these factors imply some degree of mismanagement. This bears further examination.

the concept of normal R&D spending

As you may have gathered by now, no single strategic factor functions *in vacuo*. R&D is no exception. It has to fit in with a multiplicity of other strategic factors. Obviously, it wouldn't make any sense for the local sand-and-gravel pit operator to spend as much on his R&D as the biotech pioneer. But most businesses fall between these two extremes; so, prior to deciding how much is too much, you have to know what is "normal" for your situation. This is the key that unlocks the door to the ultimate R&D and new-product strategies.

Let us look initially at the situation where very low spending on R&D (we'll define that as no more than 0.5 percent of sales for our present purposes) would be normal for a business.[13] The strategic profile of such a business goes like this: it's in the mature phase of its lifecycle, has about average (close to the GNP) growth going on in its market, is pretty limited on the degree to which it has managed to vertically integrate itself, and, as a natural consequence of that, has a fairly low level of investment intensity (i.e., it has suppliers selling it much of what goes into its products—components, packaging, etc.—at the one end, and uses external channels of distribution at the other end), has fewer new products than its competitors, and is just middling on market share magnitude. In other words, there isn't much in this strategic thumbnail sketch that says it could really capitalize on an ambitious R&D program. Hence, such a business would be wise to *downhold* its R&D spending.

In sharp contrast, the business that regularly spends a whole lot more than normal on its R&D (let's say anything at or beyond 4.0 percent of its sales volume) will still be in the peach-fuzz phase of its lifecycle, and, of course, the market will be growing at a handsome clip. It'll have both higher-than-average vertical integration and investment intensity. Its market share will be quite high, and finally, it'll be very active in new-product launches.

Just to drive this home a bit more, let's study each of the main factors separately. Take vertical integration first. It should be obvious that the more complexity you have in your operation (i.e., the more you make instead of buy), the more opportunities you have to do some of it more efficiently or even to produce a superior product. So, it should come as no surprise to learn that the combination of high R&D spending and high levels of vertical integration produce the highest ROI plateau. In fact, you can regard the R&D high-rollers as belonging to an exclusive club in which one of the benefits of membership—for those with high vertical integration—is an ROI three times as big as their low vertical integration cohorts. In the not so exclusive R&D low-roller club, the difference between the high and low vertical integrationists is hardly noticeable at all.

So, the first lesson about R&D strategy is this: If you're thinking of going into it in a big way, check first to see what your vertical integration level is. If your operation is humming along at only an average or low level of vertical integration, your strong commitment to R&D won't produce any higher ROIs than for a business with a much lower R&D burden. The principle: If your business doesn't have the complexity, it doesn't offer the necessary scope for R&D to be effective. To impose it on the low vertically integrated business makes R&D—which is always a high risk game at the best of times— even more risky, sometimes causing it to eventually lose all management support.

Almost the same story can be told about the courtship of R&D and market share. In a sense, this courtship is an indication of a mutually rewarding romance between marketing and science. Though it occurs all too seldom, there are some excellent matches involving these two usually loggerheaded forces, and it seems reasonable that the occasion of such happy marriages is marked by glowing happiness in the form of substantial market shares. The businesses that succeed in the market—those with the big shares—are usually the ones that have learned, better than their competitors, how to benefit from shared accountabilities between marketing and R&D, while their faltering rivals put all their chips on marketing. In the R&D high-roller club the chaps with the low market shares receive a miserably tiny ROI while their fellow members, who are well-heeled with fat market shares, experience an ROI level about six times larger. In the R&D low-roller club the differences in ROI levels are much less dramatic, though indeed they are present to a lesser extent. The message, besides the fact that big market shares are healthy, is that a business also needs a large market share to get decent mileage out of its R&D. Some of the reasons for this will seem obvious. For one thing, whenever the small business's R&D does come up with a great idea, and it's put on the market, the bigger businesses have the resources to quickly copy it—or to go the smaller business one better; hence, the saying: "The pioneers are the ones with the arrows in their backs!"

Corporate size is also a strategic factor here; the bigger company is the one that can use its R&D more effectively to produce higher ROIs. Its overall human, physical, and financial resources are more formidable; they can be used to make more certain that the fruits of its R&D are adroitly implemented, and such a company is less likely to be enraptured by the verbal vampings of its headstrong tacticians. Big companies can also afford to hire and keep the best graduates of our engineering schools, which is becoming a more critical factor all the time as the size of the graduating class (only one-fifth that of the Soviet Union and equal to Japan's) in most years fails to keep up with demand. Furthermore, in many cases, the big company with the hefty market shares to protect can justify having better lab equipment— another incentive to bright scientists who, in another era, may have elected to remain in teaching, but who are now disenchanted with the academic setting where typical laboratory facilities are 20 to 30 years old and obviously dreadfully obsolete. Only the bigger companies can dangle that kind of lure.[14]

But these are only fragmentary glimpses. The successful strategists always orchestrate their R&D efforts in concert with many other strategic factors. We were talking about the question of normality and how it should be used to determine how much you invest in R&D. Our point was that the absolute amount you elect to put into R&D has no real bearing on your financial performance, but that what does count is how you veer away from what is normal for your set of strategic conditions. So, in order to arrive at some nonfustian insights into what level of R&D makes the most sense, we plumb the copious SPI data bank looking for what transpires when you invest in more, or less, R&D than is normal for a business with a given strategic profile (e.g., magnitude of vertical integration, market share level, etc.). The beauty of this exercise (just in case all my relationships and possibly tedious quibbles over definitions are starting to annoy you) is to isolate R&D from the distracting noise of stronger factors, like market share, so we can see it in its naked state.

(Off hand, you're not expected to know what amount of R&D is normal for you. I'm sure an elaborate computer program could be brought to bear on the problem, but that's hardly necessary to get through the rest of this chapter. In the preceding sections, I spelled out most of the traits of the normally low and the normally high R&D spender; you can readily come to a rough, but good enough, determination on where your business fits and whether your current R&D budget, as a percent of net sales, makes you an *overspender* or an *underspender* compared to these rough benchmarks. For definitions, let's say spending beyond what is normal by 1 percent of sales makes you an overspender, below by 1 percent, an underspender.)

R&D overspending has a sodden impact regardless of market share. In one analysis, the SPI showed that low market share overspenders had an ROI of 11 percent, but their underspending counterparts had a 16 percent ROI. Even if your market share is high, overspending still nets out with a lower ROI than underspending by the same margin (27 percent vs. 32 percent). While the overall higher level of ROI somehow makes the penalty feel less severe, in truth, market share does not rescue you from the excesses of overspending.[15] But the key point may be that the SBU with a weak market share isn't going to find salvation in R&D overspending.

Keep in mind, however, that this is not an indictment of the serious, ambitious developmental effort, but rather a recognition of the limits adjacent strategic (or circumstantial) factors can impose on its chances of successful carry-through into the market. Picture, if you will, the dilemma that Westinghouse found itself in when it stepped back and took a long, hard look at its ceramic gas-turbine blade developmental progress and asked itself if it should continue to plow more R&D money into it. Westinghouse knew it was going to take about another $80 million in R&D to get the blades to where they would be acceptable for use in the high-temperature turbines that were slated to become the future's big market. They also figured by 1990 blade sales would bring in $205 million more than the additional R&D would consume. But it didn't take much arithmetic to show that, when they discounted this at 15 percent a year (to cover the cost of the capital, etc.) the project did not pay out. Worse yet, after 1990, the project's return on its invested capital would be only 11 percent, which strictly speaking meant that for Westinghouse to proceed further in developing its ceramic blade business would have been an example of gross R&D overspending. And it is often the case that the early allure of R&D can later be transformed into a powerful suction from which it is difficult to escape with career unscathed.[16]

Consider for a moment the following line of thought: If R&D is fruitful, it should, as one of its principle tasks, give you some new products. If successful, these new items should help you build market share. That's a pretty reasonable scenario, which is why you're going to be surprised when you find out what the analysis shows. Amazingly, it says that the most awesome gains in market share are made by businesses that bring out lots of new products while (somehow) underspending on R&D![17] When your strategy is concentrated on aggrandizing your market share, clearly the new product route is a safe bet for helping to achieve this. But the decision to grease the skids with a higher with normal application of R&D is not a wise one. All things being equal, virtually any business will see its market shares rise if it embarks on a serious new-products program. For example, with a high ratio (10 percent or over) of new products to total sales, the average SBU can expect to see its share go up about 3.5 percent annually. But the R&D underspender will have a 4.8 percent increase in its share, while the overspender garners only a 3.2 percent increase. What these data suggest are that the new products that come about by (ahem) *reverse engineering,* or any other method besides lab work, are going to be more beneficial. While legal fees and court decisions can rapidly deprive you of any nefarious profit when you infringe on someone's patents, there are less scruffy ways of copying. In fact, with good consumer intelligence and a round of concept research, you may be able to improve on the competition's idea without ending up in the defendant's dock. Additionally, a small bit of creative thinking can lead to unusual combinations of heretofore discrete objects and concepts.

- Electronic circuitry plus a wrist watch produces the digital watch with limitless possibilities and applications.
- Even better than copying, some companies find it more profitable to combine the best features of many diverse products or services, for this, after all, is what the creative process really entails: the talent, or accidental good fortune, for associating or nourishing the links between things and ideas that normal people see as totally distinct or irrevocably separate.
- When this won't work, some companies turn to licensing arrangements to maintain their flow of new products without the need of their own R&D task force.
- Sometimes *new* means exactly that. It's an idea that requires no R&D at all. To cite a previous example: The founder of Federal Express *saw* that a parcel's fastest way from Los Angeles to San Francisco was via Memphis in the dead of the night. Ideas like that probably occur in instantaneous flashes of inspiration and creative energy. Being unusual, they often get killed off by attacking drones; significantly, the Federal Express founder first unveiled his idea in a college paper, for which he got only a "C."

Whether they come from someone's ostensibly deranged mind or from some enchanted R&D laboratory, new products and major improvements in old ones are indisputably precisely what this country needs to enliven its sputtering economy. But this kind of positive thinking wilts in head-on opposition to the popular "rock-'em, sock-'em," short-term emphasis on quarterly profit increments.[18] New-product thinking is, by definition, long-term thinking. It is now so unfashionable to do anything about this that it even has become a matter of concern for the United States Senate, where it is regarded as a major national problem.[19] (What the government can do about it, besides tinkering with a few patent regulations and some FDA approval procedures, is a big question. The answer will have to come from a complete recasting of our management incentive programs; see Chapter 11.) Too much of our nation's R&D comes about as a request from marketing departments. The R&D group in most companies waits to be told what to do. The problem with this is the narrowly conceived, "sis-boom-bah" requests from marketing ignore whole regions of scientific discovery. Ideas are not going to be very inspiring when they drift up and down the distribution channels, like decaying effluvia in a city's sewers, running back and forth through several *refinements,* from consumer to marketing product manager, until all seminal value is leached out. In the last 20 years we've seen a thumping decline in R&D (from 2.07 percent of GNP to 1.76 percent) as an influential force in our industrial milieu.[20] Since the 1950s the U.S. global share of inventions brought to market has shrunk 25 percent.[21]

It's easy to yield to the temptation to travel the most convenient route, free of virtually all risk, bringing out those tired, old, predictable line-extensions and spinoffs until the retailers' warehouses are clogged with "me too" items. This has become the stop-gap cure for spent intellectual resources, and it presents a profound danger to any enterprise encountering major market changes or foreign competitors suddenly springing the unexpected—radial tires, smaller cars with front-wheel drive—that no amount of relabeling, restyling, reshaping, repackaging, or repositioning will successfully combat.

new products and market share

Continuing current new-product strategies help companies with big market shares repeatedly replenish their product lines to stay on top. New-product programs are also bastions of hope for business units with lowly market shares. One SPI analysis shows that those businesses can double their ROI by increasing their commitment to new products.[22]

new products and life cycle

New products are especially useful when your market sheds its peach fuzz. When the market was booming ahead, there were much fantod and excitement and not much elbow room for obscure product innovation. But, now that the market has greyed and a big yawn has gripped the customer, you will get bigger ROI benefits from energizing your new-product muscle.

new products and market growth rate

As noted above, when the market is growing, the consumer is not mentally ready to absorb an array of product innovations; this will start to happen only when the market arrives at its somewhat duller mature phase. Accordingly, it is only logical that underspending on your R&D effort toward the development of new products would be the wiser course during periods of rapid market growth; and that, naturally, R&D overspending would be ill-advised. For example, in the high growth market the underspender will get, on average, a 25 percent ROI vs. the overspending cohort's 18 percent. In the low growth market the relationship is much less divergent: 21 percent vs. 18 percent. Interestingly, it is the normal R&D spenders who do even better than either the overspender or underspender in growth markets; they get the highest ROI of all (28 percent)—probably because they have managed to maintain a long-term, balanced R&D program that is exactly right for their kind of strategic profile. In other words, in this case, there is nothing at all wrong with being normal.[23]

dividing the R&D task

The really committed endeavor to keep up with every scientific development, perhaps even to blaze new trails, needs—as B.F. Goodrich has now recognized, as Hewlitt-Packard professes, and as forward thinkers like Procter & Gamble have known for over a century—the unshakeable support of top management. In fact, there is even a compelling argument to make in favor of breaking R&D into two separate organizations: one to handle the implementation of new scientific concepts, working closely with the marketing folks, and another to dedicate its unflamboyantly industrious talents to opening up new frontiers on the scientific horizon, even if these do not currently have an obvious market niche awaiting them. P&G splits its research in this manner; it's far-out group is located at Winton Hills, many miles from the company's sombre downtown Cincinnati Vatican. Bottom-lining product managers seldom rub shoulders with the eggheads from Winton Hills, but eventually (sometimes it can take up to 20 years) their pursuits merge, as Procter has routinely demonstrated in its unending parade of *genuinely* new products over the decades. It's a healthy situation, one that many large firms might consider and one that could provide an impetus for a major shift in our global new-products fortunes.

out of whack

Doesn't it seem like things are badly out of whack? Remember when you were a kid? If business intrigued you at all, it was probably due to the stories you heard about the inventors—how Tom Edison invented the light bulb, how Henry Ford managed to make Model-Ts affordable for the common man, how Alexander Graham Bell invented the telephone. In the 1930s and 1940s Hollywood was busy shooting films on the lives of history's great scientists. The saga of technology, though necessarily watered down for popular consumption, made good drama; it had all the suspense, disappointment, despair, achievement, and humor Hollywood needed. Today the romance of space, biotechnology, telecommunications, and computers continues the drama. Today's kids are weaned on personal computers. But, in spite of this and in view of the status of the scientist in industry, would you urge your own children to plan a career in R&D? Though they may find beauty and pleasure in their high school science courses, would you want them to commit the rest of their lives to it, knowing that, as interesting as their jobs may become and as important as they will always be to society, they will seldom receive any laurels for their contributions, won't get nearly the financial rewards for inventing that the sales personnel get for selling their inventions, and almost certainly will not end up running the company unless they completely turn their backs on their profession (where they are derided for being naive about finance and marketing, which in fact is the very blessing that gives their creativity full rein) and go into general management?

Yes, something is out of whack.

1. *Encounter,* March 1981, p. 12.

2. Charles W. Stevens, "U.S. Auto Makers Are Trying to Put Some Zip in Small Cars," *Wall Street Journal,* January 22, 1982, p. 23.

3. Michael L. King, "Poll Suggest U.S. Industry Mismanaging Technology," *Wall Street Journal,* September 3, 1981, sect. 2, p. 1.

4. Bill Abrams, "Study of New-Product Failures Refutes Basic Premise of Growth," *Wall Street Journal,* June 26, 1980, p. 23.

5. Ibid.

6. Ibid.

7. Bill Abrams, "Despite Mixed Record, Firms Still Pushing for New Products," *Wall Street Journal,* November 12, 1981, p. 27.

8. On the sunnier side, one thing that has improved in recent times is that the ratio of ideation to actual new products has dropped quite a bit. Today only seven new ideas need to be assessed in order to produce one really successful product; back in 1968 it took 58 ideas. This is probably due to better concept testing methods. Idea screening has become more effective. Still, this has not improved the success rate of new product introductions. Nor has it led to a higher proportion of truly new products.

9. Ibid.

10. Robert Jaztro, "The Steve King Show," WIND-Radio, Chicago, January 29, 1982.

11. Mark J. Chussil, "How Much to Spend on R&D?" *PIMSLETTER,* no. 13 (Cambridge, MA: The Strategic Planning Institute, 1978), p. 1.

12. Ibid, p. 2.

13. Ibid, p. 4.

14. Jeremy Main, "Why Engineering Deans Worry a Lot," *Fortune,* January 11, 1982, pp. 84-90.

15. Mark J. Chussil, "How Much to Spend on R&D?" p. 6.

16. Tom Alexander, "The Right Remedy for R&D Lag," *Fortune,* January 25, 1982, p. 61.

17. Mark J. Chussil, "How Much to Spend on R&D?" p. 7.

18. People will argue that things have speeded up, that product lifecycles are now so short that the old rules don't apply any longer. In some industries this is basically true, but for most I prefer to regard these shortened lifecycles as simply a different way of looking at the "new formula" gambits that consumer goods manufacturers have employed for years. Tide detergent, the market leader among the heavy-duty laundry products since WWII, has changed its formula almost on an annual basis, thus managing to stay ahead in a changing market without despairing of being able to plan on a long future.

19. Ellis R. Mottur, "National Strategy for Technological Innovation," a report prepared for the U.S. Senate Committee on Commerce, Washington, D.C. October, 1979.

20. Roger C. Bennet and Robert G. Cooper, "The Misuse of Marketing: An American Tragedy," *Business Horizons,* April, 1981, pp. 51-61.

21. Bill Moyers, "Creativity," Public Broadcasting Service, WTTW, Chicago, February 12, 1982.

22. "Selected Findings," (Cambridge, MA: The Strategic Planning Institute, 1976), p. 6.

23. Mark J. Chussil, "How Much to Spend on R&D?" p. 7.

7

production strategies

If we are to believe what we read and hear, American "know-how" is mutating into British dithering before our very eyes. It is even suggested that, where we once could make and sell anything we wanted, we now excell only at hamburg cookery and the purveyance of information. True to our national character, this metamorphosis has been transmuted on the grand scale.

cultural root of the problem

Though our end is far from nigh, it is sobering to reflect that this ultimately fatal cultural disease has infected (and leveled) numerous past civilizations. Perhaps by probing its roots, we can appreciate some of the remedies that will be prescribed later in this chapter. For whatever the malady that ails us, it has its most symptomatic rumblings on our production front.

V.S. Naipul, for example, traces a similar cultural decline in Pakistan.[1] Once the Moslem faith got entrenched as the dominant way of thought and life (compare this to our *scientific management* orientation begun in the 1950s), Pakistani culture seemed "complete."

90

All the answers were available within the Islamic framework. Other cultures were irrelevant. People cut themselves off from external thought systems. Eventually over the years such introspection produced a pervasive religious fundamentalism that totally thwarted the intellect. The myriad problems of life had to be solved via the routes ordained by the orthodoxies of the prevailing faith. Naipul observes that, once a culture sinks to this level, when all intellectual striving ceases, society becomes parasitic; it is forced to live in the past forever and go begging to neighboring cultures for anything beyond subsistence level needs. No progress is made here. Only the unorthodox, nonfundamental society changes and advances.

symptoms of the problem

Though our progression toward industrial fundamentalism is neither fast nor steady (there are still occasional protuberances of brilliance), the essential commercial culture of the West is edging down Naipul's road. We've gotten saddled with some old ways and some pretty ancient equipment, and we can't seem to halt the advance of superior Oriental technologies. But, instead of biting the bullet and facing up to our inherent inefficacy, we have stiffened our resolve to fight a twenty-first century war with Victorian weapons tempered in the glow of our post-WWII expansiveness.

Here are signposts we see on the route to becoming the fundamentalists of the Professional Management Era:[2]

- After they get themselves fired, managers high-tail it to other companies where they perpetuate their short-term scenarios. Like true believers, they never question their basic assumptions.
- Sounding like they were scripted in the Go-Go Sixties, attitudes have atrophied and the same old, familiar objectives hold sway—career first, closely followed by next month's performance numbers.
- The more mature the industry, the greater its ostensible commitment to fundamentalism—and all of our newest industries mature at a rapid clip these days.
- Across the broad horizon of our industrial society we are stuck with plants that would be better off as museums.
- Equipment is inefficient, worn out, unable to hold tolerances, and impossible to operate with today's diminished workforce skills.
- High hurdle rates keep us from purchasing new equipment, and as a direct consequence, when each recession ends, we find ourselves with insufficient capacity to meet the recovery.
- Our workforce is often bored or hostile and, when unionized or untamed by layoffs and plant closings, at constant war against the system.

• A middle management that seems unable (or maybe afraid) to cope with the status quo is actually not kept in one place long enough to try out any worthwhile, remedial program.

making production the goat

Against this glum backdrop our ambitious friends in marketing, bewitched by the old alchemy of the *marketing concept,* have imposed on our manufacturing sector the burdens of radical new products and mandatory cost-cutting schemes. All of this is done in good faith as measures to advance the interests of the company on the marketing battlefield. The marketing team may be only vaguely mindful that a greater diversity of products means shorter production runs calling for machinery with quicker change-overs and greater flexibility, none of which is forthcoming usually. Mounting demands for newer processes baffle veteran engineers. Scheduling and materials management go askew. Operating profits plunge.

Two decades or more of head-in-sand planning and of overly cooperative plant managers kow-towing to the marketing group have led to (1) payback criteria that rule out virtually any new equipment, (2) plants so huge they become ungovernable, and (3) corrupting manpower problems resulting from miserly investments in training and on-the-line coaching.

problem affects most industries

For a long time we were saying to each other: "If it ain't broke, don't fix it." But now the hidden breakage is clearly evident. You see it all about you in disappointing ROIs, which should provoke blunt strategic questions.

The general aspects of the problem may seem remote from the average reader who has only one business requiring attention at a given time, but we must approach an understanding of where our production strategies fit in the overall picture. While none of us can be absolved of total blame, all can benefit from prompt remedies that in the end serve to reestablish American industrial ascendency.

The *rate* of growth in U.S. productivity has been sinking since the mid-1960s, according to the U.S. Labor Department; in fact, among industrialized nations, our rate is second from the bottom. Only England, where squabbles over tea breaks can erupt in wildcat strikes, looks worse. That in itself should give us pause, but there is an even worse problem. The past decade has seen job opportunities shift markedly from manufacturing to the service sector. Between 1970 and 1980, the United States created 19 million new jobs; 87 percent were in the service area.[3] While the reasons for this are varied (higher cost of investment in manufacturing than in service industries, weak markets for our manufactured products, excessive governmental regulations, etc.), no nation can do without a strong manufacturing sector. We've got to export to survive. While our maturest industries have seen crazed wage-setting deals render their wares uncompetitive in global markets, little other than fastfoods and datamation is coming along to take their place. We are drumming ourselves out of business, and we could end up the way we began—back on the farm.

The nation is in dire need of production strategies that put a stop to this trend, but it's not going to be easy. Entire industries lay on the brink of ruin because they can't compete against the more agile foreign competitor. Detroit gets the brunt of the notoriety, but that's just the peak of a giant, lurching iceberg. It isn't very long ago that we learned of the closing of the last automobile tire plant in Akron, Ohio. There are all too many other sad stories.[4]

- Steel-mill equipment made in the United States used to dominate the world market, but now most of the more advanced steel processing machinery comes from Japan.
- Valves used in oil refineries now come principally from Europe, Canada, or Japan.
- Many autoparts, including entire engine assemblies and transmissions, are made in Japan and shipped to Detroit. More recently, whole cars are made overseas for an American-based company for the U.S. market.
- No industry is spared; even basic prosaic items, like castings and fasteners, increasingly come from offshore—often at savings of 25 to 30 percent and with no sacrifice in quality.
- Even critical military articles are growing dependent on foreign parts. General Dynamics Corp. reports it has grave difficulties locating U.S. sources for the enormous steel castings in its Trident sub.
- Back in 1965 we exported five machine tools for every one we imported; now imports outnumber exports 2:1.
- Our antique, lumbering plants can't guarantee delivery dates. "It's much easier competing against U.S. firms," said an executive of Makino Milling Machine Co. of Tokyo, "In fact, I don't even think Japanese companies view American companies as competition."[5]

We are efficient *only* by yesterday's standards. By today's world-class criteria we are the 97-pound weakling trying to beat off beach bullies who just swam in from countries where Naipulian business fundamentalism has not yet taken hold.

pressed for hasty solutions

Problems always invite solutions, but not always the right ones. Pressed for solutions, plant bosses may assume they can solve such problems by a healthy application of "ass-kicking." After a dreary spate of "management by objective," motivation-engineering, and bankable incentives, a more direct, Neanderthal style reemerged from the satanic mills in the late 1970s. But in many instances its integral instability makes matters worse. Eventually most of the hard-nosed fast-trackers—who take over, fire everyone in sight (with nary a twinge of remorse), and make things hum beautifully until the next quarter—find themselves booted out.

Having been repeatedly frustrated by seeing one management theory after another come a cropper, we all should be heartily chastened now and willing to concede that it is the strategists' turn to try their luck.

obvious beginnings for the strategist

The noblest of strategists would begin with an open mind, objectivity being the prerequisite for any scientific inquiry. Once all the obvious groundwork is done and problems are defined, he or she would search for a broad construct in which to reassemble the whole manufacturing system. No longer would the strategist allow plant bottlenecks to be tackled piecemeal or makeshift measures to be appended one after another until everything ends up, once again, in operational chaos. This time, starting from scratch, flexibility would be present at birth.

No doubt, if he or she hasn't already done it, our noble strategist will want to bone up on what the Japanese have been up to lately. But, unless he or she is going to ship in a Japanese labor contingent, most of what the strategist learns won't help much. Yankee workers are just different. They're not going to bring much childish enthusiasm and serf-like biddableness to the assembly line. Ergo, the strategist's solutions will require harder thinking—not mere cribbing from the Land of the Rising Sun. Though, to be sure, what Japan has wrought is not to be overlooked, even in this book.

Before our strategist even tries to get creative and dig into his or her analytical warehouse of strategic insights, several obvious remedies would come to mind. It would be trite to say the strategist would want to modernize the company's plants; that's a bit too general. First and foremost, some basic issues need to be tackled.

- Does the situation call for special purpose, dedicated equipment; general purpose, multiple use; or a combination?
- Would robots help or hinder the strategist's efforts?
- Can material, parts, and finished goods inventories be cut?
- Should the current management incentive system be discarded and one that better serves the strategist's purpose installed?

With a slightly longer timeframe in mind, our noble strategist may want to examine the issue of *plant size*.[6] "We are keenly aware of the disadvantage of large size," says Gordon Engdahl, Minnesota Mining & Manufacturing Co.'s vice president for human resources, "and we make a conscious effort to keep our units as small as possible because we think it helps keep them flexible and vital. When one gets too large, we break it apart." The average 3M plant only has 270 workers, and the median is a lot smaller: 115, an amazingly low figure for so large a company. The numbers suggest that this has worked out very well for the company. Against a general background of a declining big company role in expanding employment opportunities, 3M enlarged its labor force 40 percent during the 1970s and, at the same time, improved productivity impressively; sales during the same period quadrupled.

If you haven't been following this incipient trend very closely, it might sound like heresy, but bigness often spawns its own downfall. Instead of giving you the economies of scale promised in the standard handbooks, mammoth operations get bogged down in bureaucratic snafuing, internecine political struggles, and just plain old organizational stupidity and stubborness. As Larry Greiner, professor of organizational behavior at USC's School of Business Administration notes, "More companies seem to be showing concern that their neat organization charts don't always reflect reality and certainly don't in themselves overcome the tensions between autonomy and control that get worse with size." The battle of wills between corporate management and the employee increases in its complexity as the size of the organization swells. In good times it may appear to function moderately well, at least in the context of U.S. standards. But, when times are tough, it becomes a millstone. Richard Edwards, who teaches economics at the University of Massachusetts and who recently made a study of the behavior within bureaucracies, says that the "specialized and highly structured workforce can become a liability when business turns sour. Labor has become a quasi-fixed-cost in many companies, difficult to adjust to economic demands. That's true mostly where unions are present, but it also holds in nonunion companies that have seniority and grievance procedures similar to negotiated ones. Big companies tend to react slower to marketplace changes than small ones and bounce back from adversity slower. The auto companies are a perfect example."

type z

The 3M organizational approach may be interpreted, if you wish, as the heavily publicized "Type Z," though in fact it was devised well before William Ouchi galvanized our attention with his hybrid Japanese-American management theory. For the benefit of E.T., or any earthling whose eyes glaze over at the hint of yet another management theory, Type Z (as I read it) is where you attempt to mix the good old Yankee virtues of self-reliance and individual effort with the Japanese ethos of group decision making, concern for workers beyond the 8-hour work day, a tolerance for work regulations, and the intent of long-run employment in the same firm. As sure as you're living, this leads to financial riches as a consequence of healthier morale, lower turnover, and so forth. Zeeness wards off the evils of bigness by having employees perceive a corporate aura of goodwill toward them that is lacking in the cold, dark gloom of alienation that is said to beset most industrial environments. Ouchi feels that companies like Eastman Kodak, Levi Strauss, IBM, and NCR have Type Z characteristics. But seriously, whether any Japanese approach can ever truly be imposed on the American workplace for long is still a big question; and, true to our impatient nature, we will probably tire of it and go on to something else before we discover the answer. Urban Lehner, Tokyo bureau chief for the Wall Street Journal, tells the story of a Frenchman, a Japanese, and an American facing a firing squad. Each gets one last wish. The Frenchman asks to hear the Marseillaise. No problem. Then the Japanese asks to be granted time to give one last lecture on management, at which point the American butts in and begs to be shot first, explaining that he didn't feel he could stand another lecture on Japanese management.

The whole western world seems to have decided that the Japanese route is the one to take. That could be a hasty judgment, and the Japanese industrial milieu needs a closer examination because, as you will see, they don't have all the answers.

japanese myths

What are the undebatable pluses on the Japanese side of the ledger? Well, for one thing, they do maintain their equipment better. They are more adept at controlling physical and manpower waste. Of paramount importance, there is this central, fundamental philosophic point of difference: While we make the mistake of thinking that high quality and low costs are polar opposites, they view them as mutually compatible goals.[7] This kind of thinking permeates everything they do.

They do have better work environments where, it is widely believed, all workers gladly stay after hours to sip tea and discuss ways to improve work flow. Some of their plants require zero inventories of raw materials and components, with vendors delivering their wares right onto the assembly line at precisely the right moment. (In all honesty, though it is being proposed seriously, does any rational person really believe that could happen on a broadscale basis in the United States or Europe?) The Japanese, with more robots at this point than anybody else, have so emerged from the pages of science fiction that they can boast of having the first case of a worker slain by a robot. Still, this is not the real reason for their productive superiority. Their auto industry is *not* more automated than ours, yet it still does a lot better, probably through their more serious commitment to quality. Quality seems to exude from the very land. They can get by nicely with fewer inspectors; faulty machined parts, for example, must be chucked out only 1 percent as often as in comparable U.S. plants.

Japanese managers can treat their subordinates as if they were endowed with functioning brains, while we have to insist on breaking every job into therbligs and soul-deadening drudgery. Yet maybe our hands are tied. It is reported that the average Japanese IQ is higher than ours (111 vs. 100). Maybe what Japan has achieved is ascribed inaccurately to its management techniques; the real reason may be that they have smarter people to operate the machines. Not everyone, of course, buys the efficacy of IQ tests; and, besides, there are several other reasons to suppose that what works in Japan will never work here.

Let's start deflating the Japanese myth by citing the *Time* magazine cover story of March 30, 1981, which delineated a number of characteristics that it thought augured well in favor of Japan's continued economic success: (1) the burning desire to excell, (2) the instinctive need for consensus, (3) the love of quality, (4) the urge to compete, and (5) a general orientation toward the future. However, these qualities are shared by Americans as well (with the possible exception of wanting to achieve consensus, which may be only a manifestation of underlying insecurity). So there's got to be something else that makes Japan so illustriously successful, perhaps something deeper and not so superficially apparent. Isaac Shapiro, long-time resident of Japan and former president of the Japan Society, thinks it proceeds from a very different and very fundamental pattern of culture that stems from a unique national psyche. At the root of this is a set of factors that would be very hard to activate in the United States.[8]

• Japan is ethnically homogeneous. We are anything but, and proud of it. Still it does leave us with a wide variance in lifestyles, personal goals, and value systems, which can be awfully nettlesome.

• Japanese workers have a sense of duty—something we haven't encountered in the western world since the Battle of Britain, D-Day, and for a fortnight following Sputnik. Because of it, the Japanese can accept authority willingly and, without embarrassment, be worse conformists than we were during the 1950s.

• By all reports their educational system is superior to ours. But when you consider that four-year-old kids must slog it out preparing for kindergarten entrance exams, you have to ask if the price is worth it. I for one would rather go back to an agrarian economy.

None of these has actually produced the harmony in the workplace we keep hearing about. Different opinion surveys indicate that Japanese workers are a lot less happy and less proud of their work than Americans. They are also, and this should disturb you, a lot less willing to fight for their country. In the final analysis, there are profound psychological factors that make the Japanese totally unlike the vast majority of Americans; these can be summed up as a *survivor mentality*. Springing from an island existence that provides little in the way of resources, they need to work a lot harder just to stay alive. This is historically imbued. In the United States we have always—at least until just recently—viewed our country as the "land of opportunity" where the future will always get better and any problems that we encounter along the way can be easily erased with a strong dose of good old American "know-how" and rugged individualism. I could go on, but the conclusions would be the same: The grass is brown on both sides of the fence, and we have to find our own solutions.

strategic solutions

So if quality circles won't make our problems vanish, what can we do to improve productivity? I'd like to propose that we start by being very careful about using the term *productivity* because it is a generally misunderstood catch phrase whose true meaning contains many different, and often unrealized, facets. To begin with, we've usually been pretty strong on squeezing productivity out of our factories; we're very efficient when things are measured in minutes and hours. But we lose out when it comes to (1) the quality of our goods and services, and more importantly (2) achieving the right kind of productivity. This must look beyond even the important issues (like big plants vs. small plants, and the payout criteria for new technology) and myriad other factors. It comes down to whether we can produce the value, and do it right, or whether we continue to decline as a world marketing force.[9] Hence, for the remainder of this chapter I want to examine these two big issues: quality and real productivity.

quality in product and process

Quality is attained in many ways. Better technology can help. But before we overreact, we must be cautious; just putting in a band of robots won't help unless there is a plan for using them in the right way, as a competitive weapon, for providing flexibility and substitutes for scarce or expensive laborers and for making lead-times on new products shorter from initial concept to production line.[10] There's probably a robot in your future, but since everyone else will have them too, they won't make you more competitive if you don't use them strategically. Robotics has become the pat answer to everything. A few years ago it was considered too "far-out"; you were crazy if you talked about robots. Today the robotization movement is in danger of becoming just another dogma of the new orthodoxy.

Production problems may need strategies that sharply diverge from corporate thinking (like when Federal Express found that the fastest way from Los Angeles to San Francisco was via Memphis), and we must ask if the innovators need always risk embarrassment, derision, and even punishment for iconoclasm—even for success itself—under the hands of those who maintain the status quo and fear change in the power structure. Those companies that are managing to achieve quality supremacy think otherwise. They have not yielded to cliché.

When I first read that some U.S. textile firms were cleaning up on the world market, I thought I was reading a reprint from the National Lampoon.[11] But it turned out to be quite accurate. In France, for example, where mechanized fabric making goes back to the very dawn of the Industrial Revolution, the hottest items are Spring Mills sheets and pillowcases made down home in South Carolina. After years of dozing, some of our textile makers have become more efficient than anyone else on the globe. Some other industries, to be sure, have also come a long way in this regard (chemicals, fertilizer, coal, electrical equipment, medical supplies, aluminum, avionics, pharmaceuticals), but it is in textiles that the most dramatic story is told. After all, it's an industry that many of us were writing off only a few years ago.

After leaving the red-brick mills to New England historic societies and heading south in the 1950s, the textile operators soon began suffering once again. The lower pay of the Bible Belt was munificent compared to the peanuts textile workers were making in

Southeast Asia. The dramatic rescue came from some remarkable new technology. Spring Mills' plant in Lancaster, South Carolina, offers an interesting study in contrasts. From the outside it still looks much as it did when built decades ago, but inside it tells the story of progress and Herculean updating: air-jet fed looms, computer monitoring, and high-speed spinning machines combining three major processes in one operation have produced its world-class uberosity. True, not all U.S. textile makers have modernized to such a degree, and not all can meld modernization into a workable production strategy, but an overall optimistic note is sounded in an industry that was once considered a goner. Now, sipping bourbon and branchwater, at least a few southern textile folks can rejoice upon hearing Norman Smith, deputy chairman of England's giant Courtaulds Ltd., say, "By and large, nowadays we take the Americans to be our yardstick on overall efficiency." The moribund shall rise again, with assured quality and value that the whole world will buy.

production strategy

To raise the discussion to a more universally applicable level, we must tower above the admittedly engaging specifics and reach for the general laws governing the strategies of production. As in our marketing treatments, there are several strategic factors to examine, and all will be based on firm statistical analysis that nicely dispenses with the popular armchair thinking frequently palmed off as production strategy, which is what got us into trouble in the first place. You might also note that all serious references to Japan are now behind us. *Sic transit mundi gloria.*

vertical integration

Vertical integration is a good, easy place to start. I've discussed it before, and I guess you know what vertical integration is. It's measured by what percentage of your net sales dollar you actually make yourself vs. what you buy on the outside. For example, farmers who plant corn from their own seed, grow the stuff, and then make and consume their own 'shine are *fully integrated;* if they have to get their neighbors to run the mash through their stills for them, they ain't. Some people, newly arrived on the business scene, think integration has something to do with how many minority group members you have on the payroll, so I thought we had better get clear what it is we mean.

For inescapable strategic reasons, vertical integration is critical in almost all industrial environments. Think back to our marketing discussion on the experience curve (Chapter 3) and recall how, with sometimes only routine mental applications, you cut the per unit value added cost on what you were making every time you doubled your output. Recall that this phenomenon made it especially rewarding to have large market shares. Now, vertical integration has virtually nothing to do with the marketing people, but it has a lot to do with operations; the two departments should work closely on the synergistic effects that can be obtained from a fortuitous combination of both. This means that the operations group should know a little bit about market shares in the various product lines and what happens when it combines a "high" degree of vertical integration (that is, when its value added is 70 percent or more of net sales) with a "high" market share, as contrasted with a "low" share. Obviously, with output that you mostly make yourself (where you control the whole experience curve as opposed to buying components from suppliers, who may be unwilling to pass on their experience curve savings, even though it is your market share that may be giving them an experience curve), each incremental unit of output gives you a higher return rate. Now then, if you are the plant manager or operations manager and you've embarked on a program of juiced-up vertical integration, you should be tracking this very carefully. If, after making more of the final product yourself and allowing for a decent getting-your-feet-wet period, you don't see any drop in unit costs, then something is amiss. You also should know that this will vary according to the product's market share. The analysis shows that, when a "high" market share jibes with a "high" degree of vertical integration, your ROI can be up around 35 percent, but then, when your market share is "low" (that is to say, your experience curve is virtually nonexistent), you would be reasonable to expect only about one-third of that.[12] If your company actually means business with its MBO system and rewards specific accomplishments with cash incentives, you may want to try to get specific mention of this listed among your MBOs, providing your company is willing to indulge in a program of increased vertical integration and has the market shares to make it effective. Alternately, you should be wary of overcommitting yourself in your MBO "promises" if the corporation has meager market shares. A lot of plant managers get themselves locked in on promises that they can't keep simply because the strategic factors that control profitability are against them. It's pretty sad when you break a gut on some major vertical integration installation to cut out a gouging supplier, but then lose your bonus because your profit center doesn't yield the anticipated increase in ROI, when in actual fact the profit center's low market share makes a higher ROI most unlikely.

In similar fashion (as we saw in Chapter 6) a heavy-up on your vertical integration program coupled with a relatively "ambitious"

R&D effort (say, 3 percent or more of net sales) can be a source of substantial ROI improvements. This is immediately clear when you consider the flipside of this: If you invest in a lot of R&D, but add very little to the product yourself (in order to make it marketable), exactly what is it you're going to apply all those marvellous R&D discoveries to? There's not much to work with. But, on the other hand, when most of the work is done right in your own shop and your value added level is real high, all this R&D process and product thinking and discovery can be appplied to a rather large wedge of do-it-yourself activities and technologies. The more you learn from your R&D efforts, the more opportunities you have to apply it when most of the product is made right at home. A kind of synergy develops. (Contrary to the popular misconception, R&D isn't just dreaming up wild new products; good R&D has much broader applications.) One processing innovation inspires another. When you have minimal vertical integration, R&D is just a wasted luxury. So, if you have a whole flotilla of PhDs with their expensive lab equipment all working on just one small aspect (the one you do yourself) of the overall series of activities needed to make your product ready for the market, then the chance of finding something that will improve your financial performance is skimpy indeed. Once you have incurred an onerous R&D overhead, it is politically difficult to get rid of it. What would Wall Street think if you abandoned it? It would not be easy to explain. Hence, unless you have the vertical integration base to begin with, you're usually better off if you don't make a large R&D commitment.

Based on this very real bond between vertical integration and R&D, you may logically assume that this should follow right on through to a concentration with new products. You're probably thinking that, since high vertical integration and a generous amount of R&D means elevated ROIs, and since R&D often coughs up a lot of new products, it follows that hyperactivity on new products also can join hands with high vertical integration to achieve the same effect. Common sense cuts several ways, and in this case it's more twisted than a pig's tail. The actual strategic experiences of most companies that have been through this is that, when you are giving birth to many new products, it's quite unwise to embark on serious vertical integration. For one thing, when you have a strong flurry of new products, you don't get much chance to travel the experience curve. Another reason: New products, to a fairly large degree, imply new production technology, and if you overdo the make (vs. buy) aspects of it too early, you will probably end up with processes and equipment that rapidly grow obsolete as the product category matures. Of course, this depends on how "new" the products really are; if you're just adding another flavor to your toothpaste in order to get more shelf space in the supermarket, it probably doesn't matter. But, as a general rule of thumb, you should depend more on outside suppliers while a product category is in its growth phase and only move on to internal production as it matures. In this way you will be more likely to have production facilities with the bugs all worked out for you. In other words let yourself benefit from someone else's experience curve.

It follows that your market growth rate, another of those strategic elements that impacts heavily on ROI when considering the marketing aspects of your business, adheres to the same line of thought. It, therefore, must be considered when wrestling with manufacturing options. The staid, unglamorous, no-growth market that stock market mavens prefer to shun is, in fact, the locale of big opportunities for the vertical integrator. Low growth gives the increased vertical integration strategy its best chance of bearing fruit in the form of higher ROI and is where the operations manager's creative muscle can really pay off. But not so with the fast moving market, where the ROI of the "low" vertical integration business (ie., value added at less than 52 percent of net sales) would be higher (24 percent) than with a "high" level of vertical integration (20 percent). The numbers run in the opposite direction with low growth situations: 15 percent vs. 19 percent.[13]

While I have trouble picturing a company eager to elevate its level of vertical integration while a recession is depressing sales and interest rates are high, it is still a good time to do it. Better yet, if you happen to be amply integrated when a recession hits, you will be better off than your counterparts who are not.[14] So, if you are in an industry that suffers appreciably during a recession, you should consider increasing your vertical integration in order to maintain your return rates. This may sound like rather cavalier advice, but here's the rationale: You will control the costs, not your suppliers—who cannot be counted on to pass along savings accruing from their internal cost-cutting. With the incentive to find ways of saving money, and with a big base of operational activities to attack with the miser's scalpel, you have a better chance of improving your profit picture. Another factor here, which gives free enterprise a bad name until you think it all the way through, is that the more vertically integrated you are, the more employees you have under your roof. Anyone with a sharp pencil knows that labor cost is the first and easiest thing to look to when the P&L statement needs fine-tuning. So you can get the benefit of layoffs during a recession, not your supplier. (They are going to be laid off anyway, aren't they?) At the same time, as I hasten to add on behalf of free enterprise, in some cases high vertical integration actually helps you provide your labor force with greater security when the recession comes. You can transfer part of the work that was formerly done by your vendors to them. As volumes decline and your own workers are idled, you would be better off, where your facilities permit, to fill their time with projects previously subcontracted so as to avoid the administrative and political upheavals encountered in layoffs. Of course, this works best with a diversified product line where your human resources can be transferred from the line hit by the recession and to the ones still doing okay.

I am not one to vote in favor of high marketing expenditures unless encouraged by several other strategic factors acting in concert, but I am anxious to specify a situation where it may be absolutely ruinous. When coupled with low vertical integration, "high" marketing costs (somewhere in the neighborhood of 4 percent or more of net sales) yield very ungenerous ROIs (as low as 4 percent).[15] When you find low vertical integration joining hands with high marketing expenses, you usually have a situation where someone has let insanity reign. Since most of what goes into your product is beyond the manager's direct control under such circumstances, your manager is not really in the driver's seat on the production side. Accordingly, he or she is tempted to try to push buttons on the marketing side, the argument being that you've got to flex some muscle in the battle against competition and, since you can't do it by governing much of the operational side of the business, you've got to swamp the customer with inducements. It is a hard temptation to resist, but yielding to it gives you a double whammy of poor strategic planning.

unions and strategy

Got union problems? If you have a unionized plant, you have problems. There isn't a whole lot you can do about it right away, but with some careful strategic management you may be able to attenuate some problems. This happens to be another opportunity for production and marketing to join forces and work toward common strategic objectives. The analytical basis for this mutual effort lies in the finding that, while it doesn't make any difference with low market shares whether you are unionized or not, when you attain ample market shares (especially in a mature industry), unionization can squeeze your ROI pretty bad. When your share is "big" (i.e., your share as a percent of the three market leaders is at least 54 percent) a "nonunionized" (i.e., a third or less of employees belonging to a union) operation will yield an average 34 percent ROI; if "unionized" (70 percent or more in union), it drops to 27 percent. Your success makes you, in union eyes, a delectable target for their intensified bargaining games. The meddlesome work rules you agree to will prove most crippling later when you've got to speed up production to fill fast emptying pipelines caused by your promotional successes. Contrary to the popular belief, propelled by horror stories of things like linotype operators featherbedding their way to higher pay than newspaper editors, the main drag on ROI from unionization is not so much due to wages as to work practices. As long as your share remains high and your periodic marketing events bring on sales spurts, the presence of the union is an immense barrier to the financial rewards that should greet your success in the market. In this sense unionization can foster its own destruction by throttling the very success that furnishes the surplus cash flow that entrepreneurs need for future growth—the very growth that supplies new jobs. Currently, organized labor is being forced to back off in its demands because most of the heavily organized industries are in decline; it is ironic that unions inflict their worst damage (on profitability and long run prospects) specifically in those businesses where stellar marketing success was once achieved. Perhaps only the dreamy-eyed would anticipate much success in trying to reason with union negotiators on this, but, given the high stakes, there is some justification for trying to build incentives into the contract that would allow both marketing and production to achieve their goals without the customary haggling. If such a framework could be ironed out, then everybody—even the people on the assembly line—would profit.

More than ever before, the climate may be almost right for more rational contracts. Decades of virtual union cartellization have driven the American Foundryland to the brink of penury. In the halcyon past, when the major industries were untroubled by foreign competition, cost vigilance was not as pressing a matter. Under the heels of strong, industry-wide unions, most companies had little taste for real battle. Putting up a heroic scrap against excessive union demands only meant seeing production halted by bitter strikes while competitors merrily plundered their markets and waited for the foolhardy to settle on a deal that the whole industry would subsequently commit itself to. The outcome was fairly easy for skilled negotiators to forecast.. Steel, automotive, airline, and many other industries all saw this happening to them at a time when offshore competition was no real threat; the resulting cost increases were simply financed by price increases since the consumer had few alternatives. But now, beleaguered by seemingly invincible foreign competition, our Foundryland enterprises are spewing buckets of flopsweat. Though doubtful that it'll be the scenario for the next Warren Beatty movie, the jobs that the self-righteous labor movement clumsily set out to make safe, happy, and secure, have disappeared. All those bullfeathers about the dignity of labor don't help the idled UAW member make his house payments on time.

The labor component of the nation's output is staggering; seventy-five percent of our economy's total costs are labor-related (40 percent of it is blue-collar). If organized labor cannot be handled with greater strategic finesse, if the plant managers cannot work hand-in-hand with marketing and planning to establish strategies that minimize the financial drag that unionization almost invariably leads to, then the business could fail in the long run, and one by one entire industries will continue to be engulfed by overseas competitors. Labor will suffer as much as capital from this internicine strategic blundering and neglect.[17]

employee productivity

Whether unionized or not, the ultimate goal of the operations staff should be to achieve very high productivity. One form of productivity comes from the employee base and the other from the asset base. Employee productivity is measured by the value added contributed by each worker.[18]

The one key finding of this section and the next is that a good worker is more important to you than costly mechanized production aids. Not surprisingly, high employee productivity gives you a higher ROI than low employee productivity, but for strategic blueprinting purposes there are some occasions when its impact is relatively better than others. For one thing, it is a nice way to alleviate the drag inflicted on your P&L statement by recessions. High employee productivity can give you a steady, comfortable return rate regardless of the state of the economy. In a recession it would give you a 23 percent ROI on average, according to the analytical studies, and in good times a not-too-different 26 percent. But low employee productivity, at no time a good thing to have, is especially damaging during recessions; during good times you might get, say, an 18 percent ROI with it, but it quickly causes your ROI to plunge down to around 12 percent in bad times.[19] High employee productivity is linked to wise resource allocation. During slumps, when cutbacks and layoffs must be implemented, the more sophisticated and better managed operation is able to accomplish this with fewer setbacks in efficiency. The poorly organized shop characteristically makes decisions and takes action under pressure, with little cerebral guidance, and is ill-fit to avert declining efficiency during economic downturns.

Although I hate looking at it in such a limiting way (see the next section for the optimum view on it), people keep wanting to know what happens when you have a fairly heavy investment wrapped up in your business or want to install some expensive capital improvements. The flip answer is that, if you keep having high employee productivity, it will help your financial performance. But it is not necessarily the only answer, and there's no guarantee it will make your business a winner. After all, your assets are the denominator in the ROI formula (operating profit/average assets) and nothing you do with work procedures can lower that figure. But it will help boost the numerator. For example, with a "high" investment (i.e., an investment to sales ratio of over 1.3) and low employee productivity, your returns would be only around 7 percent, but you can double your ROI, ceteris paribus, with an effort to bring your level of employee productivity up. In sharp contrast, if your investment intensity is rather "low" (i.e., investment to sales ratio of around 0.9 or less) productivity strides can be absolutely astounding, due mainly to the arithmetic. Based on the averages of many different types of business, your gains would take you from an average ROI of around 8 percent all the way up to 37 percent.[20] You have to remember that, if you've allowed what you're putting into the business to grow more rapidly than your per-worker value-added incremental output, your ROI is bound to plunge, even if you've obtained relative improvements in employee productivity. And if yours is a typical business, these relative gains won't be terribly impressive. Most people think that, if they invest more in technology, they should have better results. What usually happens is that the gargantuan technology commitment brings with it lots of management headaches and fears that tend to cloud one's judgment. (See Chapter 8 for discussion on the Managerial Clutch Response.) Even if you vow that this won't happen to you, it inevitably forces you to do just about anything to keep your lines humming. You can't help having night-mares about a heavy investment, and the burden of constantly having to justify it might lead you down the factory aisle into the scrapbin of fiscal disaster faster than you can say, "The Japanese are coming." That's why I said I dislike looking at the investment intensity factor in this way. It's too one-sided, and all good strategies have several dimensions.

asset productivity

So, if you shouldn't fuss a lot about your capital intensity in this context, what should you worry about?

There are two main elements the Strategic Planning Institute suggests looking at that are much more instructive when trying to set production strategies.[21]

- *Employee/asset intensity.* This reflects more than just your invest-ment level. It also brings in your concomitant labor force en-cumbrance. It is the ratio of your capital to your labor load, or the average investment per employee in the business. (This is usually given as a dollar amount of the investment per the average employee. The uneven effects of inflation make it impossible to arrive at definitive parameters that would be effective for the life of this book, but extrapolations from recent calculations suggest that, at time of writing, a "high" level would be over $58,000 and a "low" level below $34,000. Needless to say, these are quite rough, and before you try to use this form of analysis, you should investigate further and develop your own cut-points.)

- *Asset efficiency.* This expresses the "productivity" of your assets by taking your investment level as a ratio of the value added in the business. A "very productive" ratio would be 0.77 or less, and a "terribly unproductive" one would be 1.1 or more.

When these two factors (which in themselves are each bi-factorial) are cross-tabbed, true insights into what I like to call *real productivity* begin to emerge. (Don't be discouraged if you find this hard to follow. It is an up-hill passage.)

Where both are excellent—that is, when you have both very potent equipment and splendid human-physical resource utilization—you will be blessed with a colossal ROI; the analysis puts it at a whopping 44 percent.

But, looking at the darker side, if your employee/asset intensity is too hefty, and you fail to use your assets effectively (i.e., your asset efficiency reading is more than 1.1), your ROI will be paltry; the analysis gives it a 13 percent.

So you can see there is a big potential payoff in getting it right, even without mentioning the usual caveat that all calculations using these strategic profit control factors do take things out of context somewhat and that we really shouldn't make a great habit of looking at only one or two of these factors in a vacuum. Other factors that we haven't mentioned could also play an important role in determining just what the expected ROI of a business should be. But despite the caveat, you cannot ignore a difference of 31 percentage points of ROI, and I take that as convincing proof that just investing in a lot of fancy machinery and what-not won't help you much unless you also know how to make it work very hard and smart. Technology brings with itself no hard and fast guarantee. If your value added per employee is high *only* because your employee/asset intensity is also high, then obviously you haven't got such a hot operation. If your productivity seems to be getting better through time, it doesn't necessarily follow that your workforce is really performing better; you may simply be guilty of wanton overinvestment in equipment. And just in case you think these are motherhood statements, let me point out that this problem is the most commmon scenario in U.S. business today: increasingly bigger investments with overall lowered asset efficiency and higher employee/asset intensity yielding progressively lower ROIs. The lazy investment always produces poorer returns, regard-less of your employee/asset intensity. But the energetic investment lets it take on tremendous leverage. The heightened manageability of the small unit or plant, à la 3M, owes much of its success to its ability to achieve the proper balance of asset intensity and efficiency for a workforce of a given size.

The proper management and control of the employee/asset intensity factor is a way to immunize yourself against the profit erosion caused by having a union. A business with strong employee/asset features will get virtually the same ROI regardless of the level of unionization it faces; no union can hurt it. But the business with a low employee/asset ratio gets hurt when unionized.[22]

Real productivity is an especially important factor to nurture when your markets are growing. If your market growth rate is low, it doesn't make a whole lot of difference whether your employee productivity is low or high. In fact the SPI data show virtually no ROI difference at all. But when your markets are burgeoning, it can make the difference between lackluster and laudatory performance. For example, a business in a growth market achieving high productivity will get an ROI of 25 percent vs. its less productive counterpart at only 12 percent.[23] But, as you may suspect, when your business is in that frantic phase of its cycle, it is awfully hard to find the time to fuss about trying to do everything the right way. It is too easy to lose sight of the housekeeping chores, when top management's attention is riveted on the growth phenomenon and no one is pressing you to mind the store as long as the customers are lined up around the block. But we know from previous chapters that growth produces concomitant hardships in the cash flow department; overall employee productivity is one way to mollify this kind of problem. You will never overcome it entirely, but it is a welcome opportunity for operations people to share in the responsibility of assuring a safe and successful trip through the heady, but risky, trials of growth. The trick is not to be a killjoy or a stop-gapper while doing it. Good strategy should not look like something you dreamed up last night. If your overall guiding policies are soundly established, your production strategy will appear to all who must implement it as just a normal extension of standard operating procedures—smooth and sensible. But to you it will mean dramatic improvements in ROI.

capacity utilization

It should dumfound no one to state that you can get a higher return on your investment if you use your assets a lot rather than seldom. I've met people who don't even have an MBA who can figure that one out. Also, while we are in the mood for stating the obvious, it is plain that, when your capital intensity is high, you will do better if your capacity utilization rate is also high. These two nuggets of wisdom serve as an entré to a warning about the scary situation you can get yourself into when your fixed capital intensity is "high" (i.e., 65 percent or more of net sales) and your capacity utilization is "low" (under 70 percent). This, dear reader, brings you an ignominious ROI of only 7 percent or roughly what you can sometimes get in a savings account. Even if you work to get your capital utility up to a very high level (say 85 percent or better), you still are not going to be in hog heaven; your ROI will then only be around 17 percent. However, if you are stuck with a lot of assets or if your kind of industry simply mandates a lot of assets, 17 percent is a lot better than 7 percent. I realize that, as a rule, you do not have all that much flexibility here. These numbers are not all that easy to manipulate.[24] But a problem defined is better than one left undefined. In some industries this could augur in favor of asset divestitures or subcontracting during peak periods, and so on, rather than building up unwanted capacity. In others it points the way to a gradual replacement of old dedicated assets by newer and more versatile ones.

capital intensity and inventories

Speaking of capital intensity (which I discuss more completely in Chapter 8 on finance), another way of giving fast relief when it is high is to keep inventories low. This is something the entire Western world is now trying to do anyway, so the advice is not very original. Still, for readers who need reassurance on everything, it may be useful to know that a low ratio of inventories to sales is good for ROI; after all, inventory does appear in the ROI formula as part of assets. On the strategic level it is, however, just as helpful to a business saddled with a heavy investment intensity as it is to the more lightly capitalized business. For example, given a heavy investment intensity, your ROI with "high" inventories (i.e., 23 percent or more of sales) will be around 6 percent. These investment intense businesses don't shine much, do they? But it can be eked up to 17 percent by prudent inventory controls.[25] If we could utilize somehow that vaunted sumarai plan of "just-in-time" inventories, of course, it would go much higher, merely by nature of the arithmetic involved.

concluding remarks

Contrast our surly, but scuppered, national confidence level with the buoyant cockiness of the Gene Kellys and Burt Lancasters in the films of the 1940s, and you have a chilling portrayal of what we have become. But it has not happened entirely under the hands of our foreign adversaries. Largely, it has come to pass as a direct consequence of our national neglect of prudent business strategies—by management, organized labor, and government. The solutions—the strategy formulation—obviously has to start at the top. This must include your operation managers; marketing and finance alone can make little progress on the central problem of making the workplace more efficient. Then the new strategies must work their way down, motivating and involving the minds of all who participate in turning this country around. This can be achieved only with good planning, well communicated, and via the proper incentives.

NOTES

1. V.S. Naipul, "Among the Believers: Pakistan," *Atlantic Monthly,* August 8, 1981, pp. 57-65.

2. Wickham Skinner, "Manufacturing and Technological Society," *Journal of Business Strategy,* 1, no. 2 (Fall 1980),. pp. 69-72.

3. Lindley H. Clark, Jr., "Service Revolution: Too Much Too Soon?" *Wall Street Journal,* April 13, 1982, p. 27.

4. Wickham Skinner, "Manufacturing and Technological Society," p. 70.

5. Thomas F. O'Boyle, "Nuts and Bolts: Ever-Rising Imports of Machinery and Parts Raise Fears in the U.S.," *Wall Street Journal,* December 23, 1981, p. 1.

6. Frederick C. Klein, "Manageable Size: Some Firms Fight Ills of Bigness by Keeping Employee Units Small," *Wall Street Journal,* February 5, 1982, pp. 1, 14.

7. Charles Burke, "Steve King Show," WIND-AM Radio, Chicago, January 21, 1982.

8. Isaac Shapiro, "Second Thoughts About Japan," *Wall Street Journal,* June 5, 1981, p. 24.

9. Wickham Skinner, "Boosting Productivity," *Wall Street Journal,* March 15, 1982, p. 18.

10. Kenichi Ohmae, "Steel Collar Workers: The Lessons From Japan," *Wall Street Journal,* February 16, 1982, p. 20.

11. Art Pine, "Made in America: Many U.S. Exporters Compete Successfully, Especially in Europe," *Wall Street Journal,* December 21, 1981, p. 1.

12. "Basic Principles of Business Strategy," (Cambridge, MA: The Strategic Planning Institute, 1980), p. 27. (No author)

13. "Selected Findings," (Cambridge, MA: The Strategic Planning Institute, 1976), p. 14.

14. Sidney Schoeffler, "Recession: Who Gets Hurt? How to Cope?" *PIMSLETTER,* (Cambridge, MA: The Strategic Planning Institute, 1979), p. 5.

15. "Selected Findings," p. 10.

16. Valerie Kijewski and Sidney Schoeffler, "Unions and Profits," *PIMSLETTER,* (Cambridge, MA: The Strategic Planning Institute, 1978), p. 2.

17. A. Gary Shilling, "American Labor—From Cartels to Competition," *Wall Street Journal,* January 21, 1982, p. 22.

18. Since this involves a dollar value, it is difficult to specify exactly what is low or high employee productivity for the life span of any book. These values also may vary somewhat by industry and by SBU. Comparative analysis among your own SBUs may serve to provide the answer for your own specific situation. Nonetheless, across many averages as this is being written, "low" could be in the neighborhood of $35,000 or less, and "high" well above $50,000. Obviously, this will require constant updating.

19. Schoeffler, "Recession: Who Gets Hurt? How to Cope?" p. 4.

20. Sidney Schoeffler, "The Unprofitability of 'Modern' Technology and What to Do about It," *PIMSLETTER,* (Cambridge, MA: The Strategic Planning Institute, 1977), p. 11.

21. Sidney Schoeffler, "Good Productivity vs. Bad Productivity," *PIMSLETTER,* (Cambridge, MA: The Strategic Planning Institute, 1978), pp. 3-8.

22. Kijewski and Schoeffler, "Unions and Profits," p. 5.

23. "Basic Principles of Business Strategy," p. 13.

24. Ibid., p. 58.

25. Ibid., p. 57.

8

"Amazing thing. Consider the diamond: the hardest matter; so hard that whatever it touches must suffer— glass, steel, the human soul."

TOADY (PETER LORRE), ROPE OF SAND

the finance component of business strategy

When I say "finance," I'm talking more about the verb than the noun. So this chapter is not about the financial instruments and appurtenances of investment bankers. Nor is it about their kindred intramural spirits whose principal thrust is snaring tax advantages with imaginative accounting capers, and with creative floats and issues. None of these admittedly absorbing antics has a great deal to do with inflating the true economic value of the enterprise for the stockholder. Like the old joke about the boxcar of tinned sardines that cause violent illness if eaten but are fine for buying and selling, stocks and bonds, though the principle foci of finance, are linked only obliquely to the corporation's objectives. Their net contribution pales in comparison to the contribution good business strategy makes to that same end.

In a very concrete sense, all strategic endeavor is financial; there is hardly a strategic decision that doesn't require some reallocation of funds or shifting around of assets. The many facets of this are covered throughout this book; in this chapter the focus will be on the central aspect of finance as seen by the strategist: avoiding or treating the problem of investment intensity, that is, of having too big an allocation of assets devoted to a single SBU. Since investment intensity will be our only focus, this chapter will be mercifully short.

The preoccupation of most corporate finance specialists with the instruments of their trade leaves too little time for agonizing over the highest question of all: What characterizes a good investment? Most wide-awake companies, at any given time, have more capital expenditure ideas on the back burner than they can conveniently handle, and the task on which their finance executives should spend most of their waking hours is sniffing out which investment opportunity stands the best chance of enhancing shareholder value. To the strategist it is plumb crazy to spend the bulk of one's time, as is too often the case, on dreaming up slick capital raising deals and only a modicum of spare time on judging its ultimate worth.

In the pressured quotidian of commercial enterprise it is easy to lose sight of the basics. Perhaps there is much truth in the old tale of the elderly department store founder who, after several decades of steady growth, looks down from his mezzanine office one morning and notices two guys counting the shelf stock. Summoning them to his office, he asks what the hell they're doing.

"We're your accountants, and we're taking inventory," they inform him.

"What for?" he inquires impatiently.

"Well, to find out how much profit you've made," they tell him.

Beckoning them over to his desk, the founder digs into a bottom drawer, pulls out a rolled-up cloth, and unfurls it, spilling its contents of spools, needles, thimbles, and pins on his desk.

"That's the inventory," he snaps, then gesturing to the busy floor below, "and that's the profit."

In our grind to avoid taxes and to hype the profits via finessed accounting, and in our fixation on short-term results, we often lose sight of the fundamental purpose of the enterprise and of how to set the goals in order to attain it. Call it what you want, it is the increasing of shareholder value that should stir us into action, and though we need to keep books and prescribe to the norms of the investment community on many peripheral matters, we must never overlook the primordial value of strategic design. This requires an abiding long-term view of things.

To the most conservative, abstemious school of strategy, this can mean that even dividend payments are unworthy, being an admission that the enterprise is not a deserving object for investment per se. (Of course there are some pesky problems attached to selling that notion to the average shareholder or even to most brokers; see Chapter 14 for more on this.) But, whether the internal investment is funded by surplus or by external benefaction, it is the paramount responsibility of strategists to make sure no investment is too intense. This is where it is easiest to go wrong and, once having gone wrong, most difficult to extricate yourself. Strategists must be ever alert for the sibylline warnings of overinvestment.

financial goal-setting

Having decided summarily that stock prices/shareholder value is the only stately thing for a corporate executive to concentrate on, I intend to carry that assumption forward. But perhaps that is too cavalier to some unfortunate readers whose companies cling to the quainter aspects of goal-setting from the dim origins of scientific management. In deference to them a more conscientious consideration of corporate goals and objectives must be rendered before we can think about such matters as investment intensity. *Nihil sine labore* (nothin' without work), as my university grimly reminds us on its crest.

First of all, what are we looking for? We need criteria for simultaneously assessing several capital expenditure opportunities, so the end result must give us a relative evaluation. This should be expressed in dollars and cents, because that is how we measure the value of things. And, since money by no means holds its value well, it should take into account the ravages of inflation. There are nine major methods for evaluating a proposed capital expenditure, and I will rapidly cover them in order of declining absurdity.

Sales Volume

Time was when a company's sales management group was so over-bearing and persuasive that it even had the accountants (the chaps with the eyeshades) believing that all that counted was sales volume— or at least they felt compelled to profess this for fear of appearing disloyal. For several eons sales managers' mentality held sway; they were, after all, matriculants of the Dale Carnegie Institute and eminently capable of winning all the friends needed to support their version of the corporate aim. Today I don't think one has to point out the banality of using sales volume projections to grade internal investment opportunities. I don't need to point out how sales volume projections get distorted in time of inflation or how they blind you from seeing how crummy you're really doing when sales are up (but not by as much as your foe's).

Market Share

This solved the basic problems mentioned above. The fact that it's expressed as a percentage presented some minor difficulties when it was first introduced, believe it or not, but today we are all much smarter and unbaffled by advanced mathematics. As much as we strategists like market share for its direct causal link with profits, on its own it's not a reasonable method for evaluating investments. For one thing it doesn't mention money.

Net Profit

Actually *operating profit* would be better because it leaves out those ancillary financial and miscellaneous charges that most capital expenditures requestors have no control over. The idea of profit gets us a little closer to where we want to go, since it is a dollar expression and is about performance and outcome. But, because it is not relative to an investment's magnitude, you can't tell whether the projected numbers are good or bad. Furthermore, to some skeptics profit is viewed as the fictive result of creative accounting.

Payback

This method incorporates profit with the size of the investment by showing how long it's going to take to pay it back. Given an equal magnitude of profits, the faster payback is to be preferred. Payback analysis is simple and, in one sense, relativistic. That's why many companies, that should really know better, still use it today. Unfortunately, its relativity is limited to new investments; it can't be employed to compare proposed investments to those already made and on line. The next approach does just that.

Return on Investment

As a preface to this I would point out that diverse terminology gets used here by different factions. Investment to some means assets; to others it's net assets (total assets minus current liabilities); to still others it means only equity (ROE). The latter is more commonly used by Wall Street stock analysts. I like to stay clear of ROE when discussing strategy because you get all tangled up in investor equity vs. long-term debt considerations that don't pertain at the SBU-level where business strategies are formulated. ROI has a lot of faults, but it's an easy concept to explain, it's relative, and it's based on a dollar amount. An investment's return rate is the basic, conventional measurement of its worth. It is so rooted in, and commonplace to, the study of strategy that we have elected to use it throughout this book despite its substantial shortcomings, which I'll spell out here while I'm at it. For one thing, ROI makes all proposed investments look bad compared to preinflationary current investments, since obviously you must pay more for comparable productive capacity today than a few years ago. (I will explore this problem as it relates to strategy in greater detail later in the chapter.) For another thing, and while we're still on the subject of inflation, it totally ignores what economists call "the time value of money;" that is, it doesn't make allowances for the ravages that inflation will inflict on money *yet to be earned*. I'm sure every reader knows what I mean here. A million dollars earned next year won't buy as much as a million earned this year. Somehow we have to factor that into our method of evaluating investment proposals. There's one more snag with ROI: It uses *profit* as part of its formula, and some aforementioned doubting Thomases don't much care for that because it occasionally gives off a whiff of bookkeeping prestidigitation. We have to overcome that problem too, so on to the next approach.

Cash Flow

This is the purest measure of an investment's current and future value. It is cash that we are in business to earn; it is cash that we require if we want to internally fund our future; and it is, accordingly, cash that probably has the greatest impact of stock prices. Though I know everyone knows what cash flow is, just in case some readers have forgotten or have been pretending too long to be able to ask anyone now, all you have to remember is two things: (1) it's just like it sounds; and (2) it's like Mafia accounting, or what the Don means when he ask, "What's duh take?" But cash flow is only the start; it doesn't take into account the time value of money, which is why the next approach is better. (Warning: From here onward we tread on concepts executive-suite primitives think effete, which in turn causes a lot of moaning and groaning among consultants. For example, Tom Kuczmarski, a Booz, Allen & Hamilton consultant, says he's "amazed" at how few companies are using these notions to measure success; he calls those who don't "antiquated.")[1]

Discounted Cash Flow

When you think about it, there are three different costs involved in investing money. The first is the cost of borrowing it; you have to pay interest plus some handling charges to get the use of it. Then, my friend, there is the cost of inflation; as soon as you get the dough it begins to lose its buying power. (Most experts hold that inflation is already taken care of in the interest rate, but I'm not sure that's true of all industries. Take the health care field for instance.) Lastly, there could be an *opportunity cost:* If you use that money for one thing, it means you can't spend it for something else. Some companies build in a standard charge level to cover this problem, others ignore it. The task of *discounting* can take all of these into account; all it really amounts to is forecasting an investment opportunity's total cash needs and returns over a given period of time (say, ten years) and *discount-*

ing them (that is, you discount future expenditures and revenues back to today's values or buying power) using the previously mentioned charges. Discounting is like figuring compound interest backwards, but no one has to do it by hand anymore. Any decent software package embodies these concepts, or, if you don't have any executive toys, you can use published tables. If you think this is just a lot of monkey-muck, try working it out using your own anticipated income cash stream against the cost of your education as an illustration. If your inflation projection is gloomy, you will be astonished (or depressed) by how little your income will be worth after ten years compared to the investment you made getting yourself educated. Of course, by itself, DCF is not comparative, so on to the next method.

Discounted Rate of Return

After all the discounting has been done, you take what you have left at the end of the period and express it as a percentage of all the cash investment required today. What you're hoping to get is a venture that gives you a stream of cash that, in today's values, lets the inflows exceed the outflows. (By the way, whenever I talk about cash flow in this book, I'm referring to discounted cash flow, even if I fail to say so.)

Net Present Value

This is an extension of discounted rate of return. Your net present value is cash inflow minus outflow expressed in today's dollar values. When your personal computer shows "NPV" in a financial forecast, this is what it's referring to. The idea of NPV can be applied to buying a house. Suppose you have two identical houses to choose from, one with a high-rate, 30-year mortgage and the other with a low-rate, assumable mortgage but a $5,000 higher price. If you're like most people, you'd conclude the latter deal to be more favorable. With the former you'd be bothered by the extra interest you'd have to pay over the next 30 years. But to the NPV advocate, the conclusion would be flawed. The $5,000 premium would have to be paid to the seller right now in today's money while the higher interest on the former would be paid gradually in tomorrow's money, which, if inflation continues, won't be worth a hell of a lot. And don't forget that interest payments are deductible. NPV analysis could tell you to avoid the assumable mortgage deal, though you do take some risk in making your inflation forecast and in estimating how long you expect to live in the new house. (A short-term stay might make the second deal more favorable.) In business the best decisions come from a tutored economic analysis of the time value of money, and those who fail to do this cannot possibly select those strategic options that are best for the firm.

The foregoing is a pretty superficial once-over and not intended to be the last word on the subject. If you must know more about this, consult a standard text on financial analysis or capital budgeting. However, as long as you grasp the basic idea of proper goal-setting and discounting, you will not get lost anywhere in the rest of this book.

judging the investment

My preference among the nine major methods of evaluating proposed captal expenditure would be either of the last two methods, discounted rate of return and net present value—although I use ROI in this book because it is more conventional. In spite of my reservations about the soundness of both the profit and the asset measurement going into the ROI calculation, the broad strategic laws are usually the same whether one looks at ROI or DCF. The merit in thrashing out how you want your company to evaluate investment proposals and current performance is so everybody in the fold can settle on the same criteria. This would appear to be the minimal requirement for any rational group of motivated managers, but it's not always that easy to accomplish.

Assuming you can settle on one good method, you still must contend with the fundamental question of financial strategy: How do you spot the investment option that'll make the most efficient use of the grubstake, given the normal level of required investment intensity in your particular industry? In a broad sense everything in this book—the entire body of strategic studies, if you will—answers this question but there are some specific issues related to the investment intensity problem that lend themselves to the same kind of no-nonsense analysis we used in marketing and production.

introductory considerations

You start with a simple axiom no sane person would bother to argue with: Over the long haul your corporate return on assets has got to exceed the cost you invested in those assets if you wish to survive and/or deliver a favorable return to your stockholders. The rate at which your book value per share grows through retained earnings has some bearing on stock prices (though perhaps not as much as formerly thought), and your unused debt capacity will suggest to some the probable forthcoming purchase of new assets that can be put to good use in further enhancing shareholder wealth (though to others, dithering on this matter could signal managerial Hamleting); if feasible, the annual dividend decision should carefully weigh the availability of other investment opportunities against the urge to unnecessarily reward stockholders in the short term. Going on from there, you will want to be sure that the investment has some decent operating leverage in it—that is, as output increases, will your cost per unit come down a lot, a little, or not at all? (One of the problems at International Harvester was poor operating leverage coming off a prickly labor situation that made getting even an industry-average return on sales unlikely, no matter how high volumes went.) And lastly, you will want to make certain that the folks pitching a proposed capital expenditure aren't guilty of *incremental cost thinking*. This is where you hear convoluted arguments like, "Hell, we aren't using that old drumdrier, so it's free; and that building was written off ten years ago, so it doesn't cost us anything." I've seen companies propelled by that kind of planning end up consisting of nothing but an assemblage of marginal SBUs, none of which could have made it on their own and which, in the aggregate, were obviously no better. There is always some theoretical use for idle equipment, and the opportunity cost thus figured must be worked into your assessment of the attractiveness of any investment; otherwise such sloppy thinking will spell fiscal doom by-and-by.

inflation and disinflation

If you don't use some form of inflation-adjusted accounting, you'll have at least some people in your firm thinking that sales are climbing when, in fact, they might be dropping along with your market share; or they may think that profits are great (note the plethora of annual reports that brag about the Nth year of record profits) when returns are actually declining. The company could be on the brink of bankruptcy, as many today are, and unable to face up to a serious credit problem or a sudden shortage of cash.[2]

For good reason, people cheer when the country's inflation rate drops. In general, that's good news. But for some it's also bad news. Think of it in terms of home ownership (a familiar vehicle): The family that bought its home in 1965 is almost living free today and would have no trouble paying off its mortgage if it wanted to. But, if they bought the house in 1980, the prospect of a halt in income growth as inflation slows makes it doubtful the family would ever be in a position to retire its debt. Same thing for a business. Barton Biggs, a Morgan Stanley strategist, observes that "a great many companies have structured themselves to benefit from rising inflation, incurring a higher percentage of long-term, fixed-rate obligations. Some who are over-committed will be wounded, some fatally" as inflation slows down.[3] Any company's debt becomes harder to pay off as inflation slows and events prevent the company from raising its prices (as was probably planned in its cash flow forecast under the assumption that inflation would continue).

Since disinflation is often a symptom of a recession, actual net selling prices may fall in some industries as supply outstrips demand. So you are forced to kill all your expansion plans because cash flow is in a tourniquet and interest rates fail to decline fast enough to make further investment attractive. You may recall from your economics lessons that Lord Keynes once opined, "The stimulus to output depends on the marginal efficiency of a given stock of capital rising relatively to the rate of interest." But, Keynes goes on to explain, when long-term interest rates refuse to budge, you aren't exactly ecstatic about investing more in the business because there is always that nagging anticipation of eventually lowered interest rates, which bring along with them the likelihood of lowered marginal efficiency on your current capital.[4] Though no doubt, when you first came across the idea of *marginal efficiency of capital* in school, it may have had little relevancy to your lifestyle, I would hasten to suggest that it does now if you have anything to do with judging the worth of an investment. But don't let Lord Keynes' fancy Bloomsbury language intimidate you. All of this is captured by the garden-variety, desktop computer in the DCF exercises it spews out.

Looking at it in everyday terms, this could mean that the plant and equipment you got at yesterday's higher finance charges are going to be pitted against competitors who bought theirs at lower rates. This is when dreary phrases like *marginal efficiency of capital* start to arouse your interest.

So much then for the miniprimer on the economics of disinflation, which I feel is an unavoidable preamble to the strategy of investment intensity.

investment intensity

The informed strategist has discovered what a lot of people have yet to learn about high finance—namely, that the capital intensive business doesn't produce glorious bottom lines. For example, when you define investment intensity as an SBU's net investment divided by net sales, then a business with a low investment intensity ratio (say 35 percent or less) gets a resounding 34 percent ROI, vs. the high investment intensity business (over 72 percent) with its calamitous 9 percent ROI.[5] In case you're curious, or looking for an out, the same dreadful story can be told when you look at it on the basis of operating income on sales (ROS).

Maybe some of us have been brainwashed by the popular press into believing that high technology (that's what you usually associate with heavy capital intensities) automatically brings on a legacy of vast riches. But this is actually a delusion. Giving your workforce space-age tools doesn't guarantee higher productivity; the worker-tool nexus needs careful monitoring before any hefty investment pays off. The best rule-of-thumb, in lieu of any more complex analysis, is that the heavier the investment, the lower your ROI.

Skeptics might aver that this is because the hi-tech revolution has taken place only very recently, that the assets were acquired at inflated price; ergo, the ROI's denominator swells and the resultant percentage ROI has to be smaller. Hence, so their argument will go, this is only an artifact of faulty accounting analysis. The skeptics will say that, if you used inflation (replacement value) accounting, you'd get a whole different picture—one that gives the heavy investment business a deservedly handsome ROI.

Makes sense, you say? Actually, studies like this have been done, and the results still uphold my previous claim that high investment intensity spells low returns regardless of asset age.[6]

In a roundabout way, however, inflation does cloud the problem; it lets you put up your prices, then you produce more dollar profits against a base of old-value, cheap-looking assets, then comes the inevitable dawn when you've got to replace those assets, and suddenly your ROI doesn't look so good anymore. What were once healthy looking profit centers now look very ill. While the investment intense business is usually bad, failure to acknowledge distortions imposed by inflation causes careless managers to make invidious comparisons to other company profit centers, leading themselves to think that their threadbare plants are great investments because they deliver such good ROIs. This kind of manager invariably concludes that any new P&E would be financially abhorrent. I discuss the ramification of compensation incentive plans that perpetuate such malfeasance in Chapter 11; meanwhile, it is sufficient to say that it conjures up spectres of lost productivity, diminished product quality, slovenly work habits and morale problems on the shop floor, and cowardly pricing schedules that bear no relationship to replacement costs. Hmmm, that sounds suspiciously like the current American industrial scene.

why the investment intense business suffers, and what can be done about it

The investment intensity issue can't be covered in a vacuum since the strategic function mandates a thoughtful analysis of all aspects of profit generation, none of which function unilaterally.

For example, in Chapter 3 I pointed out that one way of alleviating the pains of a high investment intensity is to make sure you have a large share of the market, as this allows you to benefit from the experience curve effect and achieve more efficient use of your assets. Fair enough, but as investment intensity rises, ROI descends, regardless of market share; it's nice to know that boosting your market share reduces the damage, but it still doesn't give you the returns a low investment intensity business would get. Take a high-share business, for example, with a low-investment intensity: it's ROI would be a splendid 42 percent vs. a not-so-hot 17 percent ROI when its investment intensity is high. Compare this to the low-share business: a 25 percent ROI when investment intensity is low and a miserable 4 percent (ugh!) when it's high.[7] So there has to be something else about investment intensity that makes it such a profit drain. In examining the nature of the overly onerous investment burden, we cannot lock in only one factorial pair, like market share and investment intensity, and expect to walk away from the problem with a full understanding of how to solve it.

Let's then begin with something so obvious that it usually leads to trouble: Using an asset at low capacity, just like driving your car in low gear, means it'll give a low yield. You will get a bigger ROI out of your high investment intensity business if you get your capacity utilization levels up, but, as with market share, you'll stilll have a lower ROI than the low investment intensity business. But here's where the trouble starts: A little bit of knowledge about capacity utilization is dangerous; it is the genesis of what is probably the key reason for the weak performance of the investment heavy business— the Managerial Clutch Response, which is like Management Angst (Chapter 4) but has peremptory industry-wide diffusion and less transitory effect.

When the stage for a slump is properly set and the curtain goes up, Management Clutch Response grips entire industries. (After all, your direct competitors probably will possess roughly the same investment intensity you do.) Profits slide. Competition gets belligerent, sometimes blatantly unethical. The innocenti are swept away.

The airline business easily comes to mind as one recent example of MCR. Braniff became the victim of the more predatory competitors (so it has been alleged) who dropped Braniff flight-listings from the computerized booking services they supplied to travel agents. You see, when you have an airline's enormous financial millstone, you more than just worry about passenger volume, it becomes the principle answer to your woes. You'll lure passengers with price-cuts and other inducements or, as the bullies did against Braniff, with activities of questionable legality. I'm not just talking competition, I'm talking *rough*.

But it doesn't end here. Managers can't sleep nights. Tossing and turning, images of huge, idle plants keep them awake, and the enticement of full capacity utilization flickers on and off as a welcome beacon until it becomes the sole object of their onanistic mental fondling. These managers' decisions will run the gamut from mediocre to dreadful. "We can't put up our prices; we'll get creamed," becomes the normal response to a well-reasoned proposal for a price increase in face of inflation-driven cost increases. "Let's not stir up the union; we can't afford a strike," sums up the temerity with which bargaining sessions are confronted. Then, as a natural consequence of a whole series of bad decisions like these, productivity takes a nosedive. The refusal to keep prices up with rising costs pulls down the potential value added amount that could be obtained from each worker. In some cases you find this intensified by incredibly poor people management. In some companies it gives rise to the addition of administrative fat as specialists are lugged in to solve the problem; or, conversely, you get a purge of wholesale firings. In neither case is much careful planning evident, the whole focus being solely on keeping the wheels of industry grinding out products regardless of what little sense any of it makes.[8] The MCR can take on its most vehement form in the family-owned enterprise, especially if the founding entrepreneur is still securely in charge of day-to-day affairs. But not all such companies fall victim to it. Some are in hog heaven, oblivious to the elitism of tracking ROI, and never get in a tizzy over capacity utilization. They are only too happy to show a profit—of any magnitude—at the end of each fiscal period, especially if the accountants have worked out some interesting tax shelters during that period. But where the progressive manager is involved, the pressures of having a spotless record on the career scorecard produce the hothouse climate for MCR. Once it is planted, MCR spreads like kudzu across the industrial wasteland.

preventing MCR

What can be done to prevent MCR from taking root in the first place? Generally, the answer lies, where it always does, in good strategic management. Specifically, with reference to investment intensity, the progenitor of MCR, there are five things to do.[9]

- *Develop intestinal fortitude.* Think long and hard about the overall strategic effects of a P&E investment, then ask yourself if you have the guts to resist the MCR. Or will your ulcers force you to bow to it, with the key benefits going to your employees in the form of cushier jobs and to your customers in the form of lower relative prices, brought on respectively by your inordinate and twisted fear of strikes and price resistance.

- *Resist hi-tech hankering.* Beware of going overboard on advanced technology unless you can pick it up at an industrial "garage sale." If it's really advanced, it's going to be expensive. Never let a salesman talk you into accepting the delusory idea that the automated plant is best for you. Sure, I know you have to replace tired, old equipment. Sure, we all know robots cost less than people. But as strategist, you should be enamored less with being technically up-to-date than with the need to balance employee/asset intensity with asset efficiency. Aim for the very best kind of productivity, as explained in Chapter 7.

- *Selective segmentation and niching.* Remember the limited but positive impact of the larger market share? You may want to go after a bigger share, not through costly category-wide competitive activity, but by pulling in your horns and doing battle only in market segments where you trust that your efforts will reap a substantial, perhaps a dominant, market share. Some steel companies are electing to follow this course. Working out in fewer segments, or in fewer geographic markets, and so on, may mean a leaner, but stronger, company.

- *Broader line in a narrower market.* At the same time you might want to give some thought, once narrowing your sights onto a few segments, to expanding your product offering within that framework so as to serve those segments better than the competition. The wider product line invariably offers a higher ROI than the narrower; among high investment intensity SBUs it can double the ROI, that is, make it go from weak (around 7 percent ROI) to average (around 15 percent). Having bigger inventories may be part and parcel of this strategy. As a supporting adjunct to this, you should consider the role of value. Value, as we found in Chapter 5, is an exceptionally good way to gain a high ROI. For the capital-intensive business, high value offers you a 20 percent ROI, while low value gives only 12 percent.[10]

These are all modest remedies in themselves. The investment intensity problem is very sticky, one or more of the foregoing strategic suggestions may turn it from an investment that earns less than a savings account to one that makes an average ROI, which, in the case of the heavy investment, isn't just chopped liver. (Obviously the best strategy is to avoid the investment intense business in the first place—but this gets us into the broader views of Corporate Strategy, and we're saving that for Chapter 13.)

investment intensity and cash flow

Since the people responsible for the firm's finance function watch over cash flows like hawks, they'll be eager spoilsports in commenting on the effects of any strategic decision on the long-term cash flow; they will be quick to stress that any internally funded investment, by definition, subtracts from corporate cash flow. You will find them quite unimpressed by your needs or by your own profit expectations. It will be up to you to talk around this negative mind-set that shies away from any measure that diminishes cash flow. This can become an obsession in some companies. If left to grow to extremes, it can block your ability to compete. After all, as we have already pointed out, it's obvious that neither you nor the nation can go on forever without eventually replacing run-down plants and machinery, regardless of inflated prices and outrageous financing charges. And if competition is doing it now, you've got to get on with it too.

The thinking of the hawks, the negative mind-set against any investment whatever its merits, can bring on corporate-wide attacks of MCR. Investment intensity is terrible, but it's going to make matters worse if you totally mishandle it. A modicum of spending might get you out of the woods if you play your cards right.

For example, as a basic strategic imperative in a growing market, you must keep your productive capacity well ahead of the market, lest you find yourself conceding share to your rivals. At the same time you may find it propitious—as many companies have—to increase your normal inventory levels in order to serve the customer better than competition and thus build the business; for the same reason, you may wish to deploy a more generous receivables policy. All of these asset-managing moves will cause a temporary dip in ROI and cash flow, but will be worth it nonetheless, in spite of what the financial hawk may think.[11]

In the end analysis, your investment policy should be dictated by the strategic impact it will have on your ability to compete. Underspending can weaken you; overspending leads to ruin. The main point is not to do it in a vacuum but within a studied framework of strategic analysis with all factors being thoroughly assessed and weighed. It is not a job for people with a singular compulsion to regard finance as an exercise in instruments. Rather, it is an assignment for the tough-minded, farsighted asset manager, someone who really knows how to "stook the sheaves," as they say in the Midwest.

notes

1. Bill Abrams, "Marketing: Liquor-Rating System Shows Sales Don't Tell Whole Story," *Wall Street Journal*, March 26, 1981, p. 23.

2. Peter F. Drucker, "A Corporation Should Be Inflation-Proofed," *Wall Street Journal*, May 28, 1981, p. 20.

3. Charles J. Elia, "Deteriorating Corporate Liquidity, Especially in Manufacturing Sector, Concerns Economists," *Wall Street Journal*, July 9, 1981, p. 31.

4. Lindley H. Clark, Jr., "A Kind Word for John Maynard Keynes," *Wall Street Journal*, May 18, 1982, p. 25.

5. Sidney Schoeffler, "The Unprofitability of 'Modern' Technology and What to Do About It," *PIMSLETTER*, (Cambridge, MA: The Strategic Planning Institute, 1977), pp. 1-3.

6. Mark J. Chussil, "Inflation and ROI," *PIMSLETTER*, (Cambridge, MA: The Strategic Planning Institute, 1980), pp. 1-8.

7. Sidney Schoeffler, "The Unprofitability of 'Modern' Technology and What to Do About It," p. 2.

8. Ibid., 7.

9. Ibid., pp. 7-10.

10. Mark Chussil and Steve Downs, "When Value Helps," *PIMSLETTER*, (Cambridge, MA: The Strategic Planning Institute, 1979) p. 4.

11. Bradley T. Gale and Ben Branch, "Strategic Determinants of Cash Flow," *PIMSLETTER*, (Cambridge, MA: The Strategic Planning Institute, 1980), pp. 9-10.

"Speaking for myself, I have an enormous antipathy to dying."

ARTHUR MARTINGALE (CLAUDE RAINS), ROPE OF SAND

the corporate wars: mergers, acquisitions, takeovers

There are two kinds of movie fan: the kind who goes for form, and the kind who goes for substance. The formists are a superficial lot who incline toward the gossip and the frivolous side of filmdom. Though their interest in films may be quite pervasive (even to where they call their company cafeteria the "commissary" and make pointless but *knowing* jokes about the William Morris Agency), it is still just trifling. Those who go for substance, on the other hand, seek deeper satisfactions from films, and their conversations may be sprinkled with such phrases as "mise-en-scène," "montage," and "auteur."

Similarly, there are two types of merger fan. The formist is drawn to it by a fascination with dollar signs, intricate financial pie-in-the-sky, the artful posturings of the players. Those who are more concerned with substance, a minority unfortunately, view mergers as just another strategic scenario that may, or may not, enhance ROI and cash flow.

Recent years have brought us some of the most spectacular, noisy, and controversial shotgun corporate marriages the industrial world has ever witnessed. Many of these unions have stimulated considerable head scratching among investors and strategists alike. (If anyone out there really understands what happened to Bendix in 1982, please clap your hands.) In following these unfolding dramas in the press, it is hard to resist becoming absorbed by the superficial

127

impedimenta of tender offers, counter offers, and of who said what to whom. It's no different than the movie fan who gets mentally embroiled in the new blockbuster film's budget excesses or the coke-snorting peccadillos of its above-the-title stars but never experiences the slightest curiosity about the film's potential artistic merits.

The primitive, armchair observer will continue, of course, to be enraptured by the players and inevitably will confuse their extravagantly overstated press handouts with strategic insight. More cerebral strategists, however will, take all this for what it is—carefully calculated battle tactics—and they will seek their own comprehension of the proposed union from the strategic management angle.

track record and merger skills

No doubt about it. Mergers have been, and always will be, popular items in the business press. To reporters they make juicy stories, to the investment community they make money, to readers (some of whom fear they may one day be merger victims) they make intriguing copy. But, in spite of the gallons of ink expended in covering them, the press is not too free in leveling with us on the general outcome of mergers and takeovers.

Lately the Wall Street Journal (along with a few others) has put some reporting effort against this; by its reckoning a third of all acquisitions are failures.[1] Of course, others think the figure could be higher. One of them, John Arnold, a merger consultant who should know, claims that "as many as seven out of ten acquisitions don't meet the expectations of the acquiring parties." The reason: inadequate, hurried research. "Investment bankers have been very honest with me about this," Arnold says. "They say if they take the time to do a major study of a company or industry, it could slow down the acquisition and kill the deal." No deal, no fee. A study by a couple of Harvard professors, Malcolm Salter and Wolf Weinhold, confirms this view: "Swift, decisive action—not sustained planning—is thus the hallmark of many diversifying acquisitions," says their study.

Readers, who by now are surely well-steeped in the strategic laws of business, must find this exasperating. If the takeover is so damn important, they will be asking themselves, then surely some semblance of strategic analysis and research should be conducted. If the investment banking community were really on its toes, it would have most of the spade work for this sort of thing already on file for all key industries before the first whiff of a merger wafts over their transoms. If not the investment bankers (who would not be agog with this as a business building device, I'm sure), then surely *someone* should be doing it. But, with rare exceptions, they are not; in many ways merger mongering seems, to the strategist, like a cottage industry. It is, one could say, theater-of-the-absurd writ large:

At first Pan Am's idea of engorging National Airlines must have looked like one of those cartoon lightbulbs that suddenly appears over someone's head—a glowing case of synergy if ever the Street had seen one. How sweet it was going to be when National began feeding its domestic passengers to Pan Am's international routes. But the flaw in this hasty pudding was that the two airlines' labor forces were so totally incompatible (in job classifications and seniority provisions, etc.) they just couldn't be combined. Furthermore, the domestic line's need for on-time performance didn't exactly jibe with an international's goggles-and-white-scarf notions on performance (jetting in on roughly the same day as scheduled). In the end, Pan Am frankly acknowledged that this ill-planned merger contributed to the financial woes that forced it to unload its magnificent Intercontinental Hotels subsidiary.

The personal chemistry of the merging parties can acidify even the most credible chances for synergy, like when Pillsbury gulped down the Green Giant in 1979. This blend of flour and vegetables emerged from the oven tasting like bad blood. Insiders vented their jealousies by keeping tabs on how each marriage partner fared in garnering the top jobs. People really got cantankerous. So much so that Tom Wyman, the head Green Giant (who later became Paley's heir at CBS), attempting to quell this, mounted the stage at a management confab wearing a custom-made sportcoat, half green (the Green Giant color, get it?) and half blue (the Pillsbury hue), proclaiming he was "tired of people keeping score." But to strategists the marriage was on the rocks before it was consummated. It wasn't just bad chemistry. Said Stephen Carnes, former head of Pillsbury's investor relations, "Green Giant is a strategic mistake." The frozen food portion of Green Giant, previously hit by and then suffering from high energy and carrying charges, had long before relinquished its claim to being a promising business of the future. And canned veggies have long been notorious for their wobbling margins.[2]

There's a conglomerate south of the border whose size is (or was) only outdone by its swollen Mexican ego. Grupo Industrial Alfa S.A., whose sales volume was a thumping 1.2 percent of Mexico's entire GDP, fell into so many strategic traps in its merger activities that it became a national issue. "We had a lot of bright people who could analyze cash flows, but they didn't know a thing about the commodity business," said Carlos Santacruz, former executive in Alfa's acquisition department. They thought they were special. They thought they could turn any acquisition into pure gold. They had this god complex. "It horrified me," said Caroline Trotter, Alfa's former strategic planning manager. "I recommended liquidating as many acquisitions as possible, but they proceeded to do their empire-building....They'd make huge front-end investments with no immediate returns, paying for it all with short-term debt. And they didn't want to hear anybody who said no." The banks that blessed Alfa's vaulting scenarios with loans should have known better; most now admit they didn't mess with the details. "It goes to show that most bankers don't know finance," says Ingolf Otto of Mexico City's Banking and Finance Institute. "If you tell me your child has grown one inch in a year, I'd say he is healthy. But if you tell me he has grown a yard, I'd say he is very sick. Alfa was very sick." The lesson: When you do not have a coherent strategic plan to give your acquisitive instincts form and shape, and when you don't bother to listen to your own inside strategic planning experts, you can expect trouble in River City.[3]

Mighty Exxon is having more than its share of troubles in this arena. Since the mid-1960s it has tried to carve out a position in mining, fecklessly investing over $1 billion to search out and develop uranium, copper, and other metals and losing approximately $600 million in the process. In 1979 it picked up Reliance Electric for a cool $1.24 billion, hoping to launch a new market in energy saving electric devices, which it later abandoned. Exxon Office Systems is a distinctive loser. According to Robert Stebbins, a former manager of minerals at Exxon headquarters, the company's decision making "is somewhat analogous to grasping Jell-O. Authority is usually vested in numerous ... committees rather than in individuals who can and want to be held accountable. A bureaucracy does things collectively so nobody can single out an individual for making the wrong decision." Committees can't formulate strategy. They always end up in compromise.[4]

reasons for mergers

So, if it is so bad, why do companies want to merge or make acquisitions? There are many obvious reasons, such as getting into some attractive businesses otherwise closed to them. Procter & Gamble seems to do it to pick up some quick "know-how" before it decides what kind of M.O. to use in its own resources orchestration once it really pulls out all the stops in going after new markets.

Of course, many other considerations are presented to the investing public to justify a takeover. A few take on metaphysical airs straight out of Philosophy 101, prompting Wall Street wags, who see irreversible doom in the offing, to jibe that the predator is "putting

Descartes before the hearse." One such lofty pretension is the handy claim that the formation of such a union will spread or balance the risk. This is usually explained by showing how the products of the two companies are mirror images of each other, which would allow the combined enterprise to survive, regardless of which way the economy lurches in its cyclical flipflops. Stock analysts and business strategists seldom are gulled by this argument: Why reward companies for just trying to divvy up the risk by entering new types of businesses? Stockholders with a pinch of commonsense already do the same thing for themselves! Such arguments really pall when the predator has to pay a huge premium for the prey. The stupendous $7.5 billion Du Pont coughed up for Conoco happened to be, at the time, a not-to-be-sneezed-at $3.5 billion more than Conoco's market value—a very hefty sum to stir into the pot on the bottom side of the ROI formula. Even before hydrocarbons bit the dust, the market refused to react as kindly to this merger as Du Pont had expected. The biggest merger in history, it has received its share of postmortems, some claiming Du Pont simply failed to explain clearly the beauty of the merger's strategy story; others, with the benefit of hindsight, claim there was no strategy story to tell, ergo no worthwhile rationale to support the merger.

Another reason mergerists deploy to justify their deeds, especially when the price is right, is that they are picking up a bargain. When the stock price of the victim company is suppressed to a fire-sale level, why not grab it? But, in the frenzy to consummate a merger, the bidding can get out of hand and the offered premium can soar above the true worth of the acquired assets—so much so that it's better sometimes to put the money into modernizing the acquisitive firm's own plants and go for enhanced (real) productivity (see Chapter 7).[5]

Finally some companies are encouraged to merge just because they sense there is less danger these days that such action will attract antitrust charges. This may change at Washington's whim, but the fact that something is legal does not make it prudent; there must be a more sufficient justification for a merger than this. There must be a strategic rationale.

drucker's rules

One can always count on Peter Drucker for a few bons mots on most business subjects. Recently he came up with five rules for a successful acquisition:

- Think it through. Besides money, what do you, the acquirer, contribute to the union—management skills, technology, marketing advantages? Forget synergy. And forget what the acquired company gives you.

- Be sure you have something in common.
- Show respect—for the acquired firms products, markets, and so on. Significantly, no pharmaceutical company ever made a big success out of any cosmetic firm they picked up, and no show-biz company (a TV network, for example) ever did much with any book publisher it acquired.
- Be aware that you'll lose the top people in the acquired firm. They just won't stay.[6]
- Make some key cross-pollinating promotions in the first year. This shows people in both companies that genuine opportunities lie ahead.

These are certainly critical factors that were largely lacking in all of the preceding examples. And among them is the first hint at a valid strategic approach to such activities.[7]

strategic approach to takeovers

It would be a cheap shot to point out that a few of Japan's industrial giants got that way via a whole bunch of mergers. The fault, anyway, is not in the concept of merging but in its common forms of execution. Lord knows that something must be done to make the process less than a crapshoot. The stockmarket is not consistently thrilled by mergers. While the target company's stock price usually jumps at the first rumblings of rumor, thanks to arbitrage and speculation, the predator's often falls.[8] And the postmortem discourses from security analysts and commentators frequently point up so many obvious strategic flaws in these unions as to make a rational thinker wonder how they ever came about.

It would be naive to suppose that the principal players are going to halt their zaniness and all the ego-stroking pleasures that ensue. I mean, what would you rather do? Fly around the country in your company jet, consort with big-time investment bankers, and hit the front page of your old home-town newspaper with every utterance? Or closet yourself with a brace of business strategists who can offer you nothing better than ham sandwiches from the downstairs deli and piles of printouts, grids, and bubble-charts? I'd definitely choose the latter, but I'm not sure about you. Most executives find making acquisitions more fun than ropin' 'n brandin' steers. And that's why mergers fare no better than anything else in the business world; that is to say, the probability of success is lower than it need be, the fault lying mainly in the shallowness of the analysis that paves the way to the merger. And I don't buy the excuse that there is not enough time. Chief executives who claim it all has to be done in nanoseconds are the same usually stodgy people who will spend an entire day with a PR staff learning how to flex their tongue muscles with Brobingnagian menace on their acquisitive intent. Their time would be better spent with their strategic planning experts. These experts could make a more serious contribution than anyone else inside or outside the company.

I don't feel there is any strategic message to give on the subject of takeovers except this: Mergers should pursue the same ends as in one's own corporate strategic management, which are outlined in Chapter 13. The ability of the grids displayed in that chapter to encapsulate the diverse, sometimes confusing, strategies of seemingly unwieldly and unmarriageable SBUs would benefit any strategist journeying to the imperial Land of Acquisition.

If you are merely an observer, or a potential investor, do not be deceived by the professions of the executives who are party to all the merger merriment, frolicking, and romping. Some executives blithely credit themselves with superhuman powers and will inform anyone within earshot that they can mold any assemblage of acquired assets into a superior and invincible profit-producing force with their bare hands. Some see themselves as a living metaphor—a giant tree, themselves the mighty trunk, forming many branches in an ever expanding canopy. A leading merger broker, who declined to be identified, was quoted in the Wall Street Journal as saying "American businessmen wear these large 'hero badges,' and they don't realize that their heroism isn't automatically extensible to all companies they buy."[9]

Just remember that the best of intentions—even when propelled by genuine and impressive Executive Hall of Fame leadership qualities—can't produce synergy out of thin air. The overall strategic rationale must be there first, as it must for all else that we do.

notes

1. Thomas Petzinger, Jr., "Troubled Couplings: To Win a Bidding War Doesn't Ensure Success of Merged Companies,"*Wall Street Journal*, September 1, 1981, p. 1.

2. Lawrence Ingrassia and Meg Cox, "Dowdier Doughboy: Sluggish Green Giant Slows Pillsbury's Pace from the Frenetic '70s,"*Wall Street Journal*, November 4, 1981, p. 1.

3. Lawrence Rout, "Fading Miracle: Conglomerate's Plight Hurts Mexico's Image, Hampers Its Recovery,"*Wall Street Journal*, June 10, 1982, p. 1.

4. Maria Shao, "Metal Fatigue: Exxon's Mining Unit Finds It Tough Going After 16 Years in Field," *Wall Street Journal*, August 31, 1982, p. 1.

5. Adam Meyerson, "Merger Mania and the High Takeover Premiums,"*Wall Street Journal*, July 20, 1981, p. 12.

6. A letter from Henry G. Van der Eb, retired chairman and CEO of Container Corp. of America, in the*Wall Street Journal*, October 21, 1982, p. 33. "Too frequently, the momentum and intangible strengths of an acquired company are taken for granted. Ultimately the dead hand of a superimposed bureaucracy takes its toll, stultifying

initiative and inhibiting innovation. Morale and productivity wane. Much of the economic rationale of buying underpriced physical assets in the first place can later be negated by the loss of motivation and sense of identity in the acquired company. Enlightened management is essential in the successful integration of any acquisition. While some companies do this very well, America's industrial boneyard is surfeited with examples of this ironic management failure."

7. Peter F. Drucker, "The Five Rules of Successful Acquisition,"*Wall Street Journal*, October 15, 1981, p. 22.

8. Adam Meyerson, "Shareholders Often Say No to Takeover,"*Wall Street Journal*, November 16, 1981, p. 22.

9. Petzinger, "Troubled Couplings," *Wall Street Journal*, September 1, 1981, p. 1.

10

using strategic laws to reduce international risk

To the stateside, deskbound landlubber the word "international" drums up visions of boondoggle junkets, rich foods, and exotic sex, with little to worry about in the business line except escaping from banana republics under seige or figuring out how to plunder some pitiful, undeveloped nation with new marketing ideas. To mention "strategy" and "international" in the same breath would provoke hoots of incredulity.

From the strategy-minded executive's point of view the fact that a business is somewhere offshore makes little difference; strategic principles, more or less, are applicable anywhere on the face of the globe, and in theory an international business should get the same analytical and planning treatments the domestic ones get.

But in actual practice few companies bother to do this, they just aren't all that internationally minded.[1] As a rule they have only a few decision makers on board who feel comfortable with the foreign scene—most corporate executives exuding confidence only on their own domestic turf. To these executives the company's international division is far from a routine portfolio of SBUs, but a slippery collection of suspect ventures with unquantifiable elements of risk. Risk always seems to hang by a hair, like the Damoclean sword, over their heads. It is the issue of risk that they often harp on and use to deny the international division's access to capital funding. Yet the

135

term "risk" is used willy-nilly, and few who use it would actually be able to define it if asked.

a better definition of international risk

Perhaps risk is seldom defined because everyone thinks the term is self-explanatory. In casual discussions on international business it is usually spoken of in terms of its various manifestations, such as "Canada is too risky because Ottawa is on one of its antiforeign investment binges" or "Brazil is dicey these days because inflation is out of control." In other words, emphasis is usually put on the reasons *why* risk exists, rather than on the *nature* of risk itself. Such imprecision makes the determination of foreign risk rather cumbersome and fruitless.

I have found it more useful to delineate between two different types of risk:[2]

- Profit and cash flow risk
- Asset risk

The first type of risk is clearly a strategic one. You can avoid it or lessen it by sound business strategies and by staying out of markets that are inherently unhealthy in terms of low margins, high V.A.T. taxes, and so on. The second type of risk emanates from political action (nationalization, sabotage, war), or from natural occurrences (earthquakes, drought, typhoons). These are quite separate issues and must receive distinctly individualized treatment.

Since risk is governed by both qualitative and quantitative factors occuring in both the specific industry and in the general sectors of the economy, any systematic method of international risk assessment must examine the micro and macro sources to produce a composite determination of risk for each foreign business unit you are examining.

determining profit and cash flow risk

The traditional means of gauging your international profit or cash flow risk include things like making projections based on past performance or transposing the known track-record of an SBU from one country to a similar unit in another. In other words, it's pretty much like the old fashioned notion of planning that culminates in little more than long-range budgets.

Unfortunately, the past is not always a perfect guide to the future, and these days most forecasts are hard to swallow. Transnational computations are not always safe either; the microeconomic factors having a pronounced impact on business performance are not necessarily transferable from one country to another. What you really need is some form of analytical machinery that can weigh and balance all the factors controlling the profitability of your foreign business units so you can come up with a probability determination of their profit and cash flow risk. I like to break this down into three parts for maximum clarity: (1) SBU profit risk, (2) geographic profit risk, (3) marketing profit risk.

SBU profit risk

To counterweight the often habitual radiant optimism or excessive gloom in the corporate sentiments about its international gambits, the issue of business unit profit risk can best be seriously addressed by conducting a comprehensive analysis of all the strategic profit control factors of each current (or proposed) SBU under study.

Several computer programs and mathematical models are available for this, but, for our purposes here, let's stick with the one we've attempted to use consistently throughout the book—the PIMS Program. A typical PIMS analysis would facilitate a quick but exhaustive study of the business unit's profit control factors and, based on its amply validated model, compute the SBU's likely forthcoming ten-year ROI and DCF. Since the future can bring any number of altered circumstances and situations, you also may want to consider what the program has to say about profitability under varying rates of inflation, sales volume, market growth, and market share level. Additionally, key internal factors (such as investment intensity, and vertical integration, and all the others that we've been talking about) can be studied to see if any feasible changes in them would have a significant influence on your profit.

In the end, after assessing all of the data obtained from the previous exercise, you would be able to draw unwooly conclusions regarding the potential risk for each SBU. Basically, the higher your projected return rate, the bigger your cushion and the less risk your business will face on those dimensions. The only remaining risk it can encounter would arise from that which is later outlined under asset risk.

geographic profit risk

Because of the way they organize their international divisions (and consequently their time), some companies prefer to view international risk from the aspect of geographic areas. However, as you pan back from the specific business unit, your analysis necessarily becomes both less precise and less salient. Nonetheless, it is true that there are certain broad differences between some nations, other than socio-political ones, that affect the performance of the business in general. In one country, for example, retailers demand such onerous trade allowances that no business there would be capable of rising above a mere perfunctory return rate; hence, that whole nation would have greater profit risk attached to it. Thus, I suppose it is tempting and convenient to analyze by geographic area when the corporate organization chart calls for it. Here again the PIMS Program could be utilized to detect and measure these differences. One method would be to select a random sample of corporations in each geographic region and, using PIMS' speedy *Limited Information Model* (LIM), attempt to see if any major variations exist between regions regarding ROI and DCF. (It will, of course, be necessary to have access to, or be able to make reasonably good estimates of, certain data regarding these sampled corporations. If, for example, you can obtain their financial statements and know something about their market penetration, the input requirements of the LIM model would be satisfied.) Once this has been done for the regions you are interested in, they can be ranked by average ROI and DCF rates of return to determine relative geographic risk probabilities.

marketing profit risk

The marketing function is often selected for special treatment in the examination of international risk because, unlike many of the other functions of an enterprise, marketing is often the only flexibility you have for quick response to competitive situations.

The risk that stems from the marketing situation is handled only partly in the PIMS analysis, or in any other program for that matter. A more thorough study of it is done by any number of SBU portfolio matrix devices, as described in Chapter 13, in which you factor together such aspects as the attractiveness of the market (lifecycle slot, segmentation opportunities, experience curves, etc.), competitive posture, and any meaningful technological pluses or minuses you might have. Where available, market research studies (e.g., product attitudes, corporate image, etc.) should supplement this analysis, but only if you feel you can trust them. In many nations the local consumer research is no better than astrology.

determining asset risk

The risk of having your overseas assets seized, destroyed, blockaded, or otherwise rendered useless, arises from a number of macro factors. Chief among these would be those with a political origin. Some foreign governments have been known to nationalize entire industries, or pass hostile legislation making corporate assets less productive. (Announced in triumphant voice, such nefarious deeds may be intended to win electorate support, but, as Canadians found after Pierre Trudeau's machinations against the provincial governments, they can result in lowered investment incentives and flights of capital from the country.) Managers of your international SBUs do not have exactly surgical control over such factors but, understandably, want to be able to assess them more rationally.

Sophisticated techniques have been developed to predict political risk. Employing multivariate analysis, these techniques attempt to foretell internal instability or conflict and the general long-range political/economic climate. Some international observers, however, feel such mechanistic approaches have yet to be perfected, and, until more is known about their ability to predict the kind of turmoil that would actually endanger a specific company's assets, I believe that judgmental, rather than multivariate, techniques would suffice to assess the elements influencing a nation's political risk profile.

The Delphi method, mainly a subjective form of analysis, is often employed here with some success. With Delphi you can include not only the political culprits involved in asset risk, but three other chief contributors as well: consumers, industry factors, and the economy.

While the procedure is quite straightforward, it works best if you organize a strong team effort between both overseas and headquarters people. Briefly this is how you can do this form of analysis:

- Produce a very exhaustive list of factors from each of the macro contributors.
- Rate each factor on the importance of its impact on company performance or survival using a 0-10 scale, with 10 representing "extremely important." Do this for each region.
- Next, further quantify each factor (for each region) to determine whether it is favorable or unfavorable (to the SBU under study), using a -5 to +5 scale. (The double-rating method offers a degree of flexibility that will be useful as various regional conditions change through time.)
- Then multiply the importance rating by the favorable/unfavorable rating to obtain the net score for each factor. Add up the net scores for all factors to produce the overall rating for each region (see Table 10-1). Naturally the same thing also can be done by business unit, but the expected variances by SBU within a given region would probably be small.

As the team progresses through several business unit analyses, patterns will emerge that should produce a consensus of thought and judgment.

Table 10-1. Illustration

	REGION A			REGION B		
	Import.	Fav/unfav	Net	Import.	Fav/unfav	Net
FACTORS (*Simplified*)						
Middle class growth	9	-3	-27	9	4	36
Worker absenteeism	6	-1	-6	6	1	6
"OSHA"-type rules, and enforcement	7	5	<u>35</u>	7	-5	<u>-35</u>
Totals			2			7

Interpretation: High score indicates lower risk. Region B, although it has tough safety regulations re plant operations, etc., presents lower overall risk because it has a better market (faster growing affluent class) and a more dedicated work force....

conclusion

The summarized results of both profit and asset risk assessments can be plotted on a matrix to produce an easily understood comparative portrait of the overall risk facing the corporation in each SBU or region (see Figure10-1).

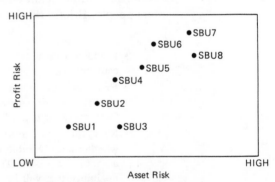

FIGURE 10-1. GENERAL RISK MATRIX

Comparative international risk can be determined and measured by the application of known strategic laws governing profitability and by coupling this to an informed and systematic treatment of the macro factors. Of course, if this still leaves your international division clouded in mystery as far as your deskbound domestic executives are concerned, the whole process could be repeated for your domestic business to show how their risk profile lines up with international's. But that opens up a whole 'nuther can of nightcrawlers.

140

notes

1. The importance and allure of international ventures vary by industry and by nationality of the parent company. With U.S. companies, for example, the value of the dollar on foreign markets and the relative cost of home labor have been major factors in determining the level of interest in overseas activities.

Accordingly over the long term, as far as American corporations are concerned, there has been a decline in international focus. In the 1950s, when overseas labor was cheap and U.S. technology comparatively more advanced, international expansion was aggressively pursued. In the 1960s an overvalued dollar also made it more profitable to import finished goods from overseas subsidiaries. Then in the 1970s the U.S. dollar declined, the labor climate at home was relatively more congenial, and international ventures were no longer as attractive as they had been. Foreign divestitures increased: For example, in 1971 there were over three times as many U.S. foreign subsidiary formations as there were divestitures, but by 1975 the ratio was about even. As of this writing, the dollar is once again strong, domestic labor costs too high, and imports once again have tremendous pull. During the entire period referred to, the global picture changed in other ways, too. The scene became more crowded with formidable enterprises from countries other than the United States or Western Europe. In the automotive field alone, there are now around 40 multinational producers vs. only five in the 1950s.

11

people,
strategy, and incentives

As a universal principle, Jane Austen (1775-1817) postulated that all men were "haughty and affected or not." I always find it hard to believe that anyone, the literati excepted, takes Austen's views on real men (and women, for that matter) seriously. Though she wrote extensively and laboriously about men and women, she seldom viewed them as vocational animals with economic motivations. (Well, what would you expect from an author who never wrote once about the then current Napoleonic menace?) No doubt this chapter would come as a profound shock to her, based as it is on the proposition that people do not automatically do the job they're supposed to, that pressure must be applied lest they slough off.

And to those who understand this fundamental flaw in human nature, and thereby have devised or subscribed to elaborate incentive systems to spur on the uncomitted worker, it may also come as a surprise to learn that, in the main, such systems are counter-productive.

Worse yet, to the broad stream of managers who have seen one management theory and organizational concept after another come and bite the dust, only to be replaced by yet another notion promoted by an army of consultants with fresh insights on organization and motivation, it must have dawned that there are no pat answers at the end of an organization chart or revised job descriptions. Many of these

142

managers have found, after repeated disappointments, that these vain attempts at achieving enhanced efficiency and group harmony succeed only in altering the corporate vocabulary, without deeply affecting the cast of characters or its financial performance. It is almost as if there exists parallel, but separate, universes: one where organizational form is the central issue, the other where the daily slings and arrows of the commercial world must be borne. Neither seems to be in real contact with the other.

My friend, this is due to the fact that the personnel experts and their wage-and-salary minions have been thinking wrong thoughts. You see, when it comes right down to it, they are tactical folks. Their very orthodox, standard formulations leave no room for the more noble strategic view you have in mind; and, if I may speak frankly, it is highly unlikely that they would have a valid, comprehensive conception of strategic management. Thus, when you ask them for a plan to improve worker/manager performance, they immediately see a problem with only two elements: the company objective (profit, ROI, etc.) and the day-to-day tactics that can be deployed to achieve it (number of shelf-facings the salesmen get in each store, calls per week, new accounts opened, etc.). They impulsively neglect to include the prime cause of all profit (strategy—in case you haven't been paying attention) and all of its detailed components. Accordingly, they flub the opportunity of devising systems that get everyone to work lockstep toward the implementation of your strategies and which can be the best vehicle for communicating the company's business strategies to its managers (in itself, not an easy task).

Your company is a big nothing without its strategies. Alone, they account for its overall performance. Alone, they increase or subtract from shareholder value. There is no point in organizing and rewarding your personnel for any purpose other then to ensure that they are cognizant of what these strategies are and to make certain they are implementing them. And for the Jane Austens of the business world, it is worth reiterating that employees are not always inclined to perform as expected; they have to be induced.

But even if you happen to be blessed with an incentive system that does everything it should (and shortly I will unravel such a plan in unsparing Austenian detail), you still have to contend with people. No strategic plan can work if you put the wrong people in the little boxes on your organization chart.

problems and people

The arcane art of deploying people can be carried to excess. I, for one, wouldn't be quite ready to subscribe to a gene analysis service, for example, nor would I willingly accept some of the more prevalent dogmas about people management. In particular, I don't feel you can treat people with the inflexibility some of these shibboleths mandate. I think most people have a fairly broad range of "stage personalities." If someone doesn't seem right for a job he's trying to do, I can't see why it hurts to tell him he's displaying the wrong personality profile for the role he's supposed to be playing. There's a good chance he can put on a different mask; *and* if this succeeds, you save yourself a lot of money compared with sacking him and training someone new. Aggressive individuals can soften up when required; even accountants can summon forth submerged and suppressed humor if assured by authority symbols that, not only is this permissable, it is perhaps a better approach for dealing with their clerks.

Other personnel management maxims are assailed as easily. For example, Freddy Heineken, whose marketing success made him a good exemplar in Chapter 5, doesn't buy the old chestnut that ideal executives must be supreme delegators. Heineken believes the boss actually should entangle himself in day-to-day affairs. Heineken himself directly supervises his firm's R&D, public relations, and finance, and he keeps at least one eye trained on all the other departments as well.[1] (Though it works for Heineken, I suspect few senior level readers would want to risk doing this in their own corporate environments.)

Even if my illustrations here, for the sake of vividness, only touch the petty periphery of the problem, the simple fact is that the orthodoxies of personnel selection may be the wrong way to go. For many strategic situations considerable flexibility in people selection and management may be more appropriate—or even essential.

Hay Associates, a prominent compensation planning consultancy, would, for example, prescribe quite widely divergent personality profiles in the different quadrants of the market matrix we used in Chapter 3.

- The high-share cash hog business would, according to Hay Associates, need the entrepreneur—someone who willingly accepts risk, has a sense of adventure, is innovative, opportunistic, and effective, someone they describe as "minimally controlling." This entrepreneur also has to have charisma.

- The cash cow, on the other hand, needs a totally different sort of person, one that they call the "sophisticated manager," someone somewhat conservative and only mildly venturesome, a good team player who would be both effective and, at the same time, efficient.

- For those cash dwarfs you are trying either to harvest or dump, Hay says you need "the critical administrator." This would be someone who is conservative, a risk-shunner, coldly pragmatic, and only minimally participative. What they are talking about here is your hard-nosed autocrat.

Personnel management can be weakened by one's unconscious attraction for conformity. Soichiro Honda, founder of the company bearing his name and considered by some to be Japan's Henry Ford, thinks American hiring and promotional practices often stomp out individualism. He says, "If you hire only those people whom you understand, the company will never get people better than you....Always remember that you often find outstanding persons among those you don't particularly like."[2]

Extending this thought to a broader perspective, conformity and the overall corporate climate may conspire to impede the very pursuit of corporate excellence. Every company has a peculiar management style that, inevitably, accrues from the idiosyncrasies of the people it hires. These management styles can produce roadblocks that are hard to circumvent. These roadblocks take many forms: They will cover the gamut from slow decision making to rash, hasty, unanalyzed decisions; from day-late-and-a-dollar-short copycatism to absurd, far-out, don't-do-it-unless-its-different thinking. Some are just reactive; they never do anything until forced by dire circumstances. Others search for PR blankets or excuses to justify their every deed.

Harvard Business School professor, Abraham Zaleznick, had an interesting thought on this: he suggested that many companies garb themselves in so much excess rationality that the human feelings get all bottled up, and unexpected inefficiencies develop. In some firms the expected norm of "pure reason" makes it imperative to shun anything smacking of personality or emotion. All management roles are defined in punctilious detail. But, below the surface, silently, insidiously, with damaging potential, everyone is seething. In the process, all the joy, thrill, and sense of mission are lost, and "the culture of passivity rules."[3]

Whatever form it takes, there is something that can be done about wayward corporate cultures. A sound incentive plan can work wonders. Bluntly speaking, there is nothing like good, old-fashioned fear to induce an effective performance. Fear exists in all companies, but it's usually the wrong kind. The fear involved in the case of an effective incentive plan is a more wholesome kind—not getting paid as much as top performance permits. Such fear can be a positive, strongly motivating force if communicated clearly. The effectiveness of an incentive plan in ridding a legacy of ill-advised hiring and promotional policies, and a resulting captious corporate culture, rests on goal congruence—when your objectives as a manager and those of the shareholders can be attained by the same sets of actions.

With this in mind, I would now submit for your approval my ideas about how you can use incentives to ensure that all company

145

strategies are properly understood and implemented. Even though you may not be involved directly in devising the incentive system in your shop, this may not prevent you from launching the concept; most plans allow incumbents (as personnel folks like to call you) to share in developing the annual document outlining the goals and guidelines. Consequently, you may have an opportunity to introduce some of these concepts for yourself and subordinates.

the strategic management incentive plan

background

Most management incentive systems are what compensation professionals call *discretionary*—that is, incumbents in particular positions do not know until year end what criteria their incentive awards will be based on. This approach is more appropriately known as the *bonus system*. It has virtually no role in motivating performance and is deemed nonproductive by most compensation experts.

The nondiscretionary systems, which are considered by the experts to be productive, generally award the incumbent on the basis of set performance criteria. The simplest of these will focus on profit or sales volume, or on a more detailed list of factors. It is agreed universally that the factors must be measurable, and simple accounting data are used as the source of this measurement.

The growth in this form of executive compensation over the years has been phenomenal and, to a large extent, both unwarranted and misguided. Of glaring interest to us, as strategists, is the huge dichotomy that has developed between executive pay and concomitant benefits to shareholders. From 1971 to 1981 in the Standard and Poor 400, pay to senior management in all forms went up 10 percent (real dollars), but salaries actually only gained 2 percent. Bonuses were up 12 percent, and incentives (i.e., those pegged to specific earnings performance) skyrocketed 25 percent. But, as those who nursed their own sickly investments during this period already know, stock prices (with dividends included in the calculation) dropped 2 percent.[4]

problems

Most nondiscretionary incentive systems force the worker to focus his or her effort on tactical, day-to-day considerations. They overlook the long-term exigencies of concentrating on the major issues that must be addressed in order to implement a business strategy that is of a long-term duration.

The basic reason that strategic factors are overlooked is because they require criteria that are economic in nature, rather than being based on standard accounting practices, and these are not usually accessible or understandable to the administrators of the incentive plan.

It is therefore necessary to develop an incentive plan that incorporates these economic goals—and which, at the same time, provides an equitable basis of measurement—if management personnel are to be actively and effectively motivated toward the successful implementation of corporate and business unit strategies. To reiterate an important point, any good incentive plan must have unmistakeable goal congruence—that is, the aims of both the officers and the troops must be satisfied by the same action plans, and the overall goal should be the ultimate creation of shareholder value.

basis of strategic management incentive plan

I suspect that faithful readers know what I am about to say here, but just in case some readers intend to copy this chapter and send it on to their firm's compensation managers (who, persumably, will not have had the benefit of exposure to the principles in preceding chapters), I'll spell it all out.

You begin with an examination of the strengths and weaknesses of a business unit that impact on strategic goals. A determination is made as to which factors must be changed, and by how much, in order for the business unit to achieve its strategic objectives. (In the formulation of your strategic business plan, you obviously have carried out this particular part of the analysis.) It goes without saying that most of these factors are going to be *strategic* rather than *accounting*, although their measurements are usually readily available (perhaps with some adaptation) within the company. These include such economic considerations as

Capital and Production Structure
- investment/sales ratio
- fixed capital intensity
- vertical integration level
- value added per employee
- capacity utilization level

Market Environment
- share of business vs. top four contenders
- number of customers accounting for 50 percent of sales

Competitive Position and Action
- market share
- relative product quality
- relative price
- relative value to customer

- R&D expenditures/sales
- marketing expenditures/sales

Those factors that the employee can control (with either shared or direct freedom to act), and that the strategic analysis shows to be in need of change in order to achieve the desired goal, will form the components of the incentive plan.

advantages of the strategic management incentive plan

All business strategies, as we've said until we're blue in the physiognomy, ultimately seek to enhance the wealth of the company's shareholders through such means as improvements in cash flow or ROI. Not all of your miscellaneous managers, however, fully understand all the implications of the strategies they are given to implement, and not all managers contribute to the formulation of these strategies. It is apparent that, if incumbent managers are to pursue a successful course of action in implementing a given strategic scenario, they must do so with full cognizance of the determinants of business success (as viewed by none other than the modern applied science we know as *strategic planning*). In other words, they should not be expected to work in the dark; they have to know the components of a business strategy to judge how well they are executing it.

It is true that managers could be rewarded, as a simplistic expedient, for achieving end results—for simply improving cash flow or ROI—without regard to the determinant steps in achieving this. There are two flaws in this approach, however.

One flaw is that short-term measures may be used to achieve these goals, which would not be good for the corporation long-term. The second flaw is that there is little assurance that such goals can be achieved without due regard for the variables that determine the attainment and perpetuation of these objectives in the most efficient manner. To deny this is tantamount to going back to the dark ages of prestrategic-management muddling and "watching your quarters."

It has become rather a commonplace observation these days that managers are inclined to try to jack up their quarterly earnings with actions that eventually harm the company's future. Even boards of directors are not always free of such legerdemain, often deciding to raise dividends while badly needed capital improvements go unattended. Line managers neglect things that have no bearing on their near-term performance, like R&D, or things with big price tags, like new technology. Some product managers may cut down on their sustaining advertising knowing that they'll be working other brands by the time their successors run into the eroding Nielsens of declining consumer demand. Why should the perpetrators care when their compensation is based on their quarterlies? In like manner, many managers refused to switch to LIFO because their reported earnings would have been depressed, even though that was generally the logical move to make if they were seriously trying to cope with the inflationary times. Some canny managers delay paying bills until after the fiscal period ends in companies using something called "assets net of financing" to figure the incentive award, despite the fact that by so doing they cause their company to relinquish cash discounts.

The overemphasis of the short term can easily induce unscrupulous marketing executives to find ways to jimmy the numbers. As I write this, news of internal corporate ripoffs is fresh in mind. Marketing managers have been fibbing about sales that were merely factory shipments diverted to a public warehouse in order to satisfy the requirements of a short-sighted incentive plan. A major ad agency, J. Walter Thompson, claims someone in its hottest profit center was faking sales volumes for years, again just so the incentive plan would pay off big. Chase Manhattan Bank, with over 35,000 employees, discovered it took only nine of them to generate a shattering $135 million writeoffs in the Drysdale Government Securities Inc. default. Analysts blamed an incentive plan that followed the customary habit of tying remuneration to short-term performance factors: Chase's Integrated Securities Services group was tempted accordingly to dish out money on instruments that more prudent banks might have fled from.[5]

A concentration on strategy protects the company from these pitfalls. Its emphasis would be on different goals—ones that would not lend themselves to elaborate ripoff schemes.

Strategy is the net result of economic factors, both internal and external, that must be ordered and allocated via the applied science of strategic management so as to achieve, in a logical, stepwise fashion, certain desired performance goals. Managers who are motivated to follow given strategic scenarios and to plan and direct the changes necessary to do so are most likely to be the ones who will achieve the desired ends.

While the other incentive plans resort to judgment and guesswork, only the strategic management incentive plan employs state-of-the-art techniques in setting realistic goals and engineering specific action programs to reach them. It is the only approach that can determine *beforehand* what specific elements need to be changed in order to achieve the goals for which the strategy was designed. It is the only management incentive system that can use accredited, computerized, empirical models to provide the components of the incentive compensation plan and their parameters. Lastly, it's the only plan that can make management compensation programs responsive to strategic needs.

I don't wish to create the impression that there are no long-term incentives currently in force anywhere. They are, to be sure, quite rare; but some prominent firms have adopted them. At the corporate level, Mead Corp. splits its incentive goals evenly between objectives to be achieved in the current year and those with a longer time horizon; in its divisions, the company uses a 75:25 ratio. However, even its one-year objectives are based on the corporation's strategic plan. Other companies, with varying degrees of sophistication, have attempted to stretch out the time horizons of their incentive systems. Koppers Co. bases its management incentive rewards on a three-year growth objective in its earnings-per-share multiple. Though some strategists may have a few qualms about using EPS because, as I discussed in Chapter 8, it can be misleading, others might feel it's still a hell of a lot better than relying on the traditional tactical quotients.[6]

Santa Fe Industries takes out the impact of inflation, thus concentrating on real growth. As these plans go, this is surprisingly unusual.[7] Other companies like to tie in their corporate performance with the industry as a whole, which would have prevented oil executives in the 1970s from experiencing a Big Casino effect and from joining the soup lines during the subsequent glut.

criteria of effective incentives

Most compensation specialists would agree that, in order to be effective, an incentive plan should have the following criteria:

- The award system should be attuned to corporate needs. In the case of the strategic management incentive plan these needs are viewed as strategic in origin, not tactical.
- Potential awards should be large enough to reflect the importance of the goals.
- The incentive awards plus basic salary should be sufficiently appealing to attract and keep qualified people.
- The awards should provide effective levels of continuous, sustained motivation.
- The system should be simple, easy to explain, and easy to administer.
- The system should be flexible so that adjustments can be made when organizational or strategic conditions require them.
- Levels of the incentive awards should be tied to preestablished goals so that the incumbent's performance can be clearly viewed by him or her in terms of direct, forthcoming payments.
- Both goal-setting and precision of measurement are vital.
- Goal-setting should be sufficiently equitable to let an incumbent in a given incentive-eligible position increase his or her total compensation via extra effort.
- Goal-setting should be such that most (around 90 percent) eligible incumbents can achieve at least a minimal level of incentive payment.

implementation

1. Position Description. For companies that maintain formal position descriptions of management personnel, a section should appear in this document outlining the strategy of the business unit in which each incumbent is employed. This statement should specify the kind of business, the agreed upon goals, and the strategic steps required to achieve them. For example: "The ABC Division is in the transportation business, and its goal is to achieve an ROI of 21 percent by (year) by penetrating the high-priced segment of the recreational vehicle market and achieving therein a market share of 34 percent (dollars), a value added level of 56 percent, capacity utilization of 87 percent, etc."

This statement of strategy should be reviewed and up-dated periodically in concert with long-term planning procedures. As seasoned strategists know only too well, no strategy goes unchanged forever.

In addition, if the company incorporates MBOs or *accountability statements* in its position descriptions, these should be amended to include the components of the strategic action plan as just outlined. For example: "The incumbent will plan and direct the activities of his or her division in order to achieve a 34 percent share of the high-priced recreational vehicle market by (year)." If your company does not have formal position descriptions, it will suffice if the strategy statement plus its detailed components are explained in a memo sent to the incumbent, to his or her superiors, and to the compensation personnel who administer the program.

2. *Various Levels in the Organization.* When the top executive of a business unit, in conjunction with his or her own superiors, finalizes the writing of strategic accountabilities, the executive can then break the components down into subcomponents and delegate them to subordinates so that they too will become part of the incentive plan.

This also ensures total communication of, and commitment to, the strategic scenario agreed to by management. (For concerned strategists this in itself makes the strategic management incentive plan worthwhile.)

The process should extend into the organizational structure as far as possible in order to maximize complete awareness of, concern for, and adherence to programs required to attain the objectives necessary for the successful implementation of the business strategy.

3. *Communication.* If you want it to work, the compensation program should be transmitted in a manner wholly consistent with the organization structure and climate in which it must operate. When communicated properly, the incentive plan becomes an integral element in the task of implementing corporate strategies. It is the chief way of ensuring unmistakeable communication of the strategy to all levels of management and of ensuring their enthusiastic cooperation in focusing their energies on the specific programs needed to successfully carry out the strategic scenario.

The following sections will strike the strategic thinker as rather tedious, but they serve to answer, in advance, all the quibbles your compensation administrators are likely to have. To the cynical reader, their very tedium may explain their attraction to the compensation specialist. The cynic's suspicion that compensationists thrive on this kind of detail is reinforced, no doubt, by reading their turgid job descriptions. How seldom they seem to reflect flesh and blood people. The truth, however, is that this seeming sterility of prose style is necessary, since anything involving such sensitive relations with employees must strive to attain a quasi-legal status. With that justification for the pained writing that follows, let's get on with the key details of the plan.

1. Overview. The strategic management incentive plan provides a long-range program (usually three years) broken down into annual segments. In each year four different levels of performance are possible— "acceptable," "commendable," "outstanding," and "distinguished"—each with its own size of cash award. These performance level criteria can be applied to one or more factors or components in the strategic plan. In the following example four separate strategic components are provided: market share, vertical integration, capacity utilization, and product quality (see Figure 11-1). These are given for purposes of illustration only, and the assumption is that they were identified as the critical elements needing attention and alteration if the goals of the strategic plan are to be met. Meeting the measurement criteria that all workable incentive plans need to do, annualized numerical values (obtained from the strategic planning procedure) are assigned to the components. For example, the strategy calls for raising market share from 12 percent to 15 percent (for purposes of flexibility I've introduced a new division here; and we're no longer talking about the recreational vehicle division) in a three-year period, or an average of one percentage point per year. Achieving this would be judged "outstanding" and would provide an award of 24 percent of midpoint base salary. Performance that came in under the 1 percent would provide less than a 24 percent award; performance in excess of it would give more, but it couldn't go over 32 percent. However, there could be a carry-forward into the next year. Exact determinations of how much the incumbent gets have to be made by management. For example, management could decide that a mere 0.1 percent increase in market share should not receive any award; on the other hand, if it reverses a declining share trend, maybe it should merit a substantial award. You have to work all these things out in advance so your employees know exactly what the criteria are. Normally, "outstanding" performance would mean achieving the objective in full and "distinguished" would mean exceeding it, but there are no hard and fast rules as long as you are consistent. The plan is meant to be adapted to specific corporate needs, and, as long as the general principles are followed, you can flex the details with considerable imagination to strike a balance between the motivational power of the plan and its overall cost.

FIGURE 11-1. Sample Incentive Plan

Incentive Plan for General Manager—Abrasives Division.			
Three-year horizon			
Goal: Improve 4 factors to bring ROI from 15% to 18%.			
Factors	% of total Incentive	Three-year Improvement	Annual Average
Market share	15	12% to 15%	1%
Vertical Integration	10	41% to 43%	0.6%
Capacity utilization	10	83% to 88%	1.6%
Product quality	25	10% to 25%	5%
Misc. tactical goals and special objectives	40	—	—
	100		

Performance Levels (Flexible)	% of Annual Goal	Award as % of Base Midpoint
Acceptable	0-33%	0-8%
Commendable	34-66%	9-16%
Outstanding	67-100%	17-24%
Distinguished	101-133%	25-32% (limit in given year)

One final tip: In goal-setting, you may want to consider putting the full goal (i.e., 100 percent) somewhat above those agreed to at the corporate level as an SBU safety cushion.

2. *Use of the Midpoint.* Any management incentive system creates discord if equal effort or performance produces unequal awards. This would make anybody mad. By basing the incentive award on the incumbent's base-salary midpoint instead of actual salary, you overcome, for example, the case of senior managers getting bigger cash awards for equal—or even less—goal attainment simply because their incentives are percented on a larger base (because they are paid more due to their seniority). Using the midpoint makes the system more equitable. Personnel departments will probably appreciate this point better than the general reader, since they are the ones who would get the flak from doing it any other way.

3. *Scope of Strategic Components.* The strategic components should not constitute all your performance criteria. Somewhere between 50 and 70 percent of total incentive factors is better. This is because the strategic components almost always involve long-term projects, while day-to-day tactical/operational efforts must continue to receive serious attention and should, therefore, be included in the incentive system. There is such a thing as being too gung-ho, even where strategy is involved. My description of the plan doesn't discuss the tactical issues, because they are the patently obvious ones most current incentive plans already use (return on sales, sales volume, cost-cutting, time lost due to accidents, etc.), and to give them serious attention in a book on strategy could create the wrong impression.

4. *Concept of the Rolling Incentive.* Although strategies are long-term propositions, conceivably an astute manager could achieve at least some of the goals in the first year. Nonetheless, to keep the plan payout within reasonable bounds (what the hell, there is nothing to be gained from overpaying anyone), no annual award should exceed a predetermined cutoff point, which I feel is somewhere around 30-35 percent of midpoint base salary. On the other hand, exceedingly good performance should not be overlooked; so you may want to consider allowing for a carry-forward credit. Example: If in the abrasive products division illustration the incumbent increased market share 1.5 points, he or she would be rewarded a 32 percent incentive on that factor for 1.3 points, but the additional 0.2 points would not merit any reward that year; instead, those additional share points would be credited to his or her performance for the next year. Similarly, negative performance (losing share, for example) would result in a debt carry-forward. (Obviously, under no circumstances would deductions be made from base salary for negative perform-ance, but prolonged weak performance would constitute unacceptable performance and would present reason for career review.)

The carry-forward concept is a device you can use to ensure the maintenance of a position once gained—for example, so that the manager would not let the market share slide once the gains were achieved. It is conceivable that in some years there would be no award, but that the fruits of long-term results would eventually be achieved in a single year following perhaps two years of concerted (and unrewarded) effort. In these cases top management discretionary powers should be invoked to see to it that (at the end of this lengthy time period) substantial, extraordinary awards are granted above and beyond the plan's official guidelines. For purposes of general corpo-rate motivation, much publicity could be attached to this.

5. *Handling Transfers and Terminations.* An individual who is transferred to another position would be eligible for the incentives earned during the time he or she served in the previous position. Handling this can take three different approaches:

- The award could be prorated according to the time served.
- It could be split with successors over a three-year period.
- If the incumbent were singularly instrumental in achieving the goal (even though it would take several years to bear fruit), he or she could be awarded it all.

There are other possible approaches, and management would have to deal with each as they arise, keeping in mind the need both to motivate all individuals concerned in the future and to keep the costs of the plan within manageable limits.

Normally, any joker who leaves the fold before the end of the plan year would not be eligible for any award. Check with your legal department first, however; they may not have the guts to endorse this.

6. *Flexibility.* The plan should be reviewed often. It is customary, as well, to make your employees understand that no contractual obligation exists and that the plan components, performance standards, and rates can be revised when strategic circumstances dictate. You may want to give your participants the option of cash vs. deferred payments—if the IRS hasn't blocked that one remaining avenue of relief by the time this book hits the stands—and, lastly, they should be told clearly that the company will be the final arbiter of awards.

conclusion

Now you know a lot more about incentive systems than you probably wanted to. Amidst all the head-scratching over the unfamiliar and awkward terminology, I am sure that some readers, at least, can see how this particular management incentive idea can be used to get the lead out in companies where strategic marvels falter upon implementation.

With very little effort any company that knows something about business strategy can put in a state-of-the-art compensation incentive program responsive to the strategic needs of the corporation and fine-tuned by the applied science of modern strategic management.

notes

1. David B. Tinnin, "The Heady Success of Holland's Heineken,"*Fortune*, November 16, 1981, pp. 158-75.

2. John B. Schnapp, "Soichiro Honda, Japan's Inventive Iconoclast,"*Wall Street Journal*, February 1, 1982, p. 16.

3. Walter Kiechel, III, "Facing up to Executive Anger,"*Fortune*, November 16, 1981, pp. 207-8.

4. Louis J. Brindisi, Jr., "Why Executive Compensation Programs Go Wrong, "*Wall Street Journal*, June 14, 1982, p. 18.

5. Julie Salamon, "Chagrined Chase: How New York Bank Got Itself Entangled in Drysdale's Dealings," *Wall Street Journal*, June 6, 1982, p. 1.

6. One trouble with using something like EPS as a performance criterion is not only that it is seldom discounted for inflationary effect, but that it is, as *Fortune* magazine (E. Meadows, "New Targeting for Executive Pay," May 4, 1981, pp. 176-77) points out, "based on possibly misleading accounting data, such as reported earnings per share or return on investment ... these numbers, subject to arbitary accounting conventions and influenced by waves and ripples in the economy, often don't say much about how well a company is building future earnings growth that will enhance shareholder wealth in the long run." We, as strategists, know that only a comprehensive strategic analysis can tell where you are heading over the long haul.

7. Ibid.

12
career strategies

If only your career could be truly moved ahead by your most prescient admixture of offensive and defensive maneuvers and by a visible and vaulting continuum of outstanding performance, you could achieve all the vocational kudos due to you in your lifetime. And you'd have no beef about the system.

But, alas, since the dawn of organized society, it has not worked out that way. Such would be a far too mechanistic view of the world. It assumes people, especially those you must impress, behave with computerlike logic. Though you may feel you can program your own performance, you cannot rely on others to assess you with unmitigated objectivity. Too often personalities and perceived loyalties will have more to do with your progress than will your actual performance on the job.

Conceivably, in some companies, personnel promotions are awarded after carefully weighing the person's track-record and studying job performance reports, and so forth, but in many companies, though the more painstaking procedures are given audible lip service, real career decisions are no more carefully reasoned out then choosing between a martini and a gimlet. For one thing, the omnipresent concept of the "team" and its need for loyal players, largely chosen by the team captain and assembled in great haste to pursue the windmills of great corporate missions, can summarily do a mean number on

157

anyone's carefully plotted career. In other cases, management selections are viewed as short-term measures, and the temptation is to give form (human packaging) precedence over substance (human content). In still others, instinct alone is the guide in judging careers and selecting future captains of industry.

If you are still in school or an entry level slot, you may not have witnessed much of this. When you've been around for a few years, you'll begin to see it affecting some of your associates. Then, perish the thought, it will touch you, and, finally your subordinates who have passed you by on the success ladder.

In this chapter I will try to offer a reflective view on career planning that could, if managed properly, capitalize on the wayward but immutable failings of those who hold your future in their palms. I will show the coordinate relation between career and strategy. But first I want to explore the terrain of modern human resource management so we can see how a workable knowledge of business strategy ties in with your career advancement.

human resource management climate

It may be interesting to begin with a story. I believe the saddest case of aborted career I have ever encountered was with the manufacturing head in a major division of a large Fortune 500 company. The moral of the story is that he ended up an innocent victim of the implementation of the team concept. Throughout his life he was a great engineer. He was also a very sound manager, profit minded, committed, and with all the other right abilities and attitudes. Years of budget cuts had deprived his plants of adequate maintenance. He hated seeing his plants decline and become so inefficient, but, apparently, he was the only one who gave a damn. His successive admonitions and formal proposals for upgrading the facilities were repeatedly rejected by an ambitious, but short-sighted, division president. By the time this president moved on to his next, and greater, corporate reward, my tragic hero had acquired a file-cabinet full of documentation on the need for plant improvements and hundreds of implementation plans. When a new president took over the division, as part of his team-building scenario, he brought in his own vice-president of operations who was "appalled" to discover "plants that exceeded OSHA decibel levels and floors too filthy to eat off of" (sic). Sadly, my tragic friend was blamed for this. The unspoken assumption was that he was not a member of the team and, therefore, the enemy. Of course, he was nothing of the sort. A true professional, and the veteran of many previous management shuffles, he would have worked gladly for any team in good faith. He offered to review and explain all those past proposals of his that were now yellowing with age in his files. He didn't get the chance. In fact, his offer backfired on him. The new leadership establishment granted that, indeed, he had confronted previously all of their current objections about the plants, but they faulted him for a lack of aggressiveness in putting forth his ideas. His former boss, the guy who was really the culprit, was never consulted about the facts of the case. In matters of this sort, there is no court of inquiry, just executioners. Eventually my friend's duties were eliminated, and he became nothing more than a paper-shuffler. Even his former plant superintendants would not return his phone calls. Too old to find another job, he lived out the remainder of his life a wasted talent.

Anecdotal? Over-dramatized? Perhaps. But this kind of thing happens all the time. And it usually is inflicted on those who have built up a great reputation as tactician, while those who are known as "strategists" seldom fall victim to it.

the personnel department

The weeping aside, in spite of all their devout talk about people evaluation and their self-serving pronouncements about being able to select the right people for any job, your personnel department will not be able to help you much with your overall career problems. They really don't have the clout in most companies to effectively impose their views on line management. Nor would they necessarily have all the answers. My assessment of the personnel department function is that, when it comes to your own career development, you'd be better off keeping them at arm's length. Personnel people are not all the scientific purveyors of human assets they'd like you to believe they are. A personnel manager once persuaded me to pass over a job candidate, whose resume made him look ideally qualified for the job, because the personnel department's investigation revealed that "he was kind of weird." This appraisal, as it turned out, was based on the fact that he collected antique automobiles. I wasn't convinced there was anything wrong with that but went along, feeling they knew something about people I did not. However, in a subsequent company I worked for, the personnel manager himself turned out to be a collector of antique cars (as well as furniture and assorted Victoriana). I realize this, too, is merely anecdotal, but such encounters with the human resource contingent lead me to suspect that any effort from them on your behalf may culminate in grave disappointment; my conclusion is that, if you want to maximize your career opportunities, you'd better resign yourself to doing it on your own. You cannot count on having any absolutely dependable allies in this endeavor.

being one of the troops

Down there with the troops in an entry-level job, things will seem fine at first. The big bosses are not too concerned about you, or the damage you can wreak, when you are in the lower ranks. They probably won't even notice you. If they do, it will be for some feature entirely divorced from your professional competence—minor things, like the fact that your suits are expensive, that your accent is unusual, or that your demeanor in delivering a presentation is good. It's not hard to keep your nose clean at the entry job level. All you really have to do is obliterate your self-concern, put the company first without complaint, work fast and accurately—none of which is too much to expect from someone, as yet unproven, who wishes to be considered executive material. In a few strangely misguided companies you would also be expected to pull in the reins on your creativity and innovativeness, as this sets off a fear response from the more stalwart, whose defensive reaction may be to pigeon-hole you as a competent, but limited, technician. In other words, learn to play the game. If "smart" is not the game, feign the "dull normal" until the opportunity to shine without punishment arises. You'll soon move out of the entry-level job, so this is not much of a sacrifice compared to what is yet to come, if you decide to stick around.

the perils of middle management

It's when you reach middle management that the real trouble commences. You may not detect it at its outset. People easily seduce themselves into imagining they are doing quite well—getting periodically promoted, getting those regular 8-12 percent merit increases and lavish stroking from the boss—but their employers may not share in this regard for their development.

Professor John Veiga, who imparts management lore at the University of Connecticut, found most people donning rose-tinted glasses to assess their own career progress. In a study of over a thousand management job changes, 85 percent of "changelings" classified their new jobs as a "promotion," only 12 percent conceded them to be "lateral moves," and a skimpy 3 percent confessed that they were "demotions." But, in studying actual corporate records, Veiga learned that, in the official view (the only view that really counts), 40 percent of these moves were considered promotions, 51 percent were said to be lateral, and 9 percent were clearly regarded as demotions. Veiga's obvious conclusion: "It's clear that serious distortions exist" when you make your own career assessments once you've joined the ranks of middle management.[1] Whether this is how the corporation conspires to keep you dumb and happy, or whether you merely try to delude yourself, I couldn't say. The fact is, at any rate, that life for the middle-level manager is fairly hazardous.

Whether you want to call it "career plateauing" or the "middle-manager squeeze," it is a plain, unvarnished fact of business life that most middle-management incumbents will peak out a lot sooner than they anticipated when they arrived on the scene with the ribbon on their college diplomas still intact. Quite simply, in the middle ranks of the organization, the numbers are against you and you need to muster up all the resources at your disposal to avert the bitter disappointments that befall many, if not most, corporate "old faithfuls" in their middle years.

For one thing, just in case your view of the business world was shaped by "Dallas" and you have failed to ponder the obvious, the pyramid gets awfully narrow at the top.[2] There's loads of room at the bottom, but the climb up the side gets increasingly difficult the higher you go—and less certain. It can make your transition from high school, where you were near the top of the graduating class, to a college, where you were then unnerved to encounter classmates who were disturbingly intelligent, poised, and competitive, resemble a church picnic. Many midlevel managers have been lulled into chasing rainbows by their immediate supervisors who facilely pontificated about career progress without having any real notion of what the corporation actually planned to do with anybody. It is easy to become placated and puffed up by a company only desirous of filling slots at this level without any true regard for the incumbent's subsequent potential. In trying to keep you in your place, they will make you think you are "the leader of the future." Further delusions are planted that lure people to think their chances are better than they really are by dispatching them to special management seminars, and so on. Professor Judy Bardwick of the University of Michigan says that studies back in the mid-1960s showed that, at the age of 40 for a person in the upper decile of the corporate structure, the odds of making it to the top 1 percent of management were 15:1, but, by the age of 45, chances dwindled to only 1-out-of-45. Prof. Bardwick says that nowadays the chances are even poorer.[3] And it doesn't help much if you are a top performer, because one glaring truth of the modern work environment is that many of the best job openings are considered fillable only by outsiders.

Clearly, the current demographics no longer favor the middle manager as they did during the 1950s and 1960s. The baby-boom spurt, now working its way into this age group, will cause the number of people between 35 and 44 years of age to swell by over 40 percent (to 36 million) during the 1980s while, according to the Bureau of Labor Statistics, manager jobs will increase by a bare 19 percent. Men and, increasingly, highly-trained women, both will be vying for a proportionately decreasing number of choice jobs.

This age cohort surplus is going to destroy the egos of millions of erstwhile managers. Some will fall into the depths of depression, which will lead to divorce, child abuse, suicide, and other manifestations of national angst. Some will drop out of the corporate world and find their ultimate salvation in some form of self-employment (preferably not in marinas, since this sector of the economy would seem to be well-staffed now). The rest of those who are deemed not in the running for greater responsibilities will have to content themselves with the humiliation of being dead-ended. Only a tiny fraction of those whose youthful dreams were of being a department head or the equivalent will make it.

answer is double-lane path

You are in grave peril if you heedlessly trust your future to the clumsy machinations of your immediate supervisor, to the personnel folks, or to just about anyone else in the company. Even trusted mentors who may have the clout to do something for you will probably not be around when you eventually need them. The most assured path to career success mandates that you put yourself in the driver's seat. This path has a double-laned approach. The first lane is style. The second is substance. You have to travel on both lanes simultaneously, and on both you will encounter some surprises.

management style

According to Charles A. Garfield, president of Peak Performance Center in Berkeley, California,[4] compared to the average Joe, high performers "are a different group in terms of skills, how they work, how they manage their stress, their risks; they are different folks." High-performance executives set goals, solve problems, and take risks in a manner quite unlike lesser mortals. Five key features delineate high performers from their nonstellar cohorts:

- They never feel comfortable with their current achievements or level of expertise. They always aim higher.
- They are urged on by internalized goals.
- They'd rather solve problems than try to pin blame on someone else.
- They're risk-takers, but they always look before they leap.
- They routinely play out different options in their minds.

It may come as a surprise to some of your more overtly ardent fellow workers who calculate to affect an air of intense effort, who strive to be the last leaving the office each evening, who appear ever on the run, to those artful and sometimes all too obvious exponents of the Puritan Ethic, that optimal performers are not workaholics and do not have Type A (heart attack) personalities. Instead, they are able to get away from it all, and they enjoy their vacations. They have no trouble with stress, and, being willing to delegate, they never get entangled in details. They don't even vaguely resemble the stereo-type notions of successful executives, and, if you reflect on it long enough, you may conclude that they are in fact (and this is the main point of this chapter) the complete strategists. This is the basis of the five features of the high-performance executive and the basic reason why their decision processes usually spell corporate success. In all candor they may not be the most eloquent fashioners of strategy but—and here's where you fit in—they know it is central to every venture they spearhead and can appreciate the talents of someone who can give substance to their impressive strategic instincts. This is your chance to join them.

substance

In sharp contrast to the old recipe for success (where you are tritely instructed to groom your future successor so you'll be freed up for the big promotion), the most logical, most assured route to the top, or at least comfortably close to it, is to become the complete strategist.

Strategy formulation, discounting the locker room version, is the one talent most people fail to cultivate in their attempted ladder climbs; yet it is palpably the key factor in one's business success. By becoming comfortably familiar with the basic laws of business strategy, and by making it very clear that you speak with considerable depth and authority on the subject, you will grant yourself a substantial and impressive advantage over the great horde of competitors snapping at your heels and vying against you for that moment in the organizational limelight. Here are some factors to keep in mind while you work on shaping your strategic strengths:

- Never pass up the opportunity to interject perceptive strategic comments in reports, presentations, and discussions.
- Part of your climb up the ladder will depend on your packaging. The assessment your company makes of you will not be solely of your inherent strengths. As I have said, the assessment process is neither systematic nor scientific. Develop a "strategic image." When your name appears on a list of candidates being considered for an important promotion, the powers that be might only be able to give each candidate a one or two minute review. If strategy looms large as your big plus, and thusly makes all the other candidates look like tacticians, there is a good likelihood you will have the inside track.

- The decision process in the personally competitive executive circle requires the support of reasoned argument, which must be not only convincing to the rational mind but also, and maybe more importantly, acceptable to certain habits of thought, commonly known as "popular wisdom." In some instances this is more tribal than civilized. In this context you are in a more favorable position for promotion if your supervisors have come to speak of you as a "strategist" because in the popular argot that means you have joined the ranks of the "big picture" heavy breathers—that is, you are one of them. If asked to explain why they have promoted you, they will be confident that their decision about you will be applauded by their peers. They know that "strategists" and "apple pie" touch off the same brainwaves among their fellow movers and shakers.

- Make sure you know your company's business strategies, then proceed to elaborate and refine them so that you become one of the most eloquent spokespersons for the party line. If you do not agee with your company's strategic course, choose carefully the right time and place to attempt to have it ameliorated. Strategies have a lot of face riding on them. Be cautious here. Keep in mind that politics is always a potent force in any human organization and, even though your strategic thoughts are pure and nonsubjective, no one is free of political entanglement. If you are clumsy in voicing criticism, the next purge may sweep you away.

- If the current management fails to appreciate the value of your strategic judgments because of its excessive tactical orientation, you may be able to recover your unrequited respect if you linger long enough for this management to lose its charmed life. Just wait in the wings. The current management—as all tacticians are wont to do—eventually will reach the end of its tether. When it runs out of momentum and begins spinning wheels, make your move.

combatting the sycophant

Honing your strategy formulation skills is your best way of coping with the struggle for control that permeates most enterprises. This struggle often involves maneuvers that would chagrin the Marquis of Queensbury but which, nonetheless, can render a devastating blow to the innocenti who feel that only business results count.

Younger readers may have rather idealistic conceptions about the maturity of those who occupy important positions in the commercial pantheon. In childhood we lived by an unwritten code of honor proscribing certain forms of behavior, such as snitching and teacher-fawning. No one liked the class brown-noser, and the main thing little boys resented about little girls was that they were shameless informers. Real kids used peer pressure to eliminate such errant behavior. It is not surprising, then, to find many, fresh off the campus, who anticipate finding the same codex on the corporate scene. Unfortunately, such is not entirely the case. The business world is rife with groveling, conniving sycophants—even at high levels—who search out opportunities to ingratiate themselves to anyone in a positon to bestow favors and to dishonestly denigrate anyone who isn't. There is no level on the organization chart immune from the most fulsome obsequy. At a conference a few years ago I saw the silliest display of this between a marketing vice president and his boss, the company president. Both individuals were well known as industry leaders, and the company they ran was, and still is, a multi-billion dollar giant. We were at breakfast. The president ordered only coffee, commenting that he couldn't understand why anyone would eat a large breakfast. Taking his cue, the vice president told the waiter he also wanted only coffee, commenting that he was never hungry in the morning. Downing his coffee in one gulp, the president left our table in order to attend a preconference meeting, whereupon the vice president called the waiter back, saying, "God, am I starved. Get me some eggs, sausage, flapjacks, and double order of toast. And make it snappy!"

Here's the point: If you think you can pull off this kind of chicanery, go ahead; flattery turns many a head, even those with crowns. If you are too proud or embarrassed to try it, you'll have to employ other methods. Your technical and tactical skills will not suffice. They are not important enough to arrest the attention of anyone at the top. When the board members gather in the executive dining room for their lunchtime lobster bisque, they aren't talking about your marketing plan (unless perhaps your advertising executions touch on things close to their hearts, like salmon fishing in Scotland), and they aren't going to waste their lunch hour talking about wimp stuff like a new marketing research technique, training programs, or media buying. Hell, no. They all will be straining to introduce okay subjects: "What's the market been up to this morning?" "Any word from the Hill on that bill?" or, if there's a lull in the conversational patter, someone may seize upon the opportunity to talk about something really important to all who have gathered for the noontime repast. Invariably, this will get around to strategy. It is not far from their minds. Strategy is the one, universally accepted topic at the loftiest levels.

It follows then that the top people are expansively receptive to any underling who can expound intriguingly on the subject of strategy. In fact, one of the complaints I hear most often from senior executives is that so few of their subordinates know anything about strategy. They see them being somewhat like teenagers who can talk at length about dermatological matters, but, once you try to get them onto a loftier subject, they are lost. So, too, do many of their staffers flounder when broaching the subject of business strategy. Unquestionably, your opportunity to fill a horrible gap in the corporate decision-making faculties resides in your ability to explicate your strategic knowledge. Nietzche said, "Whoever fights monsters should see to it that in the process he does not become a monster." Which is to say, when competing with the sycophant tactician, do not stoop to his or her level; keep your efforts glued on the higher strategic plane.

the gamesman

If you are still at a relatively humble level in the organization, then, realistically, polishing your strategic skills may not be of immediate use to you in your everyday work, but this knowledge can be very impressive to your superiors, especially if they have certain characteristics. Any executive to whom you report at least will feign an interest in business strategy, but there is, in particular, one special kind of manager that would be able to most benefit from what you can offer in the strategic formulation arena.

In 1977, Harvard's Michael Maccoby's book, *The Gamesman*,[5] made a big splash by describing the different varieties of manager. No doubt you will recognize certain of your cohorts among these and also be able to pidgeonhole yourself.

- The Craftsman. Gets kicks out of doing a good job.
- The Jungle Fighter. Power crazy. Wants to dominate everybody.
- The Company Man. Looks for security, approval.
- The Gamesman. The most prevalent kind, which is fortunate, since they are the kind who will profit most from your strategic approaches to their problems. They thirst for challenge. They are enthralled by technology (which would include sophisticated computer-assisted approaches to strategy development). They have open minds, which is crucial if you want to tell them something a little different from the accepted party line on strategy they usually hear from their troops. Hence, the gamesman also is easier to deal with than the other management types. For example, the Company Man would reel in horror at the first whiff of heretical strategic thought, guided by the philosophy of the old nursery rhyme, "Always take ahold of nurse/For fear of finding something worse." The Gamesman may not be the most friendly of sorts; this type is depicted as lacking compassion, of actually fearing emotional entanglements. They can, in short, make your life miserable, unsettled, or precarious. But (and this is my impression of the Gamesman, not Maccoby's) strategy is, as Liza Doolittle once said of gin, mother's milk to them. It gives them the informational base necessary to be successful at what they like doing best—cutting deals and gambling. Their main goal is to be a winner, and their biggest dred is being a loser. They are high-rollers, but they like the odds to be in their favor. And, most of all, they need you if you have the right stuff to be a strategist.

the uses of anxiety

Successful leaders, be they Gamesmen or not, and whether or not they have the five Garfieldian traits of the high performer, will all have one big thing in common, which should persuade them to embrace the more sanguine strategy formulation techniques you can offer them. That common trait is this: The strong tug of their jobs and the excitement that their careers frequently offer leave them powerless to satisfy the demands of their personal lives, producing gnawing guilt and anxiety.[6] Especially in middle-age, this prompts leaders to search for some semblance of balance between work and family. By their later years they will resolve this problem one way or another. It is, however, during the period of attempted resolution that you, as his self-designated strategy mentor, can instill in your leader the good habit of refined strategic thinking as a useful approach to more effective, less time-confusing, occupational behavior patterns. Smart subordinates should recognize this state of anxiety in middle-aged bosses and, with tact and subtlety, offer the solutions—if it is apparent that their anxiety and guilt can be assuaged by applications of rationality.

final word of advice

You are, I trust, perceptive enough to realize that this will require considerable effort on your part. You'll only hurt yourself if you sprightly quote passages from this or any other strategy book in your reports or presentations. The big boys have this damn fool notion that book-learnin' doesn't produce strategists. They think it oozes from the pores of the specially experienced. As we showed in Chapter 2, of course they're all wet. Nonetheless, you've got to appeal to their foibles as well as to their intellects. It will be your task to penetrate beyond the screen of immediate concrete experience. So do your homework. Scan this book to pull out the fundamental principles that apply to your company. Hell, there aren't that many, so that part of the assignment should be easy. Then do your own analysis using internal data to show how these principles form the basis for your company's success (or failure); go on from there, pulling back the prepuce of the obvious, to expound on the strategic directions your company should take. Make it look like your own and not the work of some outside theoretician. It is by such means that you can give memorable utterance to crucial corporate issues, and through which your own virtuosity as a worthy strategist and heir apparent to a corner office can be demonstrated.

notes

1. John Veiga, "Do Managers on the Move Get Anywhere?" *Harvard Business Review*, March-April 1981, pp. 21-38.

2. Mary Bralove, "On the Plateau: Nowhere to Go but Sideways," *Wall Street Journal*, December 12, 1981, p. 27.

3. Ibid.

4. Erik Larson, "Why Do Some People Out Perform Others? Psychologist Picks Out Six Characteristics, *"Wall Street Journal*, January 13, 1982, p. 25.

5. Michael Maccoby, *The Gamesman*, (New York: Simon & Schuster, 1977), pp. 50-120.

6. Paul Evans, and Fernando Bartolome, *Must Success Cost So Much?* (New York: Basic Books, 1980), pp. 27-58.

13

corporate portfolio strategies

So far, I've been examining the profit control factors governing the functions and exploits of SBUs. Being the true guts of strategic study, they accentuate the thinking and planning of all astute managers at the profit center level.

grander level

If, however, you fill space in the executive-suite, or covet such, you'll strengthen your career prospects by ruminating occasionally on a grander level—where your concerns aren't with a piddly SBU, but with the whole corporate squadron of SBUs.

Here's the problem: Even the modestly diversified firm is hard to view in one glance, yet a way must be found for shaping an efficient overview. The good forester thinks about more than one tree at a time. Only shepherds are allowed to flit off on tangents over individual sheep, and their contribution to the economy has been aborted, perhaps, by such loose strategic management.

Maybe exceptional tycoons like Freddy Heineken would disagree, but most of us lesser mortals would throttle ourselves trying to

169

follow every SBU growing in the corporate forest. You might feel more easy if you could knit the strategic excursions of diverse SBUs together compactly and coherently.

Even if not yet enshrined at the top of the corporate totem-pole, you need a sturdy grasp of the corporate strategic overview. Without warning, your CEO could summon you to a pregnant-with-meaning lunch. Knowing he or she doesn't want to hear about the kids, and already knows more than you about the NFL and the PGA, you'll be reaching for something lofty and mutually significant to chat about.

You can't go wrong with "corporate strategy." Mastering this topic could get you on the CEO's fast-track list. At worst, it might ward off banishment to the Akron plant.

At the very least, a working familiarity with corporate-level strategy gives you a defense against planning department marauders with a habit of riding rough-shod over your strategic hopes.

new approaches to corporate strategy

There are numerous ways (curves and matrices mainly) of looking at corporate strategy. Not all, of course, deserve our praise, or even our attention. The most venerable, and least bewildering, is the Boston Consulting Group's cash flow matrix used in Chapter 3. Though I still like it for a lot of reasons, the BCG matrix, unfortunately, was tiresomely overused in the past years; some disenchantment set in, and Boston Consulting, stressing that its matrix was never supposed to be a universal panacea (especially when there's no market growth), prefers to talk today about its new matrix (we'll get into it later). Adding to the already evident confusion, other consulting groups (all feverish for prominence in this $300 million business) have since had their own parturitions. Most of the writing in this field reads like translations from bad German. Predictably, none of the new curves and matrices is the ultimate answer to the CEO's dream of depicting a complex enterprise on the back of a postage stamp. Nor can any be expected to fit all strategic eventualities: Like everything else in this life, they deal in probabilities, and, while they may be generally correct, the fit may be rather loose for your company.

Before breaking bread with your CEO at that command lunch, try to bone up. But do it warily. Do not give voice, for example, to the BCG cash cow concept if, as can happen, the term "cash cow" is taboo in the executive suite. Be on guard for signs of shifting beliefs. Yesterday's dogma may be today's heresy. Your CEO may have returned just now from a conference newly convinced that his or her favorite strategic matrix is no good. In a "crisis of faith," your CEO may have spawned a new quest for a trendier strategic construct, and you'd better tread gingerly while you try to learn more about that quest.

the original BCG matrix

Before abruptly rejecting any approach, give it a fair hearing. Much of the petulance against the original BCG matrix proceeded from shoddy homework; a lot of the nitpicking was based on faulty market definitions—usually a failure to get things down to the segment level where they belong. Careful reflection and the most convincing evidence available still says market share is a mighty powerful factor, and, though it is less faddish in the "also ran" company, the smart money is still on it.

Everyone is entitled to some apprehension, but it may be relaxing to know that, as recently as 1982, General Electric's new head man, John F. Welch, placed his troops under orders to concentrate more on market share than ever before. Welch's goal: transform GE's SBUs into "world-class competitors," by putting all of the firm's 250 businesses in first or second place in their respective markets. Welch saw this strategy as the best way to ensure long-run profits and to ward off foreign rivals.[1] GE is widely considered one of the world's best run outfits, and it is reassuring to all loyal proponents that faith in market share has not been declared anathema in Fairfield, Connecticut.

corporate models and the winds of chance

Prudent business planners, working on the SBU level, will have strategic scenarios sitting on a shelf that they can dust off and mobilize at the first sign of atrabilious changes in their markets. We seldom hear about such SBU-level strategy shifts; we only read about them when they affect strategy at the corporate level:

> Consider the corporate dodging and darting that mammoth macro changes provoked at AM International Inc. (formerly the Addressograph-Multigraph Corp, or "Multigrief" as the cynics call it). When legendary Roy Ash, Litton founder and Nixon budget director, took over AMI in 1976, he concluded that its brass-bound commitment to otiose electromechanical office equipment was a one-way ticket to Palookaville. Moving toward a new corporate strategy, Ash decided to mount a sexier skirmish on the battlefield of electronics. He acquired Jacquard Systems, maker of advanced word processors. Jacquard was going to be the spearhead of AMI's "office-of-the-future." Appointed cash cow to fund all this was AMI's antediluvian line of offset printers. But there was a flaw. Analysts think Ash tried to go too fast; the offset business couldn't keep the cash flowing. Trouble ensued. Ash was unceremoniously replaced by Dick Black in 1981, and another new corporate strategy was concocted, calling for a return to basics via an ambitious divestiture program.

Jacquard was put on the block. By the time Black ducked out of AMI (so he could sue it more conveniently for misrepresentation), it was in Chapter 11.[2] Both CEOs had done what they felt necessary, but neither could devise corporate strategies that *took*. They weren't right for the micro/macro environment that then existed; the sweeping corporate strategic shifts both men had in mind were too large, and no subsequent tinkering and implementation of contingency plan was up to the bail-out task. Nonetheless, though it did not work, both men were using war-room models of corporate strategies. This chapter will show how they work and what strengths and weaknesses they have.

When external forces throw your entire industry out of kilter, all your five-year plans, your strategic matrices, and maybe even some members of your own carpool go out the window. What would you have done in early 1982 if you were making personal computers when Commodore International Ltd. announced they were introducing a model that could do everything yours could, with your software, at one-third your price? "Overnight," you think to yourself, "it turns the whole hardware scene into a commodity market." Schumpeter's Theory of the Creative Destruction of Capital comes true every time you fail to strategize for contingencies and brings down upon you the rigor of its judgment. This is one of the most serious dilemmas faced by the corporate strategists. Unless there is a carefully constructed corporate strategy model—one which is endorsed resoundingly by all the officers of the company—such events are bound to send the company spinning out of orbit.

Maybe you work in an industry the "new" AT&T pines to invade. Deciding it no longer wants to be your phone company and all wound up and ready to spring into juicier areas, AT&T, with a multitude of Bell Lab marvels up its sleeve, must be making your boots rattle. How AT&T decides what to do, and how you should react, are the meat of corporate strategy.

But even when not facing gargantuan upheaval, even if change is oddly alien to your industrial barnyard, for your own sanity and to keep your SBUs straight, an effective approach to corporate strategy will help you wisely allocate your scarce corporate resources.

the directional policy matrix

I think we already have spent enough time here and in previous chapters talking about the BCG matrix. We don't need to go through it all again. But that doesn't mean you should dismiss it, for it's still a nice, easy way of sizing up a situation. Of course, it does depend on only two strategic factors—market share and growth—so it does have some limitations. The *Directional Policy Matrix*, the name given it by

Shell Chemicals U.K. Ltd., encompasses *several* factors simultaneously. Though it goes under many different names, it is a golden oldie. GE was one of its earliest pioneers (see Figure 13-1) and Borg-Warner, known in planning circles as an unremitting proponent of strong strategic management, uses the DPM grid or something close to it.

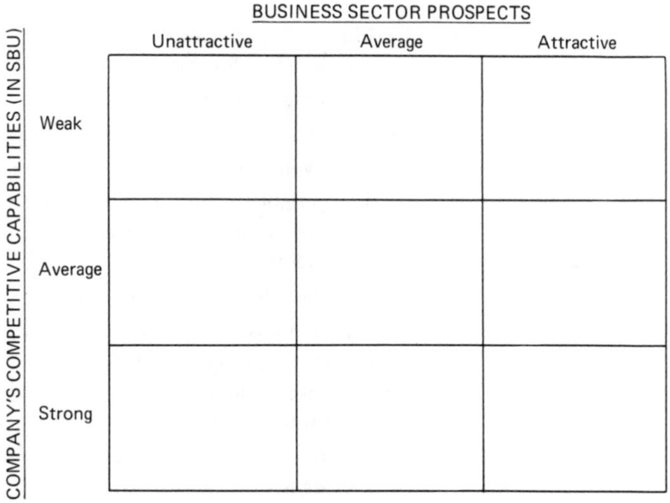

FIGURE 13-1. The DPM Grid

To use the grid, place each corporate SBU one-by-one in the appropriate box. (Most companies include competition in this by depicting each industry by a circle, its size proportionate to its dollar volume, with a sector drawn in it proportionate to the SBU's market share.) Neatness may not count, but honesty does; don't pretend an SBU is strong in its business sector or that the sector is attractive when they are not. You must use clinical objectivity for this to be effective. (In the United States I believe the GE *Business Screen* is used about as much as the DPM; it looks roughly the same, but it's turned on its side and uses the term *business strength* rather than *competitive capability*, suggesting *fact* rather than *potential*.)

Just from looking at it, it's obvious you wouldn't want to have any SBUs on the left or up near the top of the grid. But, if you've got average luck and are a typical diversified company, you'll probably have representations in those quadrants anyway.

Parenthetically, why would filling out the DPM be any better than making forecasts or slaving over long-range consolidated budgets? For one thing, forecasts and budgets don't give management any feel for why one business should do better than any other, or whether its competitive posture is gangbusters or wimpish. Forecasts and budgets certainly don't photograph the dynamic balance of SBUs across all company product lines. They also don't give much insight into possible new ventures. Forecasts and budgets are only numerical, not strategic and discursive. Besides all that, there may be no one in your circle who really believes in forecasts any more. (Come to think of it, what *did* happen to the future they promised everyone at the 1939 New York World's Fair?)

Business sector prospects are composed of the many critical factors describing the industry environment. The exact combination can vary from one industry to another, but normally includes

- Market growth rate, usually a past five-year average, although some people use a forecast of future growth
- Profit stability over recent periods
- How easy it is to hold onto margins under fluctuating demand levels
- How well the sector lends itself to product differentiation
- The number of different companies working out in the sector and whether or not it is dominated by a small coterie of elete, formidable contenders
- Whether the market is so enticing that everyone wants to jump in
- Whether customers have to bear major changeover expenses in order to use the product or service
- Whether it's likely some potential competitor could bring out a cheap substitute that leaves you high and dry
- Whether there is the likelihood of raw material or other critical shortages.

The list could be expanded for several more pages. In some industries you'd be forced to touch on environmental impact studies and other forms of governmental meddling that can transform dreams into nightmares and render a sector quite doleful. What finally goes into your definition of business sector prospects is up to you, but the list should be limited to strategic factors. Don't get into futile tactical considerations.

Your company's competitive capabilities cover three main factors:

- Your market position (yes, we're back to market share again)
- Your manufacturing capability
- Your product research talents

All of these are things that, I trust, were amply explained in previous chapters. But the Shell Chemical folks have additional refinements on this. To Shell, market position means not only share but how entrenched you are in the market. For example, are you numero uno for no good reason (luck, perhaps), or is your market share microscopic through some strange gambado? —like maybe past managers thought they could scrape by without advertising, or let their independent distributors take on competitive lines? These considerations could mean the current status quo is alterable with minimal effort. Another question you might ask yourself is whether your market share is a function of your super technical leadership or, conversely, if customers have—up to now at any rate—merely been tolerating your technical backwardness for one reason or another.

Manufacturing capability can bring to mind many related considerations, such as the *real* efficiency and productivity of your operations, the integrity and modernity of your plants and equipment, distance from market and distribution systems, union temperament, process R&D, raw material accessability, and so on. All should be couched in terms relative to competition.

If you're a numbers-man, you easily can work out some kind of index system to assign quantitative values to each factor. The one I suggest in Chapter 10 would work nicely. Some strategists hate this kind of numerical gymnastics, feeling that they can tell by eyeball judgment where an SBU should fit on the matrix.[3]

life cycle matrix

The problem with Shell's DPM (or with GE's Business Screen) is it gives short shrift to start-up businesses that have yet to develop into bona fide industries. The life cycle approach overcomes this by abandoning business sector prospects and getting directly into the guts of most strategic overviews: stage of market life cycle (see Figure 13-2).

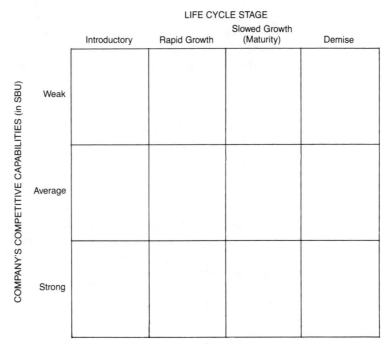

FIGURE 13-2.

With both competitive position and market size thus plotted, it is a simple matter to see at a glance where a continuation of a current strategy will take you. Such a mapping of the current and (by extrapolation) future standing of a multibusiness firm is a convenient reference point for the top-level executive wishing to ration his or her time to solving only major strategic problems and to addressing issues of central importance to the firm. But it is an important guide as well to SBU managers, serving them as a goal-setting aid and a clear device for communicating and animating common corporate strategic philosophies.

theory of shared costs

Though few dispute the efficacy of the experience curve idea—after all, repetition should make us all close to perfect—some companies found, after getting pretty far down the curve with the big market share and everything else urged on them by master strategists, they still never got to wallow in the cash gravy. Take Du Pont for example: It invents nylon, creates the synthetic fibre market, only to yield ground to cheap substitutes just when it should have been reaping huge benefits. You don't hear Du Pont complaining about this, but classic strategists think they should have gotten a much bigger reward out of nylon.

In actuality, Du Pont did get its reward, says the neostrategist. It just doesn't show up in the older strategic articles we've been looking at. To explain it, you must turn to the *theory of shared cost*, which says that different product lines often have costs that they share with one another. Even if you fumbled the ball on stodgy old Product A-1, you still benefit by unfurling Products A-2 and A-3 and producing a vibrant family of products all using the same marketing, advertising, administrative staff, factory, and even the same night watchman. One product without the other would have been a no-show.

The application of this theory requires more than just cost analysis; you easily can get swept along with the shared cost concept and end up with a very marginal operation in which no single business can stand on its own two feet.[4]

The cynic might also spot an opening here for a permanent intramural debating society, which would block all decision-making processes. In a metaphysical sense, some surely would argue, everything the company does is all linked together; in the end analysis only the company's consolidated P&L statement is worth looking at. At an intermediate stop on this *continuum absurdum* would be resurrected all those tedious controversies about cost allocation frequently advanced by accountants. The shared cost theory works best if used with reserve and only in application to closely related SBUs. Too often is it used to weasel out of culpability.

technology life cycles

Maybe this theory is more to your liking. It throws more light on what you should do when you have mounted a moving experience curve in a new technology. A passing familiarity with history shows that every new technology is doomed; sooner or later it always is surpassed by another new technology. But what may surprise you is that there is a definite pattern to this. As McKinsey strategy consultants point out, every new technology starts out real slow. What seems to be an awful lot of effort from the R&D group at first just produces a tiny advance. Then a major breakthrough occurs, followed by several more break-throughs. Finally, huge rewards are received for only meager incremental efforts. Then, alas, the innovation curve flattens out once again and very little technical progress will be seen thereafter. But, lo and behold, if you had looked closely when all those breakthroughs were going on, you'd have noticed something peculiar: a batch of *new* technologies starting off. They'd be just in their slow-development phase now, but later, when the current technology curve is flattening, one of them will be on the rise. The old and new technologies' curves overlap. Through history each new technology has taken off at a higher plateau than the one that preceded it. McKinsey cites the tire cord as a well known example: First the cord was made of cotton, then of rayon, and just as rayon's performance curve was starting to level off, nylon cord hit its rapid advancement phase—and the march of tire cord progress is still going on. Or, for a cautionary illustration on what can happen when you doze through the auspicious ribbon-cutting for the next-in-line technology, I could submit for your consideration the case of National Cash Register, master builder of the land's mightiest electromechanical cash registers, which watched from the sidelines while Burroughs grabbed market leadership with their electronic models. The commercial graveyards are chock-a-block with cadavers of companies that complacently felt their technological suit of clothes would fit all occasions the future cared to fashion.

In a sense, this is almost tantamount to saying that it's smart to keep up-to-date. The important difference is that the lifecycles of technology do appear to have constant patterns and relationships, and with vigilance you can do a better job on keeping your corporate strategies timely than if you just muddle along under the misapprehension that the future will unfold with erratic, random abandon.[5]

In his 1980 book, *Competitive Strategy*,[6] Professor Michael Porter of the Harvard Business School shows another curve—one that looks like the mouth in the "Have a Nice Day" smiling face. By putting ROI on the vertical axis and market share on the horizontal, Porter produces a smiling U-curve that seems to apply to most industries. Over on the high left end of the smile you find high-profit businesses with (and I'm blushing with embarrassment as I write this) *tiny* market shares. These are the firms that make specialization pay off "big." (Just a minute now, let me clear up the embarrassment for a second. Since this is an apparent contradiction to what most master strategists would expect, I have to offer the counterargument—which is, namely, that the very act of specialization strongly suggests the existence of segments, and that these segments must be examined separately. Having done that, you'd no doubt find that the specializers have very big shares in their unique segments.) On the high right end of the smile are the classic giant-share SBUs with their concomitant low-unit costs. They, too, are in high cotton. The poor subjacents stuck in the middle are guilty of nondifferentiation and other strategic crimes and, unless they mend their ways, will be punished with low ROI forever.

This construct provides Portor with a springboard for his thesis on *generic strategies*. He cites three. You may recognize them as eloquent variations on previously considered aspects of marketing strategies.

- His first "generic" strategy is *cost leadership*—that is, strategies like producing a standard type of product and under-pricing it vis-à-vis competition.
- Next is *uniqueness* (what we have called differentiation) wherein customers unmistakenly see your product as different, desirable, and probably well worth a premium price.
- Lastly, the *focus* strategy (what we might have termed a niche or segmentation approach) wherein you "focus" on just one geographic market, one channel of distribution, one demographic group, one narrow product line, and so one.

Porter feels your essential goal should be dominance, which is what the other master strategies were shooting for in our chapter on marketing. You want to avoid being "me too," so you have to be alerted to what is happening in the market in order to pick a generic strategy that will make you different and, therefore, give you the biggest chance of being a leader. Furthermore, says Porter, you should try to carve out a "defensible competitive position," not only against direct or potential rivals but also against other elements in the business environment, such as the supplier who may be able to exert undue bargaining power, the buyer who can get touchy without notice, and the ominous threat of something entirely new entering your market that makes you obsolete overnight. Sometimes the industry will dictate your choice of generic strategy, but normally it takes a coldly rational assessment of the forces operating in your industry before you structure your strategy.[7]

walker lewis matrix

Walker Lewis of Strategic Planning Associates sees your customer's perceptions as the pivotal consideration in strategizing; how they perceive your product and the relative importance of its features and how sensitive they are to your pricing decisions are the critical dimensions here. Lewis plots customer price sensitivity on the north-south line of a grid, with the top indicating high price sensitivity for big ticket items accounting for a big chunk of the customer's purchases, whereas on the bottom are the low price sensitive items that represent relatively insignificant dollar volumes in the customer's overall budget. On the east-west line Lewis plots a combination of how unique customers see your product or service and whether this uniqueness is, in their minds, worth paying for. In Chapter 5 I said that the last thing you want is to be stuck in a commodity category. That crops up on this matrix on the left, but Lewis gives it two different levels: price-sensitive and not price-sensitive. You have to fine-tune your marketing strategies to suit each. For example the value strategy would work where there is price sensitivity, and presumably would not otherwise. Over on the right of the grid, you have more of an opportunity for good, old fashioned marketing— adding product flourishes, value, spin-offs, and so on.

I suspect that, over the years, this marketing matrix has germinated amorphously many times in the minds of marketing people. Certainly its options have been exercised several times in the past, but whether it is novel or old-hat, the principle thing is its usefulness in corporate strategy. As a supplement to the chore of summarizing and compacting the diverse pricing strategies of all the corporation's SBUs, it has apparent merit, and many companies will find it a useful way of amplifying their five-year plans.[8]

the new BCG matrix

Just as the study of business strategy has progressed from the buzz-word level and on to a solid, permanent fixture of the daily lives of recent MBA graduates who accept it as a given, so too must it continue to develop and grow. The growth of strategic management is abetted by earnest consultants, all wishing to find that Holy Grail that satisfies all strategic twists in a single grid.

Sometimes these new approaches were welcome improvements, sometimes not. But if, as prisoners of our erudition, we begin thinking of these grids and curves (including my own with which I dramatically bring down the curtain of this chapter) as panaceas, we will fall into the traps of dogmatism and inflexibility and will surely suffer great remorse.

With that in mind, let's now take a look at what the Boston Consulting Group, one of the more creative toilers in the strategic vinyard, has been up to ever since it set dour, gray-haired executives to contemplating on "cash cows" and other fatigued metaphors. As economic conditions made slow growth endemic for many industries, as the stars and even the question marks dwindled in number, SBU-plottings on the classic BCG matrix became depressingly bottom-heavy. New hurdles had come on the scene to make planning more challenging—things like intrusive federal regulations, tough foreign rivalries, and so on. Widespread growing strategic sophistication, even among the street-fighter upstarts, made it damn hard to play the big share/low cost game with impunity. Consummate competitive segmentation and niching by even the most unlikely competitors made counter-strategies difficult to nail down.

Much of the basis for BCG's newest thinking is, once again, sedulously dependent on the marketing elements of strategy—in particular, an emphasis on product differentiation and on staking out defensible market positions. Of course it comes with a free grid (see Figure 13-3).

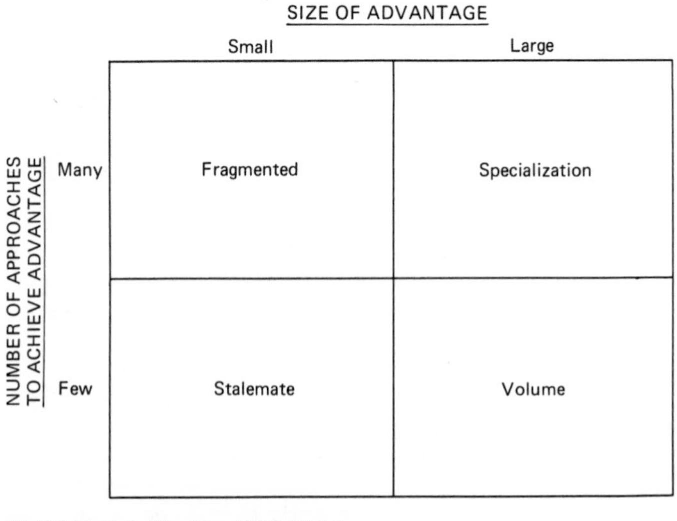

SIZE OF ADVANTAGE

	Small	Large
Many	Fragmented	Specialization
Few	Stalemate	Volume

NUMBER OF APPROACHES TO ACHIEVE ADVANTAGE

FIGURE 13-3. The New BCG Matrix

BCG's premise is that strategy development is governed by your competitive milieu and the potential for change that this offers. Affecting your success is the size of the advantage you can invoke over your rivals and the scope (or the number of practical methods) you have available to realize that advantage. As you can see by the grid's upper-left quadrant, when the potential approaches are numerous (but their appeal is negligible), you will have a fragmented industry where nobody makes out very well. You may need better R&D and a more ambitious marketing research effort to uncover hidden consumer needs, but even at that, the judgment is that your chances of success are probably limited. This is clearly not the kind of industry you want to spend much time and money on. Also unattractive is the subjacent quadrant where the scope for product differentiation is much less and you'd find it very expensive to come up with novel product ideas. Even if you succeed, the consumer just isn't going to reward you; your novel idea will not be very interesting to the consumer. Marketing effort is going to be consigned largely to the Willy Lomans with their shoeshines and febrile personalities. It doesn't offer the multipotentialities a P&G product manager would be happy with.

Over on the right you have markets where customers appreciate and want product differentiation. Accordingly, it's worth having an active R&D staff; their successful product development work will be met with customer enthusiasm. Even if you happen to be a little fellow, you can perform your niching act and succeed here. If you're a giant, then volume and its concomitant riches will be bestowed on you—providing you call the market and its needs correctly. In the lower-right box we have a kind of 1950s' look: a few companies, a few brands, all with tremendous sales volumes. You can never say for sure that this always will stay this way. The cigarette business in the 1950s looked like this, with only four brands—Camel, Lucky Strike, Chesterfield, and Old Gold—sopping up most of the market. But then came the filters and other developments, and today it is downright perplexing to keep all the cigarette brands and styles straight in one's mind.

BCG claims that "too many companies have pursued strategies during the 1970s that were inappropriate to their specific competitive environments. Market share, for example," they point out "often lacks value in stalemate and fragmented businesses. In specialization businesses, focus and superior brand image may be more rewarding than mere size."[9]

Now, before you start banging your head against a wall, I don't believe this forces us to turn our backs on all previous thinking. For one thing, strong, viable growth markets still exist in some industries and will return in others. For another, the PIMS Program continues to uphold the importance of strong market shares under practically all situations. But with BCG's latest matrix, the art and science of strategy makes another step forward, and if you could select your SBU portfolio (as you can in new product planning), you'd want to give it more than fleeting recognition.

The danger in many of these grids is that users sometimes ignore their essentially exegetical natures and make them the last word on the market. While I don't believe in companies taking too many long-shots, I'm also leery of letting models hand down repressive final verdicts. Where would Orville Redenbacher be if he had believed popcorn to be an ingrained commodity item, or Morton Thiokol's Morton Salt Division if it had really believed decades ago that salt was just sodium chloride and had never tried to create a *brand* that was unique (free-flowing, iodized) and more appealing? Virtually every consumer goods company enjoying success today is doing it on the backs of products that were once lowly commodities. The moral is that nothing is permanent; the creative mind should not be shackled, and no strategic guidance tool should be allowed to become a harness. And that goes for my own matrix, which now follows.

the basic success ambience matrix

The Basic Success Ambience matrix is one further reticulated compendium of elements giving a quick, visual depiction of an SBU array. Combining a number of marketing concepts—from both producer and (importantly) consumer aspects—with certain industry traits, it attempts to overcome the glaring shortcomings of previous matrices by recognizing both the nature of the product or service and the motivation of the consumer. It's not a veiled scheme to get back to the lurid excesses of the marketing concept, but a measured response to the reality that the scope of the product-consumer nexus has deep effects on profit boundaries. Unlike most of the other grids discussed in the foregoing, the BSA is speculative—not having stood the test of usage across a wide number of industries.

As a concession to strategic needs the BSA comes in two sections. The first is shown in Figure 13-4, and the second, which touches on the industry instead of the consumer, is shown in Figure 13-5.

The postulates on which my BSA grid is founded are that your market success potential is mainly predicated on

- Inherent product nature—the range of physical and pyschological opportunities for product differentiation
- Consumer motivation parameters—the physical and psychological scope and spectrum of consumer needs and product perception and receptivity. (For example, anything that lends itself to our traditional

FIGURE 13-4 BASIC SUCCESS AMBIENCE MATRIX-1

BASIC SUCCESS AMBIENCE MATRIX-2*

CONSUMER MOTIVATION
(Ranges from utilitarian and practical to highly
sophisticated, technically complex or advanced, and
self-indulgent.)

notions of mass advertising will by higher on the vertical line and farther to the right on the horizontal.)

- Industry personality (or "toughness")—as shown on BSA Matrix-2, deals with the relative sophistication of the market competitors, how easy it is to get established, competitive styles, market shares, and so on.

To simplify, you can see the obvious divergence in success potential by comparing a sixpack of brew to a ton of pig-iron. Even after hundreds of years the brewing industry has not come to the end of its string of new product positionings—hearty flavor, light taste or low calorie, imported or "just like imported," locally brewed,—or of emotional/image lures—appeals to vanity, machismo, urbanity, sophistication; appeals to a yearning for close personal relationships; or appeals based on lifestyle ("for weekends"). A ton of pig-iron is just pig-iron; pig-iron buyers have pretty mundane and limited ideas on how they're going to use it. Clearly, when any assemblage of sales inducements and product utilization opportunities is bigger, your chances of success are also bigger. It's simply of matter of straight

FIGURE 13-5 BASIC SUCCESS AMBIENCE MATRIX-2

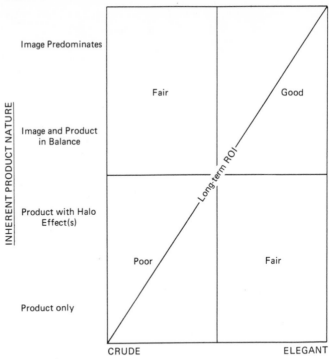

INDUSTRY PERSONALITY
(Ranges from rough, scrappy, crude, and judgmental
to smooth, elegant, and sophisticated, among other
factors described in the text.)

probability. Strategically, it is a manifestation of the product differentiation gambit: that old struggle to avoid being labeled "me too."

There is no scarcity of companies that have made this matrix work in their favor. Consider the $1.2 billion cold remedy market as a case in point. Richardson-Vicks, market leader with a 30-share, has a phalanx of over 20 different brands on the store shelf (lozenges, ointments, syrups, sprays, pills and capsules, etc.). Yet it is not solely—or even mainly—by product superiority that it manages to hold onto its position of leadership, but by image. Says Ronald A. Ahrens, president of the company's health-care division, "Frankly, our products are no better or worse than anybody else's."[10]

Products that fall high and to the right on the BSA grid characteristically appear more interesting to the consumer and, consequently, their advertising gets higher recall scores, which in turn allow a more effective use of the media at lower spending levels—in other words, substantial marketing efficiencies obtain. The philosophical underpinnings of this are quite persuasive: The thing to consider in devising your strategies is the dynamic balance of incentives that pertain at any point on the BSA grid, and whether you can increase or intensify them.

Consumers are induced toward a brand (or maker) choice by a variety of factors. At the top of the grid the scope and number of these factors is very large (that is they are both quantitative and qualitative), and they range from important to frivolous. At the bottom of the grid, the number of inducements toward brand choice narrows. But wherever you are on the BSA grid, the market will be stable when the incentives toward choice are all in balance among competitors. This is why your best offensive strategy would be to upset the balance by dramatic, communicable innovation developed through a thoroughly researched grasp of the consumer's problems, needs, and usage procedures. The wrong approach is to address the market defensively as a reaction to something a competitor has just pulled on you. It is in your own best interest to maintain constant tension in the consumer's mind regarding brand choice and to exploit this by being the sole or the major means of soothing or removing the tension through positive, unique, and profitable incentives, rather than by "me too" inducements.

The perpetuation of mere conflict between brands, rather than tension in the mind of the consumer, is insufficient. The consumer, be it housewife or industrialist, should never be viewed as a selector of brands via positive motivations alone, but rather as a vehicle for the release of tension. This applies to both consumer and industrial goods, though in the case of the latter it seldom appears to be viewed in that light. Within the industrial environment the tension is partly created by the magnitude of the difficulty faced when trying to evaluate quality in its broadest sense. Conceivably, even with the ton of pig-iron, the consummate marketer could exploit and intensify the tension in the buyer's mind by developing inducements the buyer never has had to address before.

Once having acquired the knack of exploiting the balance of incentives and turning up the tension level, your resulting leadership aura should develop its own internal energy and a momentum. In the growth market this requires regular refueling, but later, as the market matures, it needs only occasional stoking (such as modest advertising and merchandising support). The tone of your advertising, if you wish to maintain tension in the market, must serve to reinforce your leadership aura. Strategically, this means going well beyond the mere recitation of copy points about product features, which proselytize the worth of your product. Your advertising must provide continuing linkage between the end user and the strategies upon which you have entrusted the destiny of your business.

As an important extra dimension to the BSA matrix, you may overlay[11] a different horizontal parameter, as shown in BSA Matrix-2. This is a complex of factors that can be called "industry personality" or "industry toughness," which is a little more to the point. It is composed of such factors as market share, number and concentration of competitors, the traditional level of management (in particular, marketing management) sophistication, barriers to entry, and so forth.

The less favorable this composite is to your business (a value judgment perhaps), the closer you are to the left; you travel to the right as conditions become more favorable. Needless to say, when the industry personality makes it a pleasure to do business here (i.e., easy to win), then your chances of success are good and limited only by the inherent product nature you are given to play with, which is, as in BSA Matrix-1, plotted on the vertical axis.

Unlike most other corporate strategy matrices, the BSA matrix is not a mere topology—an analysis based on *types*. Its chief advantage is the provision of qualitative dimensions. Taken together, the two parts of the BSA matrix provide a veritable *mise-en-scène* for the entire corporation, giving the environments its diverse businesses function in, the forces they contend with, the opportunities they display inherently; in other words, all the elements that are key to its progress—its critical surroundings, color, and fabric. As such it can be a very critical device for promoting, at the highest level of the company, the deepest possible appreciation for the myriad strategic issues engulfing any SBU under scrutiny.

Plotting a business on either BSA grid, as with most of the alternate grids, is usually a simple matter for the manager of that business. Corporate consensus is sometimes hard to obtain when the matrix is first used, but eventually it comes about. Nonetheless it is often quite difficult to plot a business outside of one's ken—an acquisition candidate, for example. Here one must rely on consumer research and outside counsel.

conclusion

Corporate strategy, as opposed to business-level strategy, requires an ability to appreciate the principle of strategic management at all functional points in the SBU but, as well, to be able to rise above this and view the overall corporation as a changing collection of individual endeavors with varying potentials and with the possibility of constant improvements toward the end of shareholder wealth. In today's complex enterprise, one or more of the foregoing tools can make this task a little bit easier.

notes

1. Laura Landro, "Electric Switch: GE's Wizards Turning From the Bottom Line to Share of the Market, *"Wall Street Journal,* July 12, 1982, p. 1.

2. Meg Cox, "New Chairman Trying Another Strategy to Save AM International, Deep in Debt, *"Wall Street Journal*, October 12, 1981, p. 27.

3. S.J.Q. Robinson, R.E. Hichens, and D.P. Wade, "The Direction Policy Matrix, *"Long Range Planning*, vol. 11 (London: Pergamon Press Ltd., 1978), pp. 8-15.

4. Walter Kiechel, "The Decline of the Experience Curve,"*Fortune*, October 5, 1981, p. 139.

5. Ibid, p. 144.

6. Michael Porter, "Competitive Strategy" (New York: Free Press, 1980), pp. 34-46.

7. Walter Kiechel, "Three (or Four, or More) Ways to Win, "*Fortune*, October 19, 1981, p. 181.

8. Ibid, p. 184.

9. Richard K. Lochridge, "Perspectives: Strategy in the 1980s'" no. 241 (Boston, MA: Boston Consulting Group, 1981), pp. 1-2.

10. Michael Waldholz, "Marketing: Cold Cures Spread Like Flu as Companies Fight for Sales, "*Wall Street Journal*, December 17, 1981, p. 19.

11. Both matrices could be shown on the same three-dimensional chart. Computer software is available to handle this. I do not favor these depictions, however, because they are visually confusing to persons unaccustomed to them.

14

business strategy and the stock market

some problems in wooing wall street

The price of his or her stock is a matter close to any chief executive's heart, but the forces that govern stock prices are not always apparent. Much is written about it. Endless theories abound. But very strange things occur, and there often appears little rhyme or reason behind changes in stock valuations. Peculiar anomalies to popular investment wisdom monopolize our attention. Bond dealers disagree with stock analysts on market factors; one broker says "buy," another says "sell." No wonder it's confusing, especially to corporate officers endeavoring to serve in the mission of creating shareholder value.

When your own ambitions extend beyond pure survival—that is, when you have a true sense of mission about your stock price—it may help to dig a little harder at finding a more comprehensive construct on what determines stock prices than what is usually heard on the Street. This construct should include, as well, lavish footnotes on those oft' touted "causatives" whose operativeness is merely illusory. For the skilled strategist, this analytical digging would offer a rewarding perspective that could be effectively woven into his or her company's overall message to the investment community.

188

The Stockmarket   Though occasionally duped by familiar corporate gambits like loading the trade near year end, serious investment analysts take great pains to distinguish real earnings from rigged earnings. In so doing, however, analysts acquire the habit of being inordinately obsessed with these earnings figures. Hence, earnings per share becomes a central aspect of their valuation procedure. It is a common human failing that we passively accept any number of popular consensi on what makes the world tick without bothering to trace their origins or weigh their soundness. Lost in the passive acquiescence to the role of earnings is a whole host of limitations that makes much of today's stock analysis highly questionable. Some of these limitations are well known to experienced analysts, but they are forced to overlook them in face of the general failing of most companies to provide more suitable data.

For several years now there has been a rather heated controversy among investment specialists on the relative importance of earnings vs. cash flow. The more serious multivariate analyses tend to favor cash flow (anticipated, adjusted, and free) as being more closely and reliably linked to stock prices. One reason for this, of course, is the fudgeability of stated "earnings." Nonetheless, whether you happen to be an earnings or cash flow freak, a minute of uninterrupted thought would suggest that neither is the Ultimate Cause of a given stock price. They are both just lowly intervening variables. For disbelievers, consider this: If current profit had as much to do with stock price as is commonly supposed, then all P-E multiples would be the same. The truth is that both stock prices and earnings or cash flow are caused by something else—a much grander, more universal, and much more controllable power. We'll get to this shortly, but if you haven't guessed what this power is, please re-read the first few chapters of this book. Meanwhile, as a stage-setting device, I'd like to offer a more detailed critique of current stock appraisal philosophies and behavior.

the efficient stock market

Some market fans believe in the *efficient market hypothesis*, which proclaims, with considerable appeal to the intellect I think, that your stock price reflects everything that is already known or forecast about your company. Now, it doesn't claim the price is right (and, if you know your own company like the back of your hand, you may strongly disagree with how the Street evaluates your firm), but the hypothesis does purport that stock valuation is based on serious analysis and not on some crazy external pattern, as various cults and crackpots would claim.

I am not sufficiently wowed by what I see to believe that the cultists and chartists do not outnumber the efficient-marketists; so I want to take them seriously for a minute, since I've got to get rid of them before I can advance my case.

Be they sunspot theorists, or something more elegantly mathematical, their message is always the same: Externally controlled patterns can predict (therefore, govern) stock prices. Unfortunately for those with a weakness for easy answers, study after study (in particular those of Eugene Fama at the University of Chicago) has shown that prices simply do not move in patterns; they are clearly random, not patterned.

Moreover, with chilling consistency beginning with Michael Jensen's investigations at the University of Rochester back in the late 1960s and coming all the way down to the present, the most objective analysis has shown that professional fund managers and other pros who "run money," inspite of all their charts, computers, and high-priced advisors, have not been able to outperform the market. (That is to say that you may as well pick your stocks by tossing darts at a list because you will do just as well as the so-called experts with or without their funny ideas.) There is, then, something seriously amiss with the current thinking about what governs stock prices.[1]

the dividend misconception

"Ah, but Haller hasn't mentioned dividends," some will plead. "Earnings are more critical than Haller thinks; it's just that he's not looking at it in the correct way. It's what you pay out in the form of dividends that gives earnings their impact on stock prices."

This line of thought is often given expression, but it is pretty easy to deal with. Although there are many shareholders dumb enough to be unaware of the double-tax burden of getting dividends vis-à-vis enjoying a concomitantly higher stock price, or who blithely forgive any corporate board that sees no better way of investing its surplus, there is plenty of concrete evidence that dividend declarations aren't such hot ideas after all. Robert Litzenberger of Stanford and Krishna Ramaswamy of Bell Labs confirm that high dividends can be a portent of sloppy management. More to the point, their data show that a high dividend rate results in a lower share price. Rather than getting the rave reviews many would expect, this sort of thing actually weakens a company's stock price relative to competitors paying lower, or no, dividends. The reason: Stocks are priced according to their post-tax returns, and, as I said, there is more of a tax advantage to be gained, obviously, from capital gains appreciation than from a dividend payment.[2]

I think that polishes off the dividend argument. Now we can turn our attention to some of the more insidious notions on what propels stock values.

"Make your quarters, you'll make your year....Growth in earnings per share is the only real thing that counts," Harold Geneen, ex-chairman of International Telephone & Telegraph, liked to tell his troops. During his tenure, he usually achieved his goal of annual 10 percent EPS growth.[3]

In analyzing this phenomenon of excessively focusing on the short term, Michael Crozier blames computers and argues that, by bringing data on the results of corporate actions so quickly to management's attention, they've made the decision process worse, not better. "It has often become an inhibiting factor....(It) magnifies the relative influence of short-term, quantitative management as against the necessarily qualitative considerations of the long term ... producing a suffocating effect," claims Crozier.[4] Your public relations staff, who man the hot-lines from Wall Street, will vouch that this is intensified by regular, quarterly inquiries from financial analysts who also have fallen prey to the nasty habit of keeping a close eye on the day-to-day performance of your company. I would assume that the obsession with easily available short-term quantifications is likely to accelerate as the prevalence of instantaneous data spreads even further.

I would be remiss, however, if I left readers with the impression that all investors have completely sold out to quarterly analyses. This is not true; there are still occasional long-range perspectives. For example, when Lockheed decided to kill its TriStar project and take a $400 million writeoff, the stockmarket responded with a nice ($7.875 a share) run-up in its stock price, thus prompting the *Wall Street Journal* to opine, "The only explanation we can think of is that investors figured the decisions mean a bath in reported earnings this year but a much improved cash flow in the future. *Can it be that there is no truth to the old saw that the market is obsessed with the short term?*" (Italics added.)[5] Of course, I believe both the *Journal* and many other concerned observers, including myself, would be a lot happier if there were more cases like the Lockheed example—enough of them to make us really think it just "an old saw."

is growth the answer?

If not short- or long-term earnings, then how about growth? Is that what it takes to ram up the price of your stock? Well, numerous investors are lured to offerings promising growth opportunities. Common sense tells you not to invest in dying industries (or in conglomerates liberally present in such), so it follows that everyday logic induces you to gravitate toward upward bound industries. But, logic aside, does that really make sense? We saw in our marketing discourse that most new industries (or market segments to be more precise) start off with the customary bang but soon have most of their hopes punctured by the dreaded shake-out period, wherein the majority of new entrants lose their fiscal shirts. Only those lucky investors who had put their money in the top three or so surviving contenders will end up smiling. That, at least, is the strategic basis for caution on growth as a prime factor in stock valuation; but there is also an analytical approach that confirms it.

Growth anticipations are very risky, and (because they generally ignore the kind of strategic analysis mentioned above) often totally unjustified. They seldom produce the big gains investors expect from them. Moreover the "efficient market" usually *discounts* the growth factor so much that the economic gains turn out to be minimal. For example, in one study Suresh Bhirud of First Boston Corp. compared the relative P-E ratios of a sample of highly touted 1981 growth stocks to a similar grouping of 1972 selections. He found that his "representative sample of current growth stocks is discounting an average annual growth rate of 28 percent for the next five years. At year end, 1972, the previous representative sample was discounting an average growth rate of 25 percent." Bhirud's startling conclusion: "Currently, the so-called growth stocks are as overpriced as the 1972 growth stocks were." In both periods the average growth stock was traded at twice the P-E of the Standard & Poor index. (Of course, some of the favorites were going at much higher relative multiples.) Therefore, Bhirud explained, investors were expecting average earnings to grow 28.3 percent a year, compared to S&P average of only 9 percent. While no one yet knows if this is right or wrong for the current group of highflyers, you don't get much encouragement if you go back and study the results of the past decade. Because the growth factor was rapidly discounted by the time the average investor got on board, a fund consisting of the whole 1972 list of growth stocks would have yielded a price gain of only 9.7 percent through the whole decade, or about 1 percent a year.[6]

So does this mean that growth doesn't count at all? Not quite. Everyone knows of someone who struck it rich on a growth stock. But there's too much luck attached to it. Growth can never be the whole story. Informed investors are very skeptical of the unembellished growth claim. A fuller understanding of it, then, serves well at this point to provide a backdrop for the propositions that are to form the main thrust of this chapter.

Growth, as faithful readers will recall, is only one isolated profit control factor. It is neither good nor bad in itself. You have to couple it with other causal factors, like market share for example, to know exactly what growth will do for you. Followers of the stockmarket, who make a habit of focusing on only one, detached strategic factor, analytically shortchange themselves and end up seeing only a small section of a company's probable performance spectrum.

This then suggests the need and opportunity for a broader, more structured approach to the question of investments; or, if you have the desire to enhance your own company's market fortunes, a superior way of positioning it on the Street.

the story in strategy

Let us then talk seriously about the Ultimate Cause of both stock prices and earnings/cash flow. What is it that precedes earnings, that makes earnings possible, that makes them large or small, and that assures their continued existence? The answer: strategy, naturally. Clearly, your strategy is the only thing that governs your profits (or lack thereof); and nothing else can do it. If you have a fine set of business strategies in all your SBUs, and superb overall corporate strategy to boot, then you'll make a whopping big return on your investment. Barring of course the predictable caveats about rotten luck, OPEC intrigue, and so on, it is really just that simple. Your business *is* its strategy. Your strategy is the author of your profitability.

Now, even if you accept that premise, you couldn't be blamed for suspecting that its application to the investment scene may be a bit strained. You may well ask if it were not simply academic nonsense, or if serious investors, like security analysts, are really curious about your strategy. I sincerely believe the answer is affirmative; most analysts (80 percent or more) will tell you that what they really want to know (but can't get a handle on because it's either badly formulated or ill-expressed) is the official strategy of the companies they have to follow. I have personally heard this many times from analysts; moreover, if you don't want to take my word for it, the privately syndicated Greenwich Study (a periodic survey among stock analysts, brokers, and portfolio managers) confirms it scientifically.

The importance of strategy to the analyst can be demonstrated in a few brief anecdotes.

Secretive, eminently successful Procter & Gamble goes out of its way to avoid talking about itself. Its favorite comment to all inquiries is "no comment"; the investment community has more than a normal amount of trouble trying to track what P&G is up to. One prodigious analyst has gained no inconsiderable fame on the Street for the way he outshines all the others collecting data on P&G. He is Hercules A. Segalas, stock analyst for Drexel Burnham Lambert Inc.. Segalas follows Procter like Sam Spade, talking to its suppliers, interviewing its customers, travelling out to its test markets, and doing anything else he can to piece together a trenchant picture of the reticent company. Apart from the energy Segalas must expend, the fundamental reason for his success and the reason why he is the ultimate outside authority on Procter & Gamble (according to the *Wall*

Street Journal) is that "institutional clients consider Mr. Segalas particularly adept at predicting major changes in (P&G's) corporate strategy...."[7]

After spending a small fortune wining and dining a party of analysts and fund managers in a whirlwind multistate tour of its nontobacco plants—hoping of course to reap a better rating for its stock—R.J. Reynolds Industries succeeded in winning over one of its most important star analysts, Diana Temple of Salomon Brothers, with what can only be termed a very basic strategy story. Salomon issued a buy recommendation for RJR stock after Temple reported back to head office that RJR's tobacco operation had made substantial gains among young smokers (for a long while a major blemish on the firm's otherwise impeccable marketing prowess) and, furthermore, that its huge Sea-Land division was making better use of its assets—clearly a question of strategic resource deployment.[8] RJR had been trying for years to win a stronger following and acceptance on Wall Street, and feting stock analysts is a favorite way of greasing the skids here; but, in the end, it was the strategy story, pure and simple, that won over its most influential tracker.

In the spring of 1981 Mobil ran a provocative op-ed page insert headlined: "Q. What is 2nd and 192nd and kind of red all over? A. Mobil." The ad said, sure, our profits are big, but not all that big when you look at how we do on the basis of return on sales, where we rank only 192nd on the Fortune 500 list. The ad went on to say that the key thing in judging Mobil is not the numbers. "How well we navigate today's shoals is probably the true test of Mobil's performance;" or, in other words, it is strategy that tells the story better than anything else.

Simply stated, if you wish your company to be regarded in a more positive light by potential investors, look to your strategy for possible, potent financial communication opportunities. However, I do believe that this potential is infinitely deeper than in the three examples above.

It has often occured to me as bizarre that, though absolutely vital to a company's future, its financial relations program (i.e., its marketing overtures to Wall Street) generally lacks the skills found in consumer goods marketing.

While I have a great deal of admiration for the financial communicator, I would aver that he or she frequently has a rather outdated, almost quaint, understanding of business. Certainly, most financial communicators don't see it in terms of the strategic concepts covered in previous chapters. Further subtracting from their effectiveness is their imprudent reliance on unrefined "marketing" research, research that usually probes no deeper than the surface and which is often performed by practitioners who share and perpetuate the financial relations executive's limited purview. Such limitations stand in the way of enlisting an avid following from analysts and of getting them to pass more favorable judgments on the company as an investment.

It is the premise of the remainder of this chapter that substantive improvements in financial communication effectiveness could be achieved by borrowing from the field of business strategy, that there is much to be discovered in the strategic plan that could excite the investment community, and that even the research surveys conducted among your investment publics can have their utility value impressively enhanced by sharing in the strategic manager's cerebrations.

business strategy as financial communication

it's still marketing, but it's not very logical

When you ponder the consequences, it is really rather curious (to use the politest term available) that toothpaste and pantyhose get better marketing plans than do the programs geared to improving the company's stock price or chance of mustering up fresh capital. Bluntly, no conceivable product marketing activity can outrank financial communications. Can you imagine what a shareholder would say if he or she knew what was going on here? He or she would be damn miffed to discover that financial relations, which should be boosting the price of his or her stock, commonly receive the benefit of less critical thinking and planning than almost any other marketing function.

Take corporate advertising as an example. Visible by intent, by nature the summation of an intended financial relations strategy, most of it can be characterized by the passage from Tennyson's *The Lotus-Eaters*: "Like a tale of little meaning, tho' the words are strong." A professional marketing executive with a strong consumer goods background would see most corporate advertising as unobtrusive and devoid of what some folks on Madison Avenue still call the *unique selling proposition*.

But my problem with such advertising comes in at a higher level, so I like to think, where its long-term brunt, its effect on Street attitudes and stock prices, is in grave jeopardy. What troubles me most is that so few of these advertisements fit into any comprehensive thought matrix. Frequently, they seem to be guilty of addressing the wrong problems, of confusing *proximate* cause with *prime* or *ultimate* cause, and of miscellaneous infringments on serious, thoughtful inquiry. This may sound overly philosophic, but investors will not tolerate mental disorder for long. It makes them too nervous.

With a little bit of organization and with some choice contributions from the annals of strategic management, a financial relations program (with a supporting corporate advertising campaign) could be planned and implemented that would be as effective in achieving its ends as Crest toothpaste is in its marketing plans.

goal-setting queries

Before setting out to relate to the financial community, you should set a few communication goals. To this end, the following basic questions must be considered:

- Do you think your company looks better than competition to the prospective investor? To put it in more useful strategic terms, does your financial relations program make it conspicuous to the target audience that you've got the best strategic formula for generating high financial returns well into the future?
- Assuming you want more analysts to follow your company (a perennial headache for most firms), do you give them information that genuinely helps them in their work; does this information provide them with the basis for a *gut-level* confidence about your company's long-range future?
- Do you really know what needs to be communicated to get your stock price up ... and can you communicate this as effectively as Crest toothpaste does in its TV commercials?
- Does your corporate image need a total facelift?
- In your past financial communications have you lurched from one communications strategy to another, largely on cue from your ad agency? What is the exact mental residuum in the memory cells of your target audience, and how confused is it?

media targeting and shareholder wealth

Given the thesis that the essential purpose of any corporate executive is increasing shareholder wealth, then you well may ask if this perspective is reflected in corporate advertising media targeting. I believe generally it is not. Acknowledging that my view is not necessarily embraced by many advertising agencies, I feel that (a) the people you are most desirous of targeting are the analysts and brokers because they have vast influence over hundreds of other investors, and (b) that your whole financial communication program, including any corporate media advertising you might use, must be consistent. Corporate advertising usually treats analysts and portfolio money-runners as lost tribes. Though the vast bulk of nonmedia corporate financial communications (the luncheons, the one-on-ones, etc.) efforts are directed at these acknowledged opinion leaders, without whose recommendations few companies ever enjoy much action in the trading pits, corporate advertising persistently adds to their confusion by talking a different line.

Few corporate ads are designed to help analysts and other serious investment specialists form intelligent assessments about a company. The reader can pick up any magazine geared to the business community and observe that the corporate image advertising scene is seriously plagued by a paucity of fresh, serviceable ideas. A few years ago I did a "straw poll" of such ads appearing in successive issues of *Fortune* and *Forbes*, and I found that most of them (81 percent to be exact) could be lumped into only four thematic slots. The story of corporate growth, that old chestnut, accounted for 26 percent of the corporate, nonproduct, nonservice advertisements appearing in these periodicals. Boasting about new technology, usually the "cutting-edge" message, covered 24 percent of them. An old standby for the stupifyingly diversified conglomerate sans true corporate identity, the homespun list of its products, numbered 17 percent. (As an aside, an agency veteran told me he tended to create essentially the same campaign for all his medium-sized corporate clients: a big picture of their products grouped on a table and a copy line like, "We Don't Just Make Widgets/Flanges/Etc.") Lastly, we had the energy story, accounting for 14 percent of the ads tallied. Of late I have noticed energy declining in popularity and technology gaining. The diversity of expression is, however, still bleak.

"me too" advertising and communication efficiency

In the consumer goods world, where the study of advertising communications is a science, they'd call this "me too" advertising and would reject it for having a communication impact roughly comparable to wallpaper. Though both are made by P&G, you don't catch Tide making the same claims as Cheer. Each brand has its own, unique selling proposition to differentiate it from all the others. So, too, with companies trying to attract investors; they have to generate their own, internal excitement in order to secure the investment community's attention. Only after their attention is arrested does the company have any opportunity to make its points known. And only if its points are unique, only if it's not saying the same thing everyone else is (i.e., falling willy-nilly into one of the four thematic slots described above) will it succeed in scoring well within the investment community. This is a law as old as marketing itself. All consumer product managers know it; they work it into all their marketing plans. Yet, appallingly, it is widely ignored in financial communications work.

knowledge gap

My informed hunch on why so many incomplete passes are tossed in the financial relations arena is the enormous knowledge gap between the honchos managing the company and the folks running its financial communications programs. I don't think these two groups share many sentiments on what it really takes to organize and deploy corporate resources and to optimize external opportunities. Financial spokespeople usually have either financial or journalism backgrounds that have not prepared them for grappling with the potentially compelling stories of business strategy that could lift their companies above the madding crowd. Hence, most of them miss the opportunity to differentiate their communications programs with unique and compelling positioning concepts that could convince their target audience of the credibility of the company's forecasts of pending prosperity and success.

As a consequence of this knowledge gap the entire investment public is left in the dark and forced to resort to its own devices, often with unsatisfactory results.

Out of sheer desperation, analysts will exploit the most abysmally commonplace statements about the companies they follow when struggling to formulate a recommendation. One Dean Witter Reynolds analyst, for example, recommended a buy on Dart & Kraft because "not only is it broadening its product line, it is also trying to improve profit margins in its basic food business."[9] Good grief, Kraft may have accomplished as much by issuing a statement assuring Wall Street that all its food items would continue to be edible. In a company as huge as Dart & Kraft ten books could be devoted to its marketing issues alone.

It is not, however, uncommon to find analysts not quite knowing what to make of the conglomerates they survey. An analyst who starts following a company when its products are sold mainly in the dairy section can understandibly lose his or her bearings when it diversifies or merges with a totally different entity. This may explain why the market does not always cheer when a company diversifies; the analysts charged with its assessment often don't know much about its new business.

It is not realistic to place all the blame at the Guccied feet of Wall Street analysts. Many top executives fail to give coherent explanations of their corporate machinations. Confessing that, "I do not know the stockmarket, do not understand it, and I have nothing to do with it," Mr. Bergerac's impressive transformation of Revlon did not exactly sweep the stockmarket off its feet. Taking over the company in 1975, Bergerac launched a diversification program that produced sales increases at a compound annual rate of 24 percent. In five years earnings tripled. His ROE went from a good 16.5 percent to a very good 20.1 percent. Revlon acquired Technicon, a maker of medical diagnostic equipment. It picked up Continuous Curve Contact Lenses (a product category explored in Chapter 3). Both acquisitions added to sales and profit spurts in Revlon's health-care division and were nice fits for Revlon with its modest need for capital, power to generate loads of cash, high margins, and history of skilled marketing. But, alas, Revlon's highly visible cosmetic lines were not growing as fast as they used to (a below inflation 6 percent). And it was the cosmetic business that analysts following Revlon had concentrated on, not health care. All in all, by the end of 1981, Revlon was still in good shape—as for just about everyone else, there had been a few setbacks; they had the obvious obligation to pay for their acquisitions (they still looked like good long-run bets) and so forth—yet, Revlon stock had dipped to its lowest level since 1976. All the gains that Bergerac had made for Revlon shareholders were cancelled. Probable cause: Analysts following Revlon did not understand it very well beyond its cosmetic division, and Revlon management had failed to explain its overall strategic intent. "The stockmarket....I have nothing to do with it," said Bergerac.[10]

When analysts know your company just by the numbers, strange things can happen to you. Adam Smith humorously describes his "Lemming Syndrome" in explaining why stock prices often fall even farther than your temporary financial setbacks say they should. It's the portfolio manager, Smith says, who is the lemming; he or she doesn't want to get caught with any troublesome companies in his or her portfolio. Pension fund directors systematically evaluate the performance of all the fund managers they divvy up their business with, but fund managers only have to report to them quarterly. As long as they dump "bad" stocks before the quarter ends, they'll have a nice, clean record. So what fund managers do is clean house, en masse, of embarrassing stock holdings, sending prices plunging when it results in a wholesale sellout.[11]

The depth of conviction investment community specialists have about a stock is pretty much limited to a few numbers that are not gutsy enough to help them maintain their faith. Conversely, your strategy story is not so much at the mercy of periodically shifting numbers; it uses a much broader base of data to chart your company course through the future, giving you more flexibility and opportunity to seduce the nonchalant investor or analyst and hold him or her over the long term.

It is not for naught that the Quaker Oats Company likes to talk up its strategies with the investment people. Quaker knows this can, and does, generate a kind of excitement and commitment that, unless absolutely spectacular, numbers alone never will. It is not by accident that Quaker's press clippings contain statements like this one from a Dean Witter Reynold's spokesperson, trying to explain an upswing in Quaker stock prices to a reporter he deemed less informed than himself: "Investors have generally not recognized the important improvements made in Quaker's management approach and strategy in recent years.[12]

Having dismissed earnings and cash flow as mere proximate causes of stock prices and installed business strategy as the one, true, ultimate cause, I still need now to formulate a model that allows us to tackle the myriad problems presented in trying to win over investment publics. I have been writing in the ambit of business strategy but, so far, have not expounded on a paradigm that fits it all together. To put it another way, even the most cogent theory can sputter into oblivion, unless it finds a plausible, simplified way of expressing itself.

Fundamentally, without inviting too much argument, you could say all stock prices are governed by tension. The tension exists between hope and fear, between optimism and pessimism. While no ticket to a guaranteed market play, this basic premise serves as a pragmatic *sine qua non* to communications development, especially when it comes down to your basic goal-setting. Foremost among these goals should be the establishment of confidence in your corporate future. You can accomplish this by capitalizing on your internal strategic management illuminations and by keeping in mind these important points:

- Your company is not an abstraction on a ledger.
- Your company is the active realization of its strategies.
- Strategy alone is the real progenitor of your profits.
- Your strategy is your future; therefore, it strongly influences how well you can raise new equity to finance its implementation.
- You must take care how your strategy is perceived by investors torn by the tension of hope vs. fear on all investments issues.

In failing to make your strategies known, you force analysts to make assumptions—not all of which are going to be either correct or favorable. Sometimes analysts find their lonesome search for your strategies to be exceedingly frustrating, as they did in 1981 with Bill Agee, chairman of the Bendix Corporation. Prior to the Martin Marietta hassle, Agee, though frequently in the limelight for some trivial personnel matters, seemed unable to explain his corporate strategy to the analysts. Analysts started getting nervous about his acquisition strategy and began wondering whether Agee actually had a plan for getting into those technology-related businesses he kept hinting about. "There's been some frustration about the company's unwillingness to really be specific about its objectives in technology," said one analyst. "It makes them (Bendix) look like they don't know what they're doing." Eventually Agee was forced to clarify the issue by announcing that his goal was to make acquisitions with enough fiscal clout to get Bendix closer to its goal of a 20 percent ROE; additionally any acquisition to be worth considering had to fit in with

Bendix's current business lines and not be overpriced. His explanation was too undetailed to satisfy everyone, but it did remove a lot of the flak Agee had been getting for being almost mute about his strategy.[13]

Some strategy stories can captivate a stock analyst. I've seen analysts make 180-degree turnabouts on their company assessments just by gaining a more thorough appreciation of their strategies. You have to picture yourself in their shoes. Analysts aren't insiders like you. Unlike you they have not experienced what it is like when you understand all your corporate issues and plans, know exactly where the firm is going and how it is going to get there, and then read an article about your company in the paper that sounds so ill-informed that you can't imagine who the reporter interviewed besides Bill Moyers and Phil Donahue. Security analysts have the same problems as reporters. Unless you can give them almost the same feel and fervor you have as an insider, you can't expect them to be as sanguine about your company's prospects as you are. Their state of tension will continue until you give them some cerebral relief.

management evaluation and strategy

No less an authority than the *Investor Relations Handbook* says that "the most critical factor in security analysis involves an evaluation of management."[14] I'm not sure the National Investor Relations Institute had strategy in mind when they wrote the handbook, at least not the brand of strategy we're talking about. On the other hand, I don't think they meant whether the CEO "barks commands," "has vision," and is a former marine. (I'm certainly not implying this kind of thing is totally trivial; a security analyst once told me how he developed a renewed interest in one company when he read in the *New York Times* that its president was a West Point graduate; but the long-range effect of this sort of datum must depend on its linkage with managerial competence.) Management means the formulating and implementing of strategy. Good management requires a talent for recognizing the corporation's true strategic profit agents and the ability to control them; it embodies the forté for coming up with the recipe for ROIs that outperform competition.

Conventional financial communication fails here. In fact, it often blurts the wrong things when it's viewed in context of the multifactored process by which strategy delivers its ROI results. Even those seemingly innocent (if ineffective) statements about corporate growth, investment spending, new products, and so on, can cut two ways. Where you intend them to project management astuteness, they actually could signal trouble to the more perceptive analysts. I'm not convinced any company does this very well yet. Still, as timid as they might be, some modest efforts to talk strategy and hype the management image have gotten positive results.

In early 1981 Wendy's put on a big show for analysts in which they literally presented their marketing plan. Its chief points: Wendy's was going after the adult market, was bringing out many new products (chicken sandwich, breakfast menu, etc.), and was enlarging its marketing budget up to P&G proportions. With all due respect to Wendy's marketing department, it was all pretty basic, junior-level stuff, but the learned audience thought it was dynamite. Said the *Wall Street Journal* reporter who witnessed the event, "For the most part, the analysts seemed impressed." Some of them were able to play back, almost verbatim, the simple parts of the Wendy's strategy story, like Jeffrey Stein, an analyst with McDonald & Co. (strange, nomenclature coincidence) of Cleveland. "Wendy's is in an ideal situation because the population is growing into its market," he said. Stein went on to explain how Wendy's marketing and advertising strategy is to cater to adults and that the demographic trend of a gradually aging U.S. populace is moving in their favor.[15]

Other companies have approached the issue of corporate management competence with even less profundity than Wendy's and have emerged with good marks. Federal Department Stores tells the investment world that it is no longer just going to look at profits as the only performance criterion, but that in the future they would carefully track advanced criteria like return-on-investment and market share.[16] Shucks, they sound just like good old country boys.

Brokerage houses are making policy and research department staff changes to accommodate new approaches in their own work: Salomon Brothers, attempting to carve out a reputation in equities that would match their renown in bond research, recently moved philosophically away from the quantitative, numbers-oriented style of research to a brand of research giving heavy emphasis to factors, like strategy, that speak to whether a given company can expect improved profits or increased market shares, and so on.[17]

investment community "marketing research"

If your company believes in doing market research on its products or services and wouldn't dream of launching a new ad campaign without first doing a study to make sure it was effective, then, by all that's holy, it follows that your financial communications strategy and program should get a dose of its own research. After all, your financial relations effort is going to be the most important marketing activity the company indulges in all year.

Most companies that take their financial relations program seriously have no quibble with the concept of doing research to see if the program is effective; however, although probably unaware of it, they run into a problem with the research people they use. Understandably, and through no fault of their own, most research firms are ill-equipped to tackle the intricate and momentous issues governing corporate destinies. Their research methodologies are just fine for simpler things, like shampoo and razor-blades, but can't cope with the arcane complexities of business portfolios and related management issues that tax even the CEO. You will not often encounter a researcher who is really comfortable with the concepts that are stock-in-trade to strategists, corporate planners, and line managers. Research is, after all, merely an isolated staff function. Though perhaps I might have found a kinder way of putting it, I think it is unrealistic to suppose the average research technician is going to have anything other than a very narrow perspective of business. Someone told me that when you get them on the subject of business in general, researchers sound like small town barbers, but I'm unwilling to be that cruel. This is more than just gossip. A researcher who does not speak the language of Wall Street, or who is only a passive commentator rather than a line-activist, is bound to be unfamiliar with the concerns and frames of reference of the CEO, whose interests must be served in all financial relations work. Such a researcher's conclusions will inevitably lack the depth needed for developing effective communications programs.

Apart from their narrow viewing range, most orthodox researchers also employ techniques that may produce enigma rather than resolution. The issues faced by the financial spokespersons cannot be satisfactorily explored with the research profession's typically mechanistic view, its closed-ended, multiple-choice questions, and its myopic framework of attribute checklists (e.g., "How would you rate Company A's management: excellent, good, fair, or poor?"). Such approaches, though eminently standard, touch on the trifling and the obvious but completely miss the whole point of modern management and are incompatible with current theories of stock valuation. But our concern is more than theoretical. This mechanistic view of the scientoid researcher clashes with the strategist's infinite pluralism of thought, ideas, and expressions of the corporate purpose and design.

Superficial research gives further encouragement to the hapless, declawed corporate advertising plaguing the industry. Such research with its wooly platitudes and few surprises simply reinforces existing thought modes. Worse still, it's not diagnostic and consequently doesn't give you much to go on if you want to buck up your financial communications effectiveness. In brief, superficial research is hardly the right backdrop for fire-snorting copy.

Research with fund managers, brokers, and analysts is no picnic. These guys aren't just chopped liver. Researching them is an intellectual battle and the researcher must not go to them unarmed. Any researcher is going to drop the ball if he or she thinks it's just going to be a matter of asking set questions and jotting down the answers. The researcher also is going to be out in left field if he or she surmises that investor behavior is governed by the same predictable logic as Newtonian physics. (Life would be simpler if only it were.) Some awfully complex issues have to be aired, but there are no rules, and it's neither programmable, predictable, nor necessarily even organizable. The researcher must be prepared for all contingencies; this is no time for locking in on set assumptions. It is the time for the broadest possible exploration—one that will reveal how much, or how little, the analysts know and to what lines of intellectual attack they are most vulnerable. To accomplish this, it is imperative for the researcher to have intimate knowledge of your business strategies. He or she must also understand strategic management enough to know if a discussion is leading into fruitful territory or up a blind alley as far as financial communication development is concerned.

The most suitable format for such research, at least for sorting out the issues and defining some of the principles, is the roundtable discussion. The researcher who moderates a roundtable needs skills not normally endowed upon the passive technician with neither heart for battle nor background in business management. An uncommonly activist researcher must be found to serve as the moderator so that the proper talent is brought to bear on the staggeringly intricate strategic issues that inevitably must be aired. The less the researcher appears to know, the less his or her respondents (the analysts, brokers, etc.) will tell. But when the researcher appears to have a grasp of the issues equal or superior to their own, they will not hold back and will often reveal concerns that they had never before articulated to the client's own financial communicators. With this talent to bring out all the dirty laundry and the covert fears and doubts of the investors, such researchers are a rare breed. They don't come cheap, but they can make a big difference.

examples of financial communications inspired by strategic management principles

The investment community is one sector where brains do not stay baffled for long by blustering and subterfuge. So if you decide to talk strategy to this group, do not try to be simplistic. Strategy here continues to mean strategy in the fullest, most complete, scientific sense of the term—not the casual, bull session version derived from faint recall in the foxholes of the business world.

I'm going to provide several examples of what I have in mind. However, I caution you that I'm not trying to write final copy for you. It's not going to sound anything like the final copy should. What I'm giving you here are just themes—and very rough ones at that. You'll have to develop them or maybe combine several of them into one idea. No doubt you've got an ad agency that can add the words and music. All you're getting from me are the raw, uncultivated ideas.

In several cases these themes will be insufficiently synoptic to express your overall corporate thrust but would perhaps be more useful as reinforcement material. For example, rather than serve as the entire theme or message in corporate image advertising and general financial communications, they would be used only as a ten-minute insert in a slide presentation to a group of analysts. In other cases, the use of this material would start off modestly, but, as it begins to generate responses and queries from the investment community, it would be enlarged to a major role in the financial relations strategy.

One final caveat: These specimen themes are given *in vacuo*. To be effective, they must be trimmed and altered to fit the problem. You would be wise to enlist the aid of unassailable awareness and attitude research to assign precise dimensions to the problem before seeing how any of these examples can be fitted up to solve the problem.

It almost always is possible to come up with a more unique theme for your financial communications if you know the strategic components of your company well enough. I hope, when you read my examples, that something specific will gel that fits your company and solves its problem. Here then is the list (but remember, it's only a sampling and as yet unrefined).

themes to consider when attitude studies reveal street perceptions of bleak earnings outlook

- *Market position cash flow management.* Your marketing plans focus on cash flow goals, rather than the more primitive blind quest for greater sales volume and damn the torpedoes. Consider how your careful resource deployment in your diverse market segments enhances long-term cash flow and how marketing joins hands with finance to accomplish superior cash flow results.

- *Margin maintenance.* From your financial sensitivity analysis you know that the surest way to keep profits up during an inflationary spell is to maintain your gross margins. Consider how you play with your working capital (not cutting ingredient quality in order to hold firm on selling prices, etc.) so that the marketing effort's integrity is not damaged, and so on.

- *Care and feeding of cash cows.* Consider why they are critical to your operation, how you breed them, and what you do with them after they get old. Wall Street thinks of mature industries in the same way good citizens think of dirty old men; but there is a lot the Street does not understand about the strategies attached to this.

- *Productivity.* This may differentiate your company from the rest of the pack. As you know, certain profit agents will contribute to your efforts to raise employee/asset productivity, in turn making the ROI results higher and more certain. To the outsider all of the businesses in a single industry may look pretty much the same, but on the inside you may be doing something here that is worth mentioning. I wouldn't think you would want to get as complex about it, however, as we did in Chapter 7.

themes to consider when research says you are perceived as mismanaged

- *Market matrix and segmentation strategy.* Consider how you are building a virtually invincible assembly of products in several product categories by avoiding the 1960s-style sausage-factory line-extensions and concentrating on the more reliable high share/high growth spinoff philosophy. In other words, you are building a viable company, and not just filling up shelfspace in the supermarket.

- *Smarter vertical integration.* The term alone is enough to put your audience to sleep, but maybe this is because they don't know what vertical integration can do for you. Vertical integration is time-dependent; do it at the right time, and the returns can be immense. Few companies ever get it right, but, if you have, it might make a meaningful story.

- *New products program.* If most (some say 95 percent) new products fail, then you have to sympathize with the analysts who smirk when you announce your new product plans. But the strategists knows a few things here. For example, new products will pay off best when the market is in its slow-growth phase. Nonetheless, despite this and many other factorial relationships, few companies really ever learn how to manage their new products program, and they invariably end up with cash flow disasters and diminished ROIs. If you have a better approach, it will mean a lot to the stock analyst.

- *Goal-setting.* You want your management to look more than just competent. One way may be to show how management assesses its various capital expenditure options. Analysts may suspect that many firms are still holding a wet finger to the wind, rather than doing the grunt work that really is required to evaluate these investment options.

- *Organization.* Facing the future in a planned and reasoned pattern requires having the staff on board to navigate through all the shoals. Showing how your company grooms managers for different types and levels of strategic challenges could make an impressive testimonial to your company's management ability.

- *Business portfolio management.* If the analyst gets confused trying to track a multi-industry conglomerate, then he or she may think you are confused as well. Your portfolio matrix may be used to show the analyst how simple it all really is when you have your finger on the strategic guts of every single SBU. Additionally, the policy issues that you get involved in while running the portfolio could be aired (to the extent that it would be prudent) to show how buttoned up management is in addressing the opportunities and threats facing it.

themes for use when the research says you aren't farsighted enough

- *Product differentiation.* Even with miniscule market shares, you get above average ROIs when you give the customer high relative quality. One idea here would be to show some historical data on how you've been able to use this concept to improve ROI over the years. It could dismiss the notion that your company can't cut it due to small market shares.

- *R&D as profit maker.* As an antidote to the high-tech craze, assuming you are not a part of it, you might use the finding that R&D works better under some situations than others and that R&D by itself does not guarantee high profitability. If the conformation of profit agents in your firm makes it probable that your R&D efforts will pay off grandly, then this could be the source of a worthwhile one-upmanship gambit to give you better visibility vis-à-vis the high technology competitor.

- *Market growth.* As we have noted many times, growth markets are not always good for a company. Since this fundamental statement runs contrary to the popular expectation, and if you have a way of managing growth that compensates for most of the sandtraps, your explanation of how you go about it would interest serious investors.

- *Macro-micro.* Though there is the danger that this could come up sounding like a lecture on economics, the fact is that few firms spend much time worrying about the external economic forces that loom as threats (or opportunities) to the company's future. If your method of addressing the economic factors can be demonstrably linked to your profit management, it could show that you are, indeed, much more farsighted than analysts think.

- *Lifecycle games.* Not many companies do a good job in meshing their marketing strategies with the broader business strategies in order to eke out maximum returns in all phases of a product's lifecycle. Lifecycles worry the Street, but often they do not understand how good strategic management has eliminated most of the concerns.

themes for when the research says investors think you've got nothing but troubles ahead

- *Turnaround strategy.* Analysts are wary of the turnaround artists. Their deeds often turn out to be nothing more than short-term measures. On the other hand, if they have accompanied their hard-nosed actions with a sound, long-term strategic plan, maybe it would be a good idea to reveal some of the aspects of this plan.

- *Experience curve.* If you are about to reap the benefits of a carefully developed experience curve, an explanation of this, with suitable exhibits, could show convincingly that your future is good. You are being judged mainly by your current financial performance. The results of the experience curve are real, but off in the future, and unless you talk about this, an analyst's projections will be based solely on your present financial statements.

themes for when the street says you are not aggressive enough

- *Acquisition policy.* While acquisitions ordinarily receive a lot of free publicity, they aren't always viewed in the proper light. Any acquisition should be planned as an extension of good business unit portfolio management with a determined focus on the long-range impact it will have on ROI and cash flow. It's one thing to try to convince the investment community that your acquisition is good simply because it is big and you've done it aggressively; it is quite another thing to show why it makes strategic sense. Looking aggressive is more than just appearing strong, fast, and shrewd. It also has to involve an element of wisdom and competence in order to persuade the Street that it is not just grandstanding.

- *International business.* Intrusions into foreign markets may seem like an aggressive thing to do from your vantage point, but it involves a lot of risk, and oftentimes is hard for analysts to assess because of their lack of familiarity with the markets involved. Strategists have methods of reducing the risk here. (See Chapter 10.)

benefits

The foregoing is what Madison Avenue calls "copy fodder." Obviously, none of these themes are developed sufficiently to serve as finished copy. In fact, as they now stand, they are quite dull. (Of course, before McDonald's, the idea of selling hamburgers wasn't very exciting either.) But all, either separately or in groupings, contain the kernels of potent ideas that any number of companies could use to develop their own unique selling propositions for their financial communications and to spruce up their analyst meetings.

Financial communication themes borrowed from the strategic manager's perspective would easily outshine the more traditional approaches for these critical reasons:

- It happens to be what analysts say they want.
- It gives brokers something new and interesting to talk about to their customers.
- It is consonant with present day management theory and practice.
- It differentiates your company more effectively from rivals in the pursuit of capital.
- It gives your ad agency seminal new ideas to work on.
- The resulting communication pieces (advertising, annual reports, analysts meetings and one-on-ones, collateral material, etc.) would have greater impact since they'd avoid using "me too" executions.

It probably goes without saying that I am not suggesting for one minute that you reveal your entire strategic plan to the investment community and, ergo, to the snoops among your competitors. By the same token, much of it is not really as secret to competitors as you may like to think; if any of them have competent strategic planning departments, they've probably got you pegged pretty well. There's also one other way of looking at it: *Some* competitors will shake in their boots, cancel plans, or even give up when they find out what a rival is going to do, especially when a huge capital investment is announced that will threaten to over-supply the market. Suffice it to say, you do want to convey your strategy story well enough to accomplish your ends (improved stock price) and, importantly, to remove faulty perceptions about your company. It is obvious that, if you don't do something about presenting your corporate intent, distorted perceptions of your strategies are bound to develop.

What the utilization of the findings of your strategic management comes down to is an extremely thorough system that uses a totally new form of research to define your problem and give you information you've never had before—information of such depth that the solutions emerge with indisputable clarity, giving you effective and more differentiated communications programs that make investors feel confident about your future.

The investment community is a highly sophisticated, erudite market. The foregoing approach lets you sell this market with the same communication elements widely considered to be accountable for success in consumer goods marketing:

- *It has relevance*—The investor is interested in anything that removes doubts about a potential investment.
- *It is interesting*—No longer would every company sound virtually the same with 81 percent limiting themselves to the same, old four main themes. It clearly makes it eminently possible to project unique differentiating corporate entities. Thus, you get rid of that aura of sameness that inflicts a stupendous hurdle on marketing the company.

These factors will make your communications more memorable, hence more effective and more efficient. You could get by with a lower spending rate for your financial relations program.

But most importantly, it does not produce the same old puffery; it is based on a sound system of analysis, to which all conscientious investors can respond with enthusiasm and affinity. It will make them want to follow your company more thoroughly. This, of course, is fully half the battle, because if they don't follow it, they can't make positive decisions about it. Once hooked, the approach will give them a better understanding of your intentions and potentials. Provided you have more than a motley collection of dogs in your SBU portfolio, you should be able to garner a more favorable assessment from the investment community with a creative and imaginative application of this approach.

postscript for the personal investor

Few readers are in a corporate position where these worthy admonitions will have immediate relevance. Someday maybe. But not now.

Most of us, however, have personal investments. And we worry about them all the time. This chapter raises several questions for any personal investor who would love to have a greater level of confidence about his or her investment decisions—or who may wish to be able to assess more critically what his or her broker advises.

notes

1. "The Stock Market Is Efficient,"*Fortune*, June 1976, p. 147.

2. Joel Stern, "The Dividend Question,"*Wall Street Journal*, July 16, 1979, p. 24.

3. Geoffrey Colvin, "The De-Geneening of ITT,"*Fortune*, January 11, 1982, pp. 34-39. Geneen, near the end of his reign at ITT, had only a tiny fan club on Wall Street, compared to his successor, Lyman Hamilton—mainly because he shared with analysts a growing conviction that increases in earnings per share had less clout than some other factors, principally return on equity. The story is told that Geneen never had any clue as to what ITT's ROE was and never cared to find out. Maybe that's why, under Geneen, ITT limped along with lower ROEs (usually around 11 percent) than Fortune 500's median (around 13-14 percent). His successor immediately changed the whole ball game by proclaiming a 15 percent ROE the corporate target and turning his back on EPS growth, per se.

4. Michel Crozier, "Le Mal Americain," *Encounter*, (Paris: Fayard, April 1981), p. 49.

5. "Asides: TriStar's Bon Voyage," *Wall Street Journal*, December 17, 1981, p. 22. (editorial comment)

6. Charles J. Elia, "Growth Stocks Today Are as Extended in Price as Those of 1972, First Boston Strategist Finds," *Wall Street Journal*, July 6, 1981, p. 41.

7. Dean Rotbart, "Analyst Excels at Watching P&G, But Some Fault His Method, Results," *Wall Street Journal*, November 12, 1981, p. 27.

8. Gwen Kinkead, "A Low Nicotine Tour Through R.J. Reynolds," *Fortune*, January 11, 1982, pp. 76-80.

9. Gene G. Marcial, "Diversified Food Stocks Are Regaining Favor, Aided by Some Analysts' 'Disinflation' Strategy," *Wall Street Journal*, May 28, 1981, p. 46.

10. Ann M. Morrison, "Revlon's Surprising New Face,"*Fortune*, November 2, 1981, p. 72.

11. Adam Smith, "Stock Values: Notes on the Lemming Syndrome," *Wall Street Journal*, March 26, 1982, p. 22.

12. Greg David, "Quaker's Oats Attract a Crowd," *Crain's Chicago Business*, March 1981, p. 7.

13. John Koten, "Steep Prices Frustrate Bendix's Bid to Acquire a High-Technology Firm," *Wall Street Journal*, June 25, 1981, p. 23.

14. Arthur Roalman, (ed), "Investor Relations Handbook," (National Investor Relations Institute, 1974.)

15. Michael L. King, "Wendy's New Management Cooks Up Plans for Growth and Diversification," *Wall Street Journal*, March 27, 1981, p. 12.

16. "Federated Stores Sets Some New Yardsticks to Gauge Performance," *Wall Street Journal*, April 8, 1981, p. 25.

17. Tim Carrington, "Gouws Quits as Head of Stock Research in a Realignment at Salomon Brothers," *Wall Street Journal*, April 16, 1981, p. 12.

15

epilogue

Twelve Oxford dons recently scrutinized the United States, and their judgments, published as *America in Perspective: Major Trends in the United States Through the 1980s*, were not exactly uplifting. In brief, they found some very disturbing themes—a decline in our confidence and a deep sense of malfunction—which, quoth the dons, "raise doubts about the claim of 'American exceptionalism'—that uniqueness of character and society, which made the American dream a reality...." Americans, who once thought they could accomplish anything, now feel impotent.[1]

We once had a society that believed in the moral foundation of hard work. (View at random any Frank Capra film for a glint of what a lot of Americans once yearned for.) But then, it gradually transformed itself into a social order built on consumption. When times are good, this is acceptable. Unfortunately, a self-centered hedonism lacks the deep-down moral sustenance to buoy us up in bad times. That good old Puritan work ethic may strike you as both naive and dreary. But it had a power that hedonism lacks—the power to drum up enough moral allegiance to sustain our populace over the rough bits.

Some say our preoccupation with consumption spells the death of capitalism, that a system based mainly on the pursuit of pleasure inevitably produces a nasty backlash. They cite the countercultures of the 1960s. The Oxford dons claim it results in despair and fear.

211

In the worst of all possible scenarios such moral torpor could urge on a socialist ensconcement that would end any further concerns we might have about the pursuit of pleasure. Socialism also would do a "deep six" on the free enterprise system.

Most of us are inclined just to sit back and hope our sense of national malfunction blows over. That's not good enough. We've had over 15 years of industrial dithering and decline punctuated only by brief, ephemeral spates of economic euphoria. Clearly all is not well, either in business or society. As many of the illustrations in this book indicate, there is cause for a red alert.

Some jarring adjustments are in order. In the desperate struggle to regain our industrial preeminence, the role of the strategist will be exalted. It is bound to happen.

We no longer have the population growth and the eager foreign markets of the 1950s and 1960s. They once smoothed over the multitude of sins that errant professional managers, ignoring the laws of strategy, had been committing. But such benefice is gone forever. And with its passing, the day of the lucky tactician has ended. Their works lay in ruins in the rust bowls of our land.

But there is hope. With a changing demographic base this country has a decent future to look forward to, if it can deploy its resources with prudence. For one thing, the population will become more mature. The Census Bureau projects that by 1990 half of us will be over 34. With age comes wisdom—well, at least enhanced experience and judgment. And this, for starters, will, affect the consumer goods industries. To make a proper response to this, they will have to find better ways of offering quality and value. The urge for quality in products, and in life in general, will be intensified or encouraged by the increasing use of home computers, which will introduce a healthy note of organization and planning to the home. This may sound the death-knell to the consumer's inordinate reliance on brand names (seen already in the growing supermarket generic shelfspace), or at least summon a decline in the emotional hook that brand names and halo effects wield.

Such a world would be good for strategists. They already appreciate the role of quality in the ROI formula. But any world will do just fine. As we have seen throughout this book, the strategist's serious, thoughtful approach to business strategy formulation makes mincemeat of the shibboleths commonly embraced by the business community. Good strategy works in all economic environments. Its multifactored and corporately orchestrated montage is superior to error-prone human judgment. No one, in a single career or a dozen careers, can ever offer insights as profoundly reliable as a systematic approach to strategic management.

But, getting back to the moral issue, what does all this sanguineness about strategists have to do with the populace problem? The work ethic is terminally dead. What does this commitment to strategy offer to take its place? This: a true sense of purpose that everyone can share; clear-cut goals; incentives that reward salient achievement and thereby encourage effort; a truly rational base that ensures a greater likelihood of success. In short, a life with purpose—for everybody.

Consider some of the benefits of embracing strategic management.

- *The gift of common language.* Communication is the root of most problems in organizational life. The strategic approach establishes a sort of common language. With clearly expressed goals and action plans all workers would know what the game plan is. They will be rewarded for working along with it. Accordingly, they will be better team players.

- *Time savings.* Most managerial folks spend more than half their day in meetings.[2] Meetings that drag on and on (as most of them seem to do) are stifling and enervating. They drag on because the participants waste time on definitional matters and on trying to argue out strategic issues and goals. In most companies these matters seem eternally flexible. But, when you nail down your strategies, you put a quick end to all the definitional chitchat. Meetings will be shorter. As Karl Marx might have said: "Meetings are the opiate of the bosses." Shorter meetings mean more time for serious work and analysis.

- *Eyes on profit.* With everyone having specific goals involving stated improvements in one or more of the strategic profit control factors (that are part of a given strategy's structure), all eyes will be on the things that really count—cash flow and ROI. Even staff departments, who often become tangled up in the impedimenta of professional bickering and wool-gathering, will have their attention fixed on grander matters. Empire building will become largely a thing of the past.

- *Happier CEOs.* With everyone working on what really counts, the CEO's goal of achieving a better stock price for the shareholders will more likely be met. A more contented CEO is good news for all.

Contrary to the Oxford study, there is nothing we cannot do. In the old days we just put our minds to the problem. Then, that meant having the will or the ambition to carry off the solution. Now it means a fuller use of the mind. The mind can use the secrets of the master strategists—the laws of business strategy—to determine what strategy is best for any business.

Implementation has never been our problem. We are a nation of doers. Now we can become also a nation of thinkers with our minds set on the business of America and on the strategy to make it work.

notes

1. Anne Mackay-Smith, "The British Explain Americans to American Express," *Wall Street Journal*, May 13, 1982, p. 26.

2. Mortimer Adler, "Firing Line," WTTW-TV, Chicago, May 1, 1983.

index